Built on Teamwork

Sequel to *On Site*

Built on Teamwork

ALAN JENKINS

Sequel to
On Site

HEINEMANN : LONDON

William Heinemann Ltd
10 Upper Grosvenor Street, London W1X 9PA
LONDON MELBOURNE TORONTO
JOHANNESBURG AUCKLAND

SBN 434 37289 7

Printed in Great Britain by
Fakenham Press Limited,
Fakenham, Norfolk

Contents

LIST OF PLATES vii

ACKNOWLEDGMENTS xii

AUTHOR'S NOTE xiii

I The Moving Spirit 1

II Eight Years 9

III Sources of Energy 32

IV Design, Research and Development 50

V Oman 69

VI Dubai 84

VII Agro-Industry 98

VIII Homes and Gardens 110

IX Transatlantic 121

X Men of Property 140

XI Royal Occasions 164

XII The Old and the New 173

XIII The Greenham Group 185

XIV A Team is a Team 200

XV Into the 1980s 221

ILLUSTRATIONS–ACKNOWLEDGMENTS 235

INDEX 239

List of Plates

Between pages 32 and 33

Queen's Award Presentation

Seen from the air – the Southall headquarters complex

Burne House Telecommunications Centre

Council Chamber for Royal Borough of Kensington
and Chelsea

Eagle Centre, Derby

SedgeletchWater Pollution Control Works,
Houghton-le-Spring, Co. Durham.

Extension to Tower House, Aberdeen

Courage brewery extensions, Bermondsey

Motor-cycle factory, Jakarta, Indonesia

Road construction in Nigeria

Panorama Memorial Building, Baghdad

Multilateral School, Guyana

Garden Island Causeway, Australia

March 1974 – Sir Frank and Lady Taylor with their daughter Sarah on
their way to Buckingham Palace for the conferment of the Order
of Knighthood on Sir Frank.

Yorkshire Post Cartoon

April 1976 – Lady Taylor, with fellow parent board members.

Between pages 64 and 65

Constuction under way at Staples Corner Interchange

Interior, Edgley Entertainment Centre, Western Australia

Brighton Marina

The Meadows development in Sarasota, Florida

Convent, chapel, and car park, Singapore

Bedford Gardens, Brooklyn, New York

Heron's Hill Homes, Canada

Chartwell Shopping Centre, Scarborough, Canada

Greenham Concrete Delivery to Buckingham Palace

Manitowoc 4600 Series 4 crane at Graythorp

Sand and gravel winning, Kempton Park

Adam-style board room, Southgate House

British Home Stores and C & A Modes, Newcastle

Between pages 96 and 97

Lisson Green housing development

Ornamental plasterwork by Jonathan James Ltd.

St. Katharine-by-the-Tower development

Presentation to Her Majesty, Queen Elizabeth II, at St. Katharine's

Award-winning 'Rochester' home

Prefabricated Swiftplan bungalow for overseas market

Fernside Neighbourhood Centre, Alameda, U.S.A.

Tono irrigation project, Ghana

Float-out of Thistle 'A' steel jacket

Components of Thistle 'A' steel jacket

Intel factory, Malaysia

Opencast coal mining at Butterwell

Between pages 136 and 137

First prestressed concrete floating breakwater

T.S.O. Seabed Sampler undergoing trials

Taymech Aviation fuel dispenser refuelling Concorde

Pilot Plant, Glaxo Laboratories Ltd., Greenford

Hartlepool nuclear power station

Research Laboratories, Southall

Group training at Aldermaston Court

Apprentice training at Southall

Mrs. Suzanne Quentric

Teamwork sculpture by P. C. Sebastian

Risut Harbour, Oman

Housing at Medinat Qaboos, Oman

Government Offices, Dhofar, Oman

Dubai Dry Dock

Between pages 200 and 201

Sir Frank Taylor, newly elected first Life President of Taylor Woodrow

The four joint managing directors appointed on 29th June 1979

The Prime Minister, the Rt. Hon. Margaret Thatcher

All-weather flying at Fairoaks Airport, Chobham

The open air market at Newton Abbott

BNOC's Thistle 'A' platform

Maintenance work by Seaforth Maritime mechanics

'Teamwork' the original sculpture

Re-railing work in the Glasgow Underground railway

The new grandstand at Cheltenham racecourse

Queen Anne's Mansions, Westminster

Water skates used to move a 240-tonne grain barge

A Taylor Woodrow jack-up platform assisting on salvage work

Acknowledgments

THE author would like warmly to thank Sir Frank and Lady Taylor for friendly encouragement and the 'ever-open door', and countless members of the team at home and overseas, for sparing time they could ill afford to be interviewed for this book.

Among books, periodicals, and papers consulted, I must acknowledge my debt to *Achievement Magazine* (May 1976), and *Construction News* (October and November 1976); to Donald Hawley's *The Trucial States* (Allen & Unwin 1970); and to several articles in *The Sunday Times* on urban renewal, in particular one about St Katharine Docks on 23 January 1977.

Author's Note

The Taylor Woodrow Group has expanded and developed considerably since I told the story of its first fifty years in *On Site* (William Heinemann Ltd., 1971). To devote a whole new book to the eight years 1971–79 inevitably means that *Built on Teamwork* is a different kind of story; but the difference of time scale has enabled me, I hope, to look more closely at individual areas of activity.

On Site told of the growth of a major civil engineering, construction, and property group from a little band of bricklayers and carpenters in a local building business in Lancashire, led by a man of vision. *Built on Teamwork* moves straight into a highly sophisticated world of vast engineering projects valued at many millions of pounds. But I have devoted some earlier pages of this book to a quick résumé of the first fifty years so that the new reader has a chance of seeing the events of the 1970s in perspective. Much of the subsequent narrative is based on visits and interviews made in 1976 and in some cases, particularly in the Middle East, I address myself to the reader as of that time when the Group's activity there was at its greatest.

Today the Taylor Woodrow Group has some 160 subsidiary or associated companies in more than thirty different countries, a workforce of about 25 000 and an order book approaching £600 million. To avoid slowing down the narrative by parenthetic explanations or footnotes, I attempt below a very brief summary of the structure.

The holding or parent company, Taylor Woodrow Ltd.,

has its registered office at 10 Park Street, Mayfair, London. At Western House, Ealing, London, W.5, is based one of the principal subsidiary companies of the Group, Taylor Woodrow International Ltd., which manages and carries out building and civil engineering work overseas wherever there is no other local Taylor Woodrow company. Western House also contains the headquarters of Taylor Woodrow Homes Ltd., which develops, designs, and builds housing sites throughout Britain. It also has an office in Scotland and a subsidiary in Australia, and is closely linked with Taylor Woodrow's expanding interests in Florida and California.

Nearby West Africa House (the name is an historical accident) is the headquarters of Myton Ltd., specialist building contractors, acquired in 1955: they operate entirely in the United Kingdom, and have many major and outstanding projects to their credit.

At Taywood House, Southall, Middlesex, is the headquarters of Taylor Woodrow Construction Ltd., the largest subsidiary, which designs, constructs, and manages building and civil engineering works of all kinds within the U.K. (including the offshore oilfields north of the Shetlands), and has regional companies in Stafford, Darlington, and Glasgow. Southall was the original nucleus of the Group in the 1930s, and among many facilities it contains a mechanical, electrical, and process division, and atomic power department together with design, research, and architectural departments. At Southall, too, is Terresearch Ltd., soil engineers, and Swiftplan Ltd., with regional offices in Scotland and the North of England: Swiftplan designs and builds industrialized houses and offices for both Britain and tropical countries, paying special attention to insulation and noise reduction. Southall's many acres include the Group's laboratories and experimental rigs.

Taylor Woodrow Property Co. Ltd., whose offices are at Dunraven Street, has interests in America, Australia, and Belgium as well as Britain.

Based in London and Southampton, Taylor Woodrow Arcon and Arcon Building Exports supply prefabricated Arcon structures to U.K. and overseas markets respectively. Arcon are also in Singapore and Indonesia.

Taylor Woodrow have their own plant company for supplying plant and vehicles to companies in the Group, especially to Taylor Woodrow Construction. They also have the formidable resources of the Greenham Group, whose headquarters are at Woking, which hires and sells plant both within and outside the Group. The name Greenham embraces a sand and ballast company, a wholesale electrical company, workshops, a chain of ready-mix concrete plants, and companies for supplying tools, tyres, and equipment. There are Greenham companies in South Africa and Tanzania and associated companies in France, Denmark, Italy, and Kenya.

Taylor Woodrow have companies in Ghana, Nigeria, Sierra Leone, Gibraltar, and Mallorca; Australia (11 subsidiaries, including farms); and the Gulf, operating in Oman, Dubai, Jordan, Bahrain, Iraq, and Saudi Arabia.

In Canada Taylor Woodrow has a majority interest in Monarch Investments, a property group with seven subsidiaries; and along the Eastern States of America the Group operates in association with the Blitman Construction Corporation.

The Group has won three Queen's Awards for Export Achievement. When the scheme started in 1966 the Award was made jointly to Taylor Woodrow (Building Exports) Ltd. for export achievement and Taylor Woodrow Construction Ltd. for technological innovation (the Silent Pilemaster piledriver). The award has since been won twice by Taylor Woodrow International Ltd., in 1972 and 1977, for export achievement.

I

The Moving Spirit

IN the history of every great organization there are events or changes which call for a landmark, a retrospective summing up and a keen look into the future. In 1971 the Taylor Woodrow Group (or Team, as all its members say) celebrated the Jubilee of its foundation in 1921. This was the occasion for a book, *On Site*,* which tried to compress into 200 pages the story of what Sir Frank Taylor himself called 'fifty years of loyal endeavour'. (Note that word 'loyal' – it is very characteristic of the Founder of the Group.)

In October 1978 it was announced that Sir Frank would relinquish the Group managing directorship in June 1979 to be the first Life President of Taylor Woodrow Ltd, the parent company, while continuing to serve as an executive director. Nobody, least of all himself, wanted him to retire. At 74 he is in robust health, swims, plays tennis, and lives, as he has lived for the past 58 years, for the Team and its work. When the parent board, in making this announcement, acknowledged 'the tremendous contribution he has made over the years to the reputation, well-being and progress of the Group', and looked forward to 'having the benefit of his friendship, wise guidance and advice for many years to come', they meant every word of it.

It seems a propitious moment for another book about the Group, reviewing its many changes, growth and exciting

* *On Site 1921–71* (Heinemann 1971).

achievements, in the vastly more complex world since 1971, together with a shrewd but optimistic assessment of the next decade.

A number of new appointments closely followed the announcement of Sir Frank's Presidency, 'to ensure continuity of the Group's progress and philosophy'. Dick Puttick, already chairman of the parent board, became in addition chief executive, with overall power and responsibility for administering the affairs of the company. Brian Trafford, already deputy managing director, was joined by Bob Aldred, Norman Baker and Frank Gibb as joint deputy managing directors with the 'deputy' status to be dropped in June 1979 when Sir Frank became President. Norman Baker also became a joint deputy chairman of the company along with Bob Aldred. We shall meet them all again later in the book.

A few days later three more appointments were announced – the first *divisional* directorships in the history of the parent board: Peter Drew (deputy chairman of Taylor Woodrow Property Co. Ltd and chairman of St Katharine-by-the-Tower Ltd); Jim Millar (chairman of Taylor Woodrow Construction (Midlands) Ltd); and Ron Whitehouse (managing director of Taylor Woodrow International Ltd). They became full directors of the parent board in June 1979 and these too we shall meet again later on.

The Group is thus well prepared, with strong leadership, for the future. There is however one note of deep regret; and like so many things at Taylor Woodrow it is a human one. A. J. Hill (few people knew his Christian name – for some reason he was always affectionately known as 'A.J.') died in December 1978. He had been joint deputy chairman of the parent company, and was a universally known and respected figure throughout the British construction industry. In writing to his widow, Frank and Christine Taylor said: 'A.J. was a great man, a man of complete integrity and a man of action. He had great courage, physical, mental and moral. He was a concerned citizen involved in problems of community and humanitarian causes. In Taylor Woodrow he showed brilliant leadership and was a model example for the young to follow. He was a dedicated man with a zest for living, a dynamic and enthusiastic temperament, a warm and responsive personality with a disciplined and honest mind.'

One quotes this tribute at some length, not only because 'A.J.' was a much-loved co-builder of the Group but because it tells us a good deal about Frank Taylor himself. The qualities he admired in 'A.J.' were the very qualities all who have met him or worked for him find in Frank Taylor himself. This is not to say that, in picking his team over the years, Frank Taylor has looked for only one set of qualities: the sheer variety of complementary personalities you meet at Taylor Woodrow would soon correct that impression. But it remains true that moral qualities are extremely important to him.

As this book is, in some sense, a tribute to Frank Taylor himself, since he is inseparable from all that the Group has done and is doing all over the world, let us look at the man who built the Taylor Woodrow house. Frank Taylor seldom says 'I', he nearly always says 'we'. Really great men know and admit that leadership to a great extent consists in surrounding oneself with the right people – people chosen for their inner abilities, not for their outward display – and they are *people* first, not executives or crane-drivers or surveyors or bricklayers. Frank Taylor modestly attributes his success to 'luck' – 'the luck to have had this great Team of people to work with'.

He would be the first to acknowledge his debt to his parents. They were what he calls 'salt of the earth' folk – ordinary people struggling for a living, deeply committed to the Christian faith, strict towards any disregard for truth, with decent values and concern for others. Many years ago, presenting prizes at his old school in Derbyshire, he again spoke of 'luck' – the luck 'to be born of wonderful parents in a fine Christian home'. They were Methodists, and Methodism demands practical works as well as faith. A strange but appropriate coincidence: the street by which he walked to school every day was called Wesley Street. Sunday, in his youth, meant chapel twice a day and Sunday School in the afternoon. Two of the men who accompanied him to the peak of success, one of whom taught him to mix mortar and lay bricks, were friends he met at Sunday School.

The values that were inculcated in his early life are, he believes, shared in their hearts by the great majority of people. The average man and woman do *not* want a life of leisure or to be paid for not working. They want to work with other people and derive from their work satisfaction as well as money. Everyone knows there are some frankly unpleasant jobs in which this is not easy, but they are tolerable because of one's mates. These beliefs lie behind Frank Taylor's vigorous support of free enterprise organizations. All his publicly and privately expressed opinions point to his doctrine of 'work as salvation', and in this he comes close to Martin Luther's 'to work is to pray'.

His anger is rarely allowed to show itself. It does so when this doctrine of work, based on a sense of honour and mutual respect, is flouted by what he calls 'the something-for-nothing brigade'. 'Today,' he said recently in a national newspaper, 'the British industrialist has to spend too much time trying to keep his business from falling into the hands of those who would steal it.' As you would expect, he is a passionate opponent of any attempt to nationalize the building industry, which he is certain would lessen its efficiency and its spirit of service. But he is equally critical of insensitive management: 'Too many managements treat employees as

minions. Too many do not bother to say "well done" and
"thank-you" when they should. To inspire allegiance you
have to encourage effort and reward when it is due. Then,
when things get tough, you can count on them.' There must
of course be discipline and a willingness to accept that what is
good for the Team comes before what is good for an individual member, who may lose a little personal glory at a given
moment but still has the satisfaction of belonging to the
Team. 'You've got to be fair and firm,' Frank Taylor once said
in a broadcast interview, 'and it must be in that order. Give
people a square deal, and you can expect the same in return.'

We see, then, that Frank Taylor is motivated by principles
rather than mere piety. Thus his objection to bad language is
not so much moral as linguistic: people swear, he thinks,
because their vocabulary is poor, and because they lack respect
for their own language. To bring such principles into business
may seem unsophisticated, even out of date. If this is really so,
then we have lost all standards of conduct. When, more than
twenty years ago, his deputy chairman retired, Frank Taylor,
who, though a very controlled man, is not ashamed of
emotion, said of him: 'John Fenton is a fine, Christian gentleman. His life, actions and works are a model for all of us.'

These firm attributes of mind do not mean inflexibility or
lack of humour. No man is prouder of the decentralized
structure of the Group, or more receptive to the idea that
there may be more than one solution to a problem. No man
smiles more readily, enjoys having his leg pulled, laughs at
his own mistakes (there have been one or two, generally
because he gave his trust to someone who wasn't worthy of
it). No man is more willing to listen to a grievance, or – best
of all – a new and constructive idea. Hence his 'ever open
door' policy by which anyone with something on his mind
may go and talk to him personally.

How these principles are carried into daily business are

clear from a glance at the Team Handbook, a guide for new members. Among them are words of wisdom on how to *enjoy* your job and the people you work with that may look odd in the turbulent, I'm-all-right-Jack conditions of today: 'Do more than you get paid for. Be loyal to your boss and those working under you. Never withhold credit from those working under you.' Above all, 'be team-minded. It is team-work that wins games, battles and business.'

This kind of leadership is sometimes expressed in pithy bits of folk-wisdom called Taylor-Woodrowisms. They are tongue-in-cheek, but they are *meant*. You find them in the house journal, or sometimes in terse notes from the Founder himself, on whose desk Harry Truman's 'The buck stops here' is prominently displayed. They may be quotations, many of them American (Abe Lincoln, Ralph Waldo Emerson, Elbert Hubbard) or they may be invented on the spur of the moment. The earliest the author has been able to discover is from 1935: 'Pull together. If you can't pull, push. If you can't push, get out of the way.' Others are: 'Think! Think Big!' 'If you haven't got it, *get* it.' 'Profit is a *clean* word'. 'You cannot help the poor by destroying the rich.' 'You cannot further the brotherhood of man by encouraging class-hatred.' 'Education is what you get by reading the fine print; experience is what you get from not reading it.' 'Today is the tomorrow you were worrying about yesterday.'

Add to this the importance of good manners and grati-tude – the author had a letter from Frank Taylor thanking him for thanking Frank Taylor for something! It is all, perhaps, part of the perfectionism that lies behind his stan-dards of conduct and performance; such as the caution with which he greets outstanding results (and this is *not* the in-joke it is sometimes thought to be!) as 'Not Unsatisfactory'.

Not untypical of the way in which Frank Taylor himself inspires people into achieving more than they think they can, is a story he likes to relate about the huge granite sculpture of the Teamwork symbol which stands outside Western House. Created by David Wynne in 1958 (he was less famous then than now), it is thought to be the largest monolithic granite sculpture since the days of the Pharaohs.

To start with, it involved David Wynne in a visit to a quarry in Cornwall, run by a father of 84 and his son aged 60.

'David told them he wanted a piece of granite, one chunk of 100 tons: about 20 ft long × 10 ft high × 5 ft wide. The father said, "We are too busy to do that". David said, "Before I return to London, I wonder whether you and your son would have lunch with me". The father said, "I am too busy, but my son can have lunch with you".

'During the lunch David talked to the son and said, "I wonder, may I go back and tell your father that you have explained to me why you could not get out a piece of granite the size I want?" The son said, "Oh, what a good idea".

'They went back; David thanked the father for letting his son have lunch with him and said, "Of course, during lunch your son explained to me that you would not know how to get a piece of granite out the size I want". The father exploded and said "But of course we can. . . ." So David got his piece of granite, hired a caravan, lived in it for over a year, doing the first big sculpture of our four men out of one piece of granite.'

The word 'loyal' occurred in the first paragraph of this chapter. Loyalty, to Frank Taylor, is a two-way thing; it can also be a lifelong thing. He himself has never forgotten any kindness or help he has ever received from another person, be it his Hayes bank manager who financed his first housing estate in Southern England, or his doctor who became a life-long friend. Impulsively helpful himself, he was inspecting his team's work on Mulberry harbours one day when bombs were falling all around, and, without bothering to take off his City hat and coat, got down to it and poured concrete with the rest of the gang. Hat and coat were never quite the same again. . . .

Extraordinary to think that, in his twenties, he was tempted to give up the firm he had started as soon as he had made £10 000 (you *could* retire on £10 000 in those days!) and devote his life, among other things, to repairing his education. Then he realized that, in times of high unemployment, he had taken on a heavy responsibility for the Team he had created. Looking back, he knows he could not have taken any other decision than to stay; a decision that led on to the worldwide achievements that bear his name today.

Suppose he *had* decided to quit, all those years ago. What would he have done? His father had wanted him to try fruit farming. Indeed, the Group owns farms in Australia, and Frank Taylor himself has a small farm at his Surrey home. Country life has always had its attractions for him, and his favourite book is a trilogy about country life in Oxfordshire in the 1880s. The author had to go to Canada to discover this! At the home of Mr and Mrs Norman Notley near Toronto (Norman, now retired, was a pioneer of Taylor Woodrow's entry into Canada) he was looking along their bookshelves when he spotted Flora Thompson's *Lark Rise to Candleford*. It is a perfect period piece, a document of social history: an old lady's simply but vividly written reminiscences of the hard yet colourful life of farming folk. 'Sir Frank gave me that,' Mrs Notley told me, showing the author his signature on the fly-leaf. 'It's his favourite book.'

Frank Taylor a farmer? Well, no doubt he would have made a great success of it. But the twenty-five thousand members of his Team, and the world of industry as a whole, would have been the poorer in every sense. In whatever other sphere his talents might have been employed, he would have shown himself (as one of his colleagues has said) 'a master of human relations with an inspired flair for leadership'.

II

Eight Years

IN December 1972, at a ceremony in Dubai, on the east coast of Arabia, a contract worth £91 million was signed between two leading British civil engineering groups and the Dubai Dry Dock Company, representing the Ruler of Dubai. It was for the construction of dry docks, ship repair shops, and harbour works. With the extension of Port Rashid next door to it, it quickly grew to a value of £332 million. It was, and still is, the largest single overseas contract ever undertaken by the British construction industry. There is no particular virtue in bigness, and there is more than bigness in Dubai. Here history is being made at jet-speed – the kind of speed that has revived an old joke: 'What is that new building?' – 'I don't know, it wasn't there this morning.'

If the average newspaper reader of 1972 was doubtful where Dubai was, he can be so no longer: Dubai has been in the news ever since, and Her Majesty the Queen stopped there during her Arabian tour early in 1979 when she performed the opening ceremony of the huge dry docks. Everything about this contract is typical of how a major industry, here seen at its very best, works today. It is a 'joint venture' – an equal partnership, a pooling of brains and resources, between two huge organizations, both highly experienced in this kind of work and in this part of the world. It is international, designed to meet the needs of international trade, and drawing its materials, equipment, and labour from different parts of the world. It is happening in an oil-producing country whose Ruler is determined to bring trade and industry to Dubai to raise the living standards of his people. And it is happening *fast*.

Twelve years ago Dubai, one of the United Arab Emirates, was little more than a trading post, a small picturesque harbour full of dhows curving delicately against the blue sea and sky, alongside a creek that ended in a Gulf-side oasis. The picturesqueness is still there; but now, as your jumbo-jet takes off from Dubai's modern airport, you see straight roads lined with factories and houses disappearing into the desert, and a clutch of mini-skyscrapers where, quite recently, there were tents and camels.

Among the actors in this transformation scene are Sheikh Rashid bin Said Al Maktoum, Ruler of Dubai for nearly twenty years; Harry Ridehalgh, formerly senior partner in Sir William Halcrow & Partners, the consulting engineers, and the two firms who eventually won the contract, Taylor Woodrow International and Costain International. How they all met each other and worked together we shall tell in a later chapter. For the present, let us simply note that this is not a case of an oil-rich Arab chieftain spending money for status: Sheikh Rashid is a realist: he knows that one day the oil will dry up (not that Dubai is predominantly an oil state anyway), and that most of his revenue will come from Dubai's traditional role as an *entrepôt* trading centre.

Contrary to popular belief, the Arab world does not finance great enterprises by casually dipping into its own pockets. The money is raised conventionally in the City of London. Master-minded by Morgan Grenfell the merchant bankers, the Dubai loan (in Eurodollars) involved a syndicate of forty-nine banks in London, New York, and

Toronto. So interdependent are the great commercial and industrial undertakings of today's world: it cannot be otherwise.

Britain's civil engineering industry, which we are going to look at in this book through the eyes of one of its very top firms, Taylor Woodrow, is transforming the face of the earth wherever it works, and, it is not too much to claim, is bringing prosperity and a better way of life to both sophisticated and developing peoples the world over. That it does so profitably is a tribute to its skills and efficiency. Without this industry there would be no power stations, nuclear or otherwise; no hydro-electric projects; no modern factories – nowadays cunningly designed to blend with a landscaped background and free from the smoke and dirt which we associate with the Industrial Revolution. The offices we work in; the roofs over our heads; communications by land, sea and air, through desert and jungle and green countryside; the bringing of water to the parched earth for the growing of food; the building of schools, universities, hospitals, laboratories, churches, a modern cathedral – there is no progress or improvement in the human condition that does not, somewhere along the line, need this vital industry.

Taylor Woodrow are involved in every one of these things, and more besides. We have said that bigness is no compelling virtue: what is more important is how the bigness grew. Most great construction firms began by building homes for ordinary people, and it was with a pair of semi-detached houses built by a boy of 16 in Blackpool, that the Taylor Woodrow story began in 1921.

Details of the youth of Frank Taylor, founder of the group, have been told many times, often by journalists who have presented this as a 'rags to riches' story. This Frank Taylor himself strenuously denies. There were few luxuries in the terrace house at 33 Station Road, Hadfield, Derbyshire, where his parents ran a retail fruit shop – the front parlour being the shop; but 'we never went hungry'. Hard work came naturally to him: his parents habitually worked a 17- or 18-hour day, and so did young Frank when, at the age of eleven, he was left in sole charge of the shop while his parents were on holiday in Blackpool. He had the responsibility of getting up at 4.30 a.m. to drive a horse and cart to the market eleven miles away and bringing the produce back in time to open the shop at 8 a.m.

To Blackpool the family moved a year later, mainly for the sake of his mother's health. Not long afterwards, sick of living in rented accommodation, they decided to own their own home. So Frank, having been taught the rudiments of bricklaying and mortar-mixing by a Sunday School friend named Leslie Turner, drew out all his savings, persuaded a bank-manager to lend him £400, and with his own hands and the help of a few friends in the trade built two houses in Central Drive, Blackpool – one for his parents, the other for his uncle, Jack Woodrow, whom he took into partnership because he himself could not legally buy or sell land until he was of age, but who died a few years later.

Soon he was employing other men, many of whom stayed with him and rose to be top managers in his growing organization. That organization, as it is today, is the subject of our story.

Taylor Woodrow's Golden Jubilee in 1971 was really a tribute to its youthful versatility, for few big groups in this industry could look back on so swift a rise to national and international significance. They now described themselves as 'the world-wide team of engineers, constructors and developers'. This flexible breadth of skills and ancillary services stood them in good stead during the next few years. Built up through the years of crisis and difficulty, taking boom and slump, stop-go economic policies, storm and stress with an obstinate capacity for survival, Taylor Woodrow men and women looked at the decade ahead and did not entirely like what they saw.

When the history of the 1970s comes to be written, future generations of students will marvel at the speed of change Britain and the world experienced. Entering the unknown world of the Common Market, however hopefully; decimalization and metrication; inflation and labour unrest going hand in hand (1972 saw the longest strike in the history of the British construction industry); escalating costs of materials; intensified competition for contracts as the volume of building and civil engineering work shrank; an energy crisis and the highest price for oil ever known – in this atmosphere, there must be something special about a group of companies which, almost monotonously, reports annually 'record profits for the umpteenth consecutive year'.

One thing was crystal-clear to everyone in the civil engineering industry: most of the new business was going to be found abroad, generally in the 'developing' countries, and particularly in those whose new-found wealth was derived from oil.

What did the world look like in 1971? Along the Gulf, six Trucial States were forming the United Arab Emirates, and Bahrain and Qatar were declaring their independence – all of interest to Taylor Woodrow. On the moon, three American astronauts were pulling a sort of golf-cart around, collecting samples of rock, and one of them drove a golf-ball into space. The Russians placed a self-propelled vehicle on the moon, and a Russian space laboratory orbited the earth. Rolls-Royce were taken over by the Government. The Open University began. There was an ugly civil war in East Pakistan, and a certain General Amin seized power in Uganda. A world of change, no doubt about it. An American journalist, Theodore White, called 1971 'a year of watershed events – the end of the Post-War World'.

In his Jubilee message to the Team, Frank Taylor wrote: 'Our thoughts must be concerned with what we are going to make of the next 50 years. Where will we be building in 2021 – on the Moon, or some planet even further away? What new techniques and materials will we be using? Will concrete and prestressing be something to read about in dusty old books? What will have replaced computer technology and accounting?'

At Invergordon, Scotland, a £37 million aluminium reduction works was in its final stages. At Grangemouth Docks, also in Scotland, work was beginning on a £6¼ million contract for a new lock as part of the overall development of the docks. At Heysham, Lancashire, a new task for the British Nuclear Design and Construction consortium (of which Taylor Woodrow was a founder-member) to build a 1250 megawatt nuclear power station, a twin to the one at Hartlepool. In Singapore, the first 700-foot container berth in the East Lagoon wharf project was completed ahead of schedule. In Perth, Australia, the Premier of Western Australia opened the A$8 million City Arcade complex. In Birmingham, England, a new shopping centre over New Street Station, built and developed by Taylor Woodrow Industrial Estates in partnership with Norwich Union Insurance and Capital & Counties Property, was letting shops successfully. And in London, Myton Ltd. did one of their speed-and-co-ordination miracles by converting over 100 000 square feet of old warehouse into a modern office building for Babcock & Wilcox in only fifteen weeks.

No company is more familiar with London Airport than Taylor Woodrow. In 1950 they started the tunnel connecting Bath Road with the central terminal area; three years later they were working on the subways, passenger-handling buildings and the nine-storey air traffic control building; the year after that found them building the three-storey 'Queen's Building', later adding aircraft standings, taxiways, and multi-storey car-parks; and their specialist company Myton had contributed, nearby, the Ariel, the world's first completely circular hotel. Tunnelling, again, was an important contract comprising the underground link between the central terminal and the new cargo area of the airport, completed in December 1968. In 1972 Taylor Woodrow Construction started work on Heathrow Central Station, the new underground passenger terminus. For years air travellers had bemoaned the lack of Underground transport from Hounslow West, where the Piccadilly Line ended, to the airport only three-and-a-half miles away. The new station is in the centre of the airport, under the car-park between the control tower and the main terminal buildings.

Cheerfulness broke in at Samlesbury in Lancashire where, on 31 March 1972 at Whitbreads' new brewery – built in sixteen months from the receipt of planning permission to meet the vital 'brew-date' – the first brew was produced and sampled. Whitbread's chairman, Mr Alex Bennett, called it 'a triumph of good labour relations'. This success was followed by the addition of a warehouse complex and a canteen and welfare block.

At Brighton, the first of the huge 600-ton precast concrete caissons, each twelve metres in diameter, was placed in position on the western arm of the main breakwaters which were to contain the exciting (and in some respects controversial) new Marina. The placing of caissons, by a portal crane moving out over the sea on rails, was always a delicate and sometimes anxious manoeuvre. The last of the thirty-five caissons forming the western arm was sunk in July 1973, and a further seventy-five caissons were afterwards positioned to form the second breakwater. Together the two breakwaters are nearly 2 000 metres in length.

Opened on 31 May 1979 by Her Majesty the Queen, Brighton Marina, at Black Rock below the cliffs at the eastern end of the town, is one of the largest marinas in the world with over 2 000 moorings – a port-of-call badly needed by craft moving along and across the Channel. With seventy-seven acres of sheltered water, it appeals especially to the 'weekend sailor', for whom there are tethered floating 'con-courses' in the outer harbour with chalet-type living accom-modation. In the inner harbour are floating walkways. The tidal basin is connected to the non-tidal water by a lock. The French coast is only sixty-eight miles away, and Chichester Harbour and other approaches to the Solent are within forty miles.

Staples Corner, Hendon, in north-west London, used to be a motorist's nightmare. Here the A.5 from London, to the Midlands and on to Holyhead crossed the A.406, the con-gested North Circular Road In October 1972 Taylor Wood-row were awarded the multi-million pound contract (design-and-construct) by the Department of the Environ-ment to help solve its traffic problems. Motorists did not grow to love it any more during the next four years: unfortunately there is no instant or perfect way of building an interchange, involving two prestressed concrete flyovers, two round-abouts to separate through traffic from local traffic, and a reinforced concrete bridge carrying an access road from the new Brent Cross Shopping Development. The trouble was that all this had to be done while keeping the traffic moving; but as we shall see, it all came right in the end. Meantime, the team on the site did their best to help motorists who passed that way. Dick England, director in charge, was delighted to receive a letter from a lady who had a flat tyre on the North Circular and wished to thank two Taylor

Woodrow team members who changed it for her: 'How kind they were,' she said, 'and what good public relations experts you have hidden beneath hard hats!'

In Nottingham, in June 1972, the first large shopping centre of its kind in Britain was opened as part of the Victoria Centre, on ten acres of land which was formerly the old Victoria Station. Taylor Woodrow's Midland construction company undertook this for the developers, Capital & Counties Property: it includes about 100 shops in covered air-conditioned arcades, a covered market, a bus station, offices, underground parking for 1 650 cars, and 464 homes in five linked tower blocks.

Overseas, things looked difficult in West Africa, though there was fresh road, bridge, and airport work in Nigeria. In Australia, the Garden Island causeway with two reinforced concrete bridges, one 608 metres long, part of the three-miles access link between the island and the mainland of Western Australia, was nearing completion. In South East Asia, which was enjoying boom conditions, Taylor Woodrow International and Arcon (Singapore) were securing fresh contracts in Singapore itself, Hong Kong, Indonesia, and Malaysia. The event of the year in this region was undoubtedly the completion of Beecham Pharmaceuticals' penicillin factory at Jurong, the vast new industrial estate outside Singapore – a design–equip–manage contract in which the work of Taylor Woodrow International, Taylor Woodrow Construction's mechanical, electrical and process division, and Arcon (Singapore) were brilliantly blended in a £4 million project which was visited in October by H.R.H. Princess Margaret.

It could fairly be claimed that Taylor Woodrow were already 'in Europe' through their associated companies: Concrete S.R.L. of Milan, supplying ready-mixed concrete; Boeg-Thomsen Holding of Denmark, who distributed construction equipment; and Taylor Woodrow's own property company which had built and was managing an air-conditioned office block in Brussels.

But the new direction in which things were about to move was contained in two short, rather low key paragraphs of the 1972 Annual Report: 'Considerable work has been carried our during the year by Taylor Woodrow International Ltd. in the Dhofar Province of Oman for H.M. The Sultan' – and an equally modest announcement about 'a joint venture with Costain Civil Engineering Ltd. for the construction in Dubai of dry docks and ship repairing facilities'. A figure of £50 million was mentioned: it was to be more than quadrupled eventually. The adventures of Taylor Woodrow in the Gulf will be told in Chapters V and VI.

To positive thinkers, every problem begets a new opportunity. Few people expected much of 1973. The headlines used the word *crisis* with a monotony that had hardly been seen since the post-war years. Yet the very urgency of finding new sources of energy pointed to two areas in which Taylor Woodrow were particularly well equipped to take part: nuclear power development and offshore oil production. But for inflation and labour troubles, it seemed that the country was on the brink (in the words of Dick Puttick, then joint deputy chairman of the Parent Board) of 'the greatest scope for expansion since the Industrial Revolution'. So it made sense that Taylor Woodrow's research and development teams should be designing North Sea oil platforms in concrete (to establish concrete as a viable alternative to steel). This was not destined to prosper immediately, but, as we shall see, research is never wasted. When the Central Electricity Generating Board's new 2 000 megawat oil-fired power station at Pembroke, South Wales, was opened in June 1973 by Mr Edward Heath, then Prime Minister, he was surprised to discover that the Mayor of Pembroke, Alderman Charles Thomas, who welcomed him, was a member of the construction team on the site!

In Oxford, the new Oxford Central Library, part of the Westgate shopping development built by Taylor Woodrow, was opened by H.M. the Queen Mother. At St Katharine Docks by the Tower of London, Strand Hotels opened their new Tower Hotel, constructed and equipped mechanically and electrically by Taylor Woodrow Construction as part of this huge dockland revival scheme. With pageantry appropriate to the historic setting, a yeoman warder was present, together with the band of the Grenadier Guards. A new Public Records Office at Kew; a multi-million pound headquarters for IBM at Portsmouth; a new town hall for the Borough of Kensington (soon to be united, under the Redcliffe-Maud scheme, with Chelsea); a new dining centre for Eton College; an hotel in Coventry, and a theatre in Leicester – Taylor Woodrow Construction had nothing if not variety. But for sheer originality and high speed in handling an offbeat assignment, the palm must go to the Special Works Department of Myton Ltd., who in an unbelievable sixteen weeks completed a £1 million project for Dorothy Perkins Ltd., completely eviscerating the old Derry & Toms store in Kensington High Street and transforming it into a trendy 1930s-nostalgia dream store to be known as Biba. Everything had to be done between March 1973, the earliest date at which Derry & Toms could vacate the store, and September, when Biba were due to open for the autumn and Christmas trading with a complete, newly trained staff. Myton used critical path analysis to build and equip this store to the last detail – a job which might normally take up to three years. That Biba eventually failed financially was a tragedy, but Myton's performance here can never be dimmed, although they have since been back in the building reconverting half of it for their client, British Home Stores Ltd.

Abroad, the emphasis was again on the Gulf area, where the Dubai contract, then worth £91 million, was signed between the Costain-Taylor Woodrow Joint Venture and the Dubai Dry Dock Company; and in the Sultanate of Oman the Group consolidated its position by forming a joint company with a local firm of long standing in Muscat, the W. J. Towell Company. But in America, too, new developments were beginning. Taylor Woodrow's associates the Blitman Construction Corporation operated mainly in the eastern States. Now, suddenly, the Group were interested in Florida, and established a base at Sarasota, following a logic which we shall examine in Chapter IX. Here they bought 1 300 acres of land for the development of some 4 000 properties, to be administered from Britain by Taylor Woodrow Homes Ltd.

That a year of consolidation should also be a year of administrative change and internal regrouping, planned well ahead, is sound thinking. Characteristic of this was the setting up of a new holding company for the Greenham Group, to centralize control and speed up administration in this rapidly expanding part of Taylor Woodrow, which we shall look at in detail in Chapter XIII.

In September 1973 Frank Taylor announced that he wished to relinquish the chairmanship of the Group with effect from 1 January 1974, and that the Board had chosen Dick Puttick to succeed him. This meant that the functions of chairman and managing director were henceforth to be separate, and that Frank Taylor would continue as managing director. This, Frank Taylor said, was 'good policy' now that Taylor Woodrow had reached its present size as a multi-national group.

The two men are very different in character, which is

probably why they work so well together. Yet their styles of
chairmanship have much in common. Dick Puttick sees his
job as 'a sort of Group personnel officer', and he is continuing
Frank Taylor's policy of 'the ever-open door' by which
any member of the Taylor Woodrow team has access to the
chairman for consultation.

Such is Dick's modesty that it is necessary to trace his
career in brief. He joined Taylor Woodrow in 1940 as junior
quantity surveyor at Malvern, where the firm was working
on temporary offices for the Admiralty. He remembers,
'we had to rough it in those days, in crowded digs among
billeted evacuees, sometimes sleeping two in a bed!' He met
his future wife Betty in 1943 while working on Lord
Beaverbrook's new aircraft factory at Weybridge. He was
senior surveyor on the Mulberry project in 1943, and served
on an enormous variety of contracts, eventually becoming
deputy chief quantity surveyor to Taylor Woodrow
Construction in 1950, a director of the company five years
later, and assistant managing director in 1968. He was elected
to the Parent Board the following year. He has been very
much involved in the nuclear power programme, especially
as a valuer and skilled negotiator. Widely travelled, a former
Council member of the C.B.I., and a member of the Surrey
Cricket Club who can remember the great days of Jack
Hobbs . . . but there you have the man. Ask anyone at
Taylor Woodrow to describe him, and they always use the
same word: 'gentleman'.

There had been other recent changes at the top. Bob
Aldred, chairman of Taylor Woodrow International, closely
identified with Australasia and the Far East, and Brian
Trafford, Executive Board member for all the Greenham
companies, had been appointed to the Parent Board. In the
summer of 1973 Christine Taylor, Frank Taylor's wife, was
appointed to the Board of Blitman Construction Corporation:

she was the Group's first woman director, having been a director of Taylor Woodrow Homes since 1955. In 1976 Lady Taylor was appointed to the Parent Board. Brian Trafford became deputy managing director in 1974 and was joined on the main Board by Nat Fletcher, who had been with the Group for thirty-five years and had for many years headed Group marketing and publicity in addition to other responsibilities. Another promotion to the Parent Board – again in 1976 – was that of John Topping, chairman of Taylor Woodrow Property Company in whose affairs he had taken a leading role since its formation in 1963.

Team members come, and seldom go until they retire – and even then, the Group never loses touch with retired members. Over the eight years 1971–79 there were several deaths of old and loyal friends which must be recorded. In his 1972 Annual Report, Frank Taylor paid a special tribute to 'my good friend and colleague Leslie Olorenshaw'. Leslie, who was joint deputy chairman of the parent company at the time of his death, aged 60, in August 1972, had been with the Group for forty years. He had joined soon atter his 18th birthday as a wages clerk at £3·50p a week.

George Dyter, chairman of Taylor Woodrow Property Co. Ltd. and for four years a member of the parent board, had been with the Group for nearly thirty years when he died in June 1974. Originally associated with the Arcon temporary housing scheme, whose export potential he had seen while serving in Nigeria, he became the first managing director of Taylor Woodrow (Building Exports) and also of Taylor Woodrow Industrial Estates.

Had Jack Ashton not died untimely in September 1974, just after his appointment as assistant managing director of Taylor Woodrow Construction, he might have taken the lead in the Group's North Sea oil activities. Jack, who joined the company in 1943, had been in charge of the Mechanical,

Electrical and Process Division (which he had largely created) since 1960.

The Group lost two very old friends in 1977. One, Billy Burns, was manager of the local branch of the Midland Bank at Hayes, near where Frank Taylor built his first houses in the South in 1930. Without Billy those houses might never have been built: he had allowed Frank Taylor, whom he scarcely knew, an overdraft of £40 000 because he trusted him! The other old friend, Dr Barnet Solomons, had been the Group's medical adviser for more than twenty years. Dr Solomons had come to Britain in 1923, working his passage as ship's doctor, to woo and win an English girl he had met in his native Adelaide, Australia. He met and became a lifelong friend of Frank Taylor in 1935, initiating an occupational health scheme for senior executives. His adventurous and selfless character made him the kind of man likely to appeal to Frank Taylor; and he had an extra quality not always found in doctors – a belief that a patient's needs are spiritual and moral as much as physical.

Later that year came the news from America of the death at the age of 83 of Charles ('Chuck') Blitman, retired chairman of Blitman Construction Corporation, with whom the Group had been associated since 1966. And in December the sudden death, aged only 54, of George Phimister, managing director of Greenham Concrete Ltd., deprived the Greenham Group of one of its most energetic personalities. Among many achievements of his 23 years' service were the building up of the Sand and Ballast company and his pioneering of the design of gravel processing equipment.

From many retirements we must single out Harold McCue, parent board director and chairman of both Taylor Woodrow Industrial Estates and Taylor Woodrow (Arcon), who retired in 1974; and Tom Reeves, director of Taylor Woodrow Construction, who retired in 1971. Harold McCue had joined

Taylor Woodrow in 1940 as general foreman to build Admiralty offices in Malvern, was in charge of supplies for airfield construction for the American Army, and was general manager of the post-war prefabricated housing programme. Tom Reeves joined as a carpenter in 1943 and worked on Thames-side on the famous concrete caissons for the Mulberry Ports while bombs fell all around. Eight years later he was agent in charge of a £1 million contract at London Airport, and went on to direct the building of Calder Hall nuclear power station and many other large contracts.

In March 1973 the Vice-Chancellor of Salford University (twelve miles from Hadfield, Frank Taylor's birthplace) had asked him to accept the honorary degree of Doctor of Science 'in recognition of your outstanding achievements'. The Chancellor of Salford University is the Duke of Edinburgh, who, on degree day the following June, invested Frank Taylor with his Doctorate. Salford has a Department of Civil Engineering, whose head, Professor R. A. Burgess, said of him: 'Many of the technological advances for which he has been responsible result from his understanding of the need to blend academic and practical expertise – the brick with the mortarboard.' And as the first day of 1974 dawned, the day of his stepping down from the chairmanship, the New Year Honours List announced the knighthood of Frank Taylor, a tribute to one of the outstanding personalities of the industry, and – as Sir Frank himself predictably said – to 'the Taylor Woodrow team of people'.

All through 1974 there was a smell of oil in the air. In March, Taylor Woodrow formed an association with Santa Fé-Pomeroy Services Inc. of America which secured a contract to assist in the management of the design and construction of the enormous platform for Burmah Oil's Thistle oilfield in the North Sea. The total value of the project was over £250 million. (We shall have more to say about

Thistle in Chapter III.) The Taywood-Santa Fé team included a number of engineers from Taylor Woodrow's expanding mechanical, electrical and process division. And on the west coast of Scotland, Taylor Woodrow were, with John Mowlem, seeking sites for the construction of Condeep platforms, and having difficulties with planning permissions.

The big disappointment of the year was the Government decision to abandon the Channel Tunnel project. The tunnel, discussed and rejected many times during the last 125 years, had been hated by the old Duke of Wellington, who feared invasions of perfidious Frenchmen under the Channel, and it was as if his malign ghost stood gleefully by. The decision once again to abandon it came after Taylor Woodrow as members of a joint venture with Balfour Beatty, Edward Nuttall, and Guy F. Atkinson, tunnelling experts all, had had a very active year of work on Phase II, and on the very day after the new tunnelling machine was ready to make its first trials. That magnificent machine, known as the Mole, is still there, about 300 yards under the seabed, never likely to see the chance to work again. But in November the late Anthony Crosland, Minister for the Environment, announced the abandonment of British Rail's high-speed rail link from the tunnel to London, which meant an indefinite postponement of the 'Chunnel'. Rio Tinto Zinc Development Enterprises, the project managers, looking at the grim cost, withdrew. 'Once again,' said *The Sunday Times* bitterly, 'we put off what is arguably the most beneficial single project since the war because we do not have the wit to grasp an opportunity when it is there.' Taylor Woodrow had at least demonstrated that it can be done; and they have faith that one day it will be done.

At Hampstead, one of Taylor Woodrow's many hospital projects, the first phase of the Royal Free, with fifteen storeys and 871 beds, was opened and received its first patients in

October 1974; and the Maternity Unit's first baby, a boy, Salil Shenoy, was born on 25 February 1975. Ray Budd, site agent on the next phase of the contract, presented a bouquet to Salil's mother, Mrs Kundra Shenoy.

In Australia, despite increasingly difficult inflationary conditions, Taylor Woodrow International completed a complex unique to Australia, the multi-purpose 'Channel 7' Edgley entertainment centre in Perth which seats over 8 000 people; and in Toronto, the Monarch Group opened their new Chartwell Shopping Centre, their fourth in Canada, where they achieved a record year and were 'cautiously optimistic' about the future.

Iraq, Lebanon, Malaysia, Gibraltar – work in all these and other countries was going ahead; but the emphasis on the oil countries was growing. In Dubai, an 80-kilometre road was built across the Oman Peninsula for transporting more than a million tons of aggregate from quarries in the interior; and in Oman itself Taylor Woodrow-Towell were refurbishing historic buildings in the ancient walled city of Muscat, and carrying out a host of other tasks for the Sultan. Down south in Dhofar they were working on road and water supply systems, sea defence works, and irrigation and farming projects, beside government housing, military camps and – significant step in bringing Oman into the twentieth century – a television studio. Near Muscat, a new township containing over a thousand homes was growing up, called, after the Sultan, Medinat Qaboos (*medinat* means 'city').

Six hundred miles south of Muscat, a new harbour at Risut, Salalah, had been completed and, because sea conditions are treacherous during the monsoon (June to October) other work at Salalah was being supplied with everything from spare parts to high-quality furniture by airlift from Britain. And in Dubai, the Ruler entrusted the Costain-Taylor Woodrow Joint Venture with further work – nothing less than the £120 million extension of his other docks, Port Rashid, work on which began in early 1976.

At Windscale, in Cumbria, Taylor Woodrow Construction were about to start work on a number of projects associated with the reprocessing of nuclear fuel, being responsible for design, management, and supervision of construction; and at Rosyth, Scotland, they were building a £4 million high-pressure test chamber following research and development work for the Naval Construction Research Establishment.

Because construction companies are accustomed to moving earth, Taylor Woodrow have over the years done a lot of opencast coal mining, especially in South Wales, where, in 1975, they secured a £17 million order from the National Coal Board to recover coal over five years at their Trecatty site. In total contrast at Southgate, North London, Myton Ltd. was engaged in the refurbishment of the historic Northmet House – a typical careful yet rapid transformation of a minor stately home into 55 000 square feet of modern office accommodation for the Legal and General Assurance Society. We shall examine the special refurbishment skills of Myton in Chapter XII.

Overseas work included, in Jordan, new plant at El Hasa Mine for the Jordan Phosphate Mines Company; in Ghana, a £6.4 million contract for the huge (6 000 acre) Tono irrigation project. And for the Thistle North Sea Field a management team of 500 people had progressed the scheme to the point where it was possible to look forward to the floating out of the jacket in mid–1976 or shortly after, and to getting the rig into oil production by mid-1977. It should perhaps be explained that the 'jacket' in question is a steel structure nearly twice as high as St. Paul's Cathedral which forms the 'legs' of an oil-rig. A vital phase of the project was the accurate placement in the North Sea. It had to be

towed 465 miles from Graythorp, near Hartlepool. Weather
conditions were a vital factor in the float-out, and fortunately
it was calm on 10 August 1976. We will describe this
operation in Chapter III. The Greenham Group, too, were
now gearing their plant-hire services to North Sea oil and to
both on- and off-shore petro-chemical industries in Europe
and Scandinavia.

In Oman, Taylor Woodrow's 'Teamwork' symbol was
to be seen everywhere around Muscat and Salalah, and fresh
tasks of all sizes were pouring in, from blocks of offices,
shops, and flats in the capital to piped water supplies in the
mountainous northern peninsula. By now Taylor Woodrow
was referred to by Omanis simply as 'the Company'.
It is almost true to say that anyone whose roof leaked or
whose backyard well ran dry wanted to send for 'the
Company'. In October 1975 Sir Frank Taylor had made his
first visit to Oman, and been received in audience by His
Majesty Sultan Qaboos bin Said. On the same visit Haji
Ali Sultan, managing director of 'the Company's' partners
in Oman, W. J. Towell & Co., presented him with a *Khunjar*
or ceremonial dagger. By now 'the Company' was using
TWINGS, its own light aircraft service for transporting
personnel and light stores from site to site across hundreds
of miles of desert where there is neither road nor rail.

When Taylor Woodrow form a company called 'Teamwork Something' you know that they have found the right
local partner in a country; so that the formation of 'Teamwork Saudi Arabia' with Ali Zaid Al Quraishi Bros. in 1976
was quickly followed by contracts to build a warehouse, an
assembly plant, and an apartment block in the Dammam
area, where a base had been set up, and further work around
the capital, Riyadh.

What is the biggest civil engineering contract in the United
Kingdom? Not a power station, not a dry-dock complex,

not a whole city centre but a contract worth more than £130 million at Butterwell, near Morpeth, Northumberland, for the opencast mining, over ten years, of twelve million tons of coal. Work began in April 1976. This immense project is a vital factor in the nation's fuel supply, and is providing employment for 590 people from the surrounding district. Eventually the area will be landscaped and restored to fertile green fields again. So solicitous were Taylor Woodrow for the comfort of local people that they built 'baffle mounds' between the site and surrounding villages (one of which has the charming biblical name of Hebron) to lessen the noise of earth-moving equipment such as 'Big Geordie', a 2 850-ton Bucyrus Erie 1 550 walking drag-line, which can shift 4 000 tons an hour.

It was in 1976 that unimpeded traffic again flowed at Staples Corner. It had never really stopped; but Taylor Woodrow had to endure a certain amount of ribbing from the B.B.C. and cursing motorists never really understood the huge technical difficulties involved: to them, it was just more spaghetti. The smooth co-operation between the TW design team and consulting engineers, backed by the Research Laboratories at Southall, where computerized analysis programmes worked out the stresses to be borne by each span of the deck of the A.406 flyover as it crossed both road and rail, was so good that without it the job would have taken much longer.

Longer still (though not in the construction of it) was the birth of Queen Anne's Mansions, a new and instantly recognizable landmark in Westminster, overlooking St James's Park, designed by Fitzroy Robinson & Partners in consultation with the late Sir Basil Spence, built by Taylor Woodrow Construction for The Land Securities Investment Trust, and occupied by a government department. As long ago as 1959 the former London County Council had looked

disapprovingly at the original Queen Anne's Mansions, a
12-storey edifice whose sole distinction was that it was the
biggest brick building in England. Queen Victoria, whose
view from nearby Buckingham Palace had been blocked by
it, had disliked it. The new design, approved by the Royal
Fine Arts Commission, had been delayed by long discussions
among interested parties (some of them preservationist)
about whether planning permission should be given for
redevelopment as an office block. Taylor Woodrow at last
moved in in 1971, the structure was virtually complete
by August 1975, and the fitting out was finished early in
1977. The specialized skills of Jonathan James Ltd. were used
in the fibrous plaster castings to encase some of the service
pipes. The lucky civil servants who work here are among
columns and walls of Roman stone marble, use staircases
clad in Sicilian pearl marble, walk upon floors of St Louis
granite, look out upon the Queen's back garden from bronze-
finished aluminium windows, double-glazed to suit the
air-conditioning system and, when in need of refreshment,
ascend to the tenth-floor restaurant which affords magnificent
views across London. No wonder Queen Anne's Mansions
is known as 'the QE2 of Land Securities': a graceful 3-wing
11-storey block linked to an octagonal tower block of fourteen
storeys by a 9-storey building.

And just by way of contrast, among their many contracts in Singapore, Taylor Woodrow International in the
autumn of 1976 built a new convent, chapel, and car-park
for the Franciscan Missionaries of the Divine Motherhood:
of the many ecclesiastical buildings they have constructed,
this was the first *octagonal* chapel on record. But it was not
their first task for the Franciscan Missionaries, with whom
they were associated some years ago in the building of the
Mount Miriam Hospital in Penang.

As 1976 drew to a close, the construction industry at home

seemed beset with problems, yet – given freedom of action – well able to deal with them. In July, the chairman of the Labour Party's special sub-committee working on a policy for the industry, was believed to be planning the nationalization of the twelve leading construction companies and plant hire firms in Britain. This, of course, would include both Taylor Woodrow and its Greenham companies. No sane person in any efficient and successful construction company believes this is either desirable or workable. In a January 1977 interview, Dick Puttick, reminding everyone of the facts that the Group had had a series of sixteen 'record years', that lean times at home meant seeking still more work abroad, and that Taylor Woodrow International had almost doubled its turnover every year since 1970, said: 'We expect to see some improvement in the U.K. in 1978 and thereafter arising from the impact of North Sea oil on our economy. Overseas there are many opportunities for the future, and Taylor Woodrow is one of the very few companies with the resources and the experience and the team to be able to take advantage of those opportunities.'

Which, of all the projects undertaken by the Group, did he find the most exciting? Perhaps surprisingly, he answered: 'The important part we played in constructing some of the floating concrete units for the Mulberry Harbours during World War II.' Why did he choose an example from so long ago? Because the need to fight never stops. 'In 1944 we were fighting for our country's survival. Today, albeit on the economic front, we are still fighting for our freedom.'

III

Sources of Energy

AUGUST 10, 1976 – a reasonably fine day and an unusually calm North Sea, especially that stretch of it which we now know as the Thistle Field. It is an area of ocean that maps of the British Isles do not normally show because it is nearer to Norway than it is to the Scottish mainland – 130 miles beyond the Shetland Islands, on the 61st parallel, a mere 5·3 degrees below the Arctic Circle. What was happening on that day was crucial to the success of a multi-million pound engineering project involving teams of specialists from the United States, Britain, and many other countries who for many months had been working towards this deadline day. The operation was the sinking into position on the seabed of the 34 000 tonne steel jacket of the Thistle 'A' oil production platform.

Among the hundreds of people anxiously waiting for news of this complex operation was a small group of engineers on a 'semi-submersible' rig about a mile and a half away. Among them were Frank Gibb, then deputy chairman and managing director of Taylor Woodrow Construction, and John Rogers, assistant managing director and co-ordinator of the proposals (prepared over Christmas 1973!) which had gained the contract for Taywood-Santa Fé, a joint venture formed between Taylor Woodrow and Santa Fé-Pomeroy Services Inc. of America. Together they had secured the contract to assist in the management of activities con-

The 1977 Queen's Award for Export Achievement presentation.

Seen from the air – the Southall headquarters complex.

Burne House Telecommunications Centre in Marylebone.

This council chamber is part of the Royal Borough of Kensington and Chelsea's new town hall complex opened by H.R.H. The Princess Anne on 31 May 1977.

Eagle Centre, a comprehensive shopping and office development in Derby.

Part of the Sedgeletch Water Pollution Control Works at
Houghton-le-Spring, Co. Durham.

The modern design of the new extension complements the existing
granite Town House in Aberdeen.

Courage Brewery, Bermondsey.

Motor-cycle factory, Jakarta, Indonesia.

Asphalt laying in Nigeria where new and improved roads are needed to help meet the country's transportation needs.

The Panorama Memorial Building under construction in Baghdad.

One of six multilateral schools in rural Guyana – a typical project management contract.

Three-mile access link between the mainland of Western Australia and Garden Island.

March 1974 – Sir Frank and Lady Taylor with their daughter Sarah on their way to Buckingham Palace for the conferment of the Order of Knighthood on Sir Frank.

Cartoon: Courtesy of the *Yorkshire Post*, who published it to illustrate their announcement of Lady Taylor's appointment.

April 1976 – Lady Taylor, with fellow parent board members.

nected with the development of the Thistle oilfield for the Thistle Partnership, for whom Burmah Oil Developments Ltd. were the operators before the British National Oil Corporation took over. Thus Taylor Woodrow were deeply – in all senses of the word – involved in North Sea Oil, where the ultimate value of BNOC's project was more than £600 million.

The semi-submersible rig from which Frank Gibb, John Rogers and others were watching the crucial manœuvre – the slow delicate uprighting of an enormous structure through three rotations, down through the water to a safe and accurate placing on the seabed – is a sort of floating hotel for off-shore personnel containing workshops and living quarters on three decks, with a 'helipad' for commuting to and from the mainland.

In the previous chapter we said that the Thistle 'A' jacket, 630 feet high, is nearly twice the height of St Paul's Cathedral, the cross on top of which is 365 feet above the ground. Another way of picturing the size of this structure is to imagine it beside the 620-foot high Post Office Tower. It is also nearly three-quarters the height of the Rockefeller Centre in New York. It has to be, because it is located in the deepest area (530 feet) so far exploited by any North Sea operation where it must be able to withstand '100-year storm' conditions, 90-foot waves, and wind gusts of up to 152 m.p.h. And its construction was achieved in a year's less time than is normally possible from drawing board to installation.

The actual uprighting, on that August afternoon, took from 14·40 hrs. to 18·18 hrs. – 3 hours 38 minutes of anxiety. (The scheduled time was four hours.) 'If our planning hadn't thought of everything in advance,' says John Rogers, 'we could have lost the lot.' Meaning 200 million dollars worth.

Thistle 'A' Field – which is expected to be producing by

the time you read these words and will eventually yield at least 200 000 barrels of oil a day out of its total estimated reserves of 550 million barrels, delivered by Brent pipeline to the Sullom Voe terminal in the Shetlands – claims many advances in technology. None of these is greater than the ways in which the jacket was built, assembled, towed out 465 miles to sea, and sunk into position. Don Shimmon, managing director of Burmah Oil Development, has been quoted as saying that 'the installation of the platform was similar in complexity, scheduling and reliability to that required for a moon-shot'. There had to be a fail-safe mechanism for every stage, an immediate alternative to anything that went wrong. It is thus no coincidence that Santa Fé International, which in less than twenty years has acquired eighty-one rigs drilling for oil around the world, appointed Les Bitner as project manager with Taylor Woodrow's Gordon Fordyce as his deputy. Les Bitner spent ten years with Boeing of America in the development of complex aerospace systems for the Titan, Polaris, and other programmes. So twenty-two men from Boeing came to Britain to study how to use remote control, digital command and simulation techniques in the Thistle operation.

Among other things, it was important to ensure that the jacket (which eventually weighed nearly 35 000 tons) could be floated; that the steel was not thicker than it needed to be; and that the $2 million dollars worth of sensitive electronic equipment used to control the structure's descent to the sea-bed should know exactly what it had to handle. Among the many firms contributing their expertise to this operation was a consortium of British companies called Seatek who specialize in the deployment of offshore platforms. One of their members is EMI Electronics, who were able to use a computer for monitoring data, and used the five-day tow-out from the Graythorp yard on Teesside to monitor the platform systems continuously through a radio link to one of the towing vessels.

The buoyancy of the Thistle jacket was such that it could be floated out in a horizontal position. Then, by a controlled 'ballasting sequence', it slowly assumed the right attitude to stand vertically on the seabed. The uprighting team were in a 'remote control module' on the 36 000-ton derrick ship *Orca*. This, in turn, was linked to the 'tower placement control module' fixed to the structure itself. Command signals were transmitted from the first to the second, activating the control valves. The two modules were linked by two radio channels (one to back up the other in case of failure) and an 'umbilical cable' and manual control system in case all else failed.

The thirty-foot-diameter 'legs' of the structure and two 9 000 cubic feet empty crude oil storage tanks were gradually filled with water so that, 'untouched by human hand', the huge structure did what it was told to do. As the first compartments began to fill, the centre of buoyancy moved towards the top of the tower, and the tower rotated until the small legs contacted the water. It then rotated again on its vertical axis as the compartments continued to fill. After a third rotation it assumed a stable position but still at an angle. More compartments were filled with sea water and the structure became vertical while still about thirty feet from the bottom. The final landing was accomplished by continuing to fill the oil storage tanks and 'small leg' compartments until the jacket was firmly on the bottom.

The safety and reliability of the whole operation depended very much on experiments with models – both physical and mathematical – and simulation techniques. The Taywood-Santa Fé radio control team, including specialists from other companies, were trained for three months in a simulator at EMI's Feltham works. There were simulated tank tests in

America and Holland, using a one-48th scale physical model, checked by a mathematical model. Parts of the model were broken down and sent to the seventy-five major manufacturers all over Europe who were making the jacket components so that they could see the role of the section they were making. The Taywood-Santa Fé systems team, including Boeing's people made a simulation model of the control panel with a small computer, and fed every conceivable situation into it, including a deliberate mistake – 'suppose we flooded the wrong tank'. 'We even,' said one 'simulated the whole tower capsizing.'

Every little task was entered on a huge 'flow-chart' of activities – people, materials, ships, who says what to whom and when. 'The documentation was like nothing anyone had ever seen before,' says John Rogers. 'There were fifteen volumes of manuals complete with emergency procedures. No wonder the planning took eighteen months!' It is generally reckoned that by 'catching the North Sea weather window' on that August afternoon instead of having to wait until after the winter, many millions of dollars which would otherwise have gone in lost production time were saved.

Some idea of the project management services task Taywood-Santa Fé faced can be gained by looking at facts and figures. There were 45 'job sites' in Europe making 103 nodes (points in a framed structure where several members meet) ranging in weight from 10 to 850 tons. Some of them had 12 tubes in junction. Lose just one of them, and the whole operation is delayed. If there was the slightest possibility of any manufacturer falling down on a job, it was no use sitting in an office hoping that things would improve. 'It happened on a number of sites, for instance an 800-ton fabrication in Belgium,' Gordon Fordyce says. 'So we got alongside him at once. One of our senior management team like Alan Grimmett, got on a plane so that the next morning we were in their yard and could make a judgment.' Fabricators were working with high-grade steels with strict welding procedures in which defects were not to be tolerated.

Taywood-Santa Fé surveyed over sixty-five manufacturers before orders were placed, finally choosing forty different sites in Britain, France, Belgium, Holland, and Germany. Fifteen temporary foundation installation modules were built at Amsterdam, Vlissingen, Algeciras, East Anglia, and Nigg, Scotland. Twenty-one permanent oil production modules were built at Wallsend, King's Lynn, St Wandrille, Cadiz, and Almeria: all these are installed on top of the jacket. Taywood-Santa Fé bought more than £300 million worth of equipment, steel, and other materials, and expedited its delivery to fifty-five places in seven countries in 3 000 separate shipments. They included steel sections, pipe, valves, fittings, electrical components, instruments, chemicals, and oil processing equipment. Sixty per cent of these were supplied by the United Kingdom, 20 per cent from E.E.C. countries, 3 per cent from the rest of Europe, 15 per cent from Japan.

Breaking down the total responsibility into activities, project management looks like this: Planning. Engineering coordination. Procurement. Materials control. Construction management. Systems Engineering. Inspection and quality assurance. Jacket towing out and placement. Cost control; budget preparation; cash forecasting; and accounting.

In programming the work more than 150 critical-path network drawings were developed and 20 000 specific activities monitored. Working back from the 1977 target date for the start of oil production, Taywood-Santa Fé developed a master plan scheduling the 'milestones', the key points of the whole operation. There was an all-important management tool known as 'Project 2', a computer programme monitoring the progress of module and jacket fabrication. Every three weeks, planners updated the computer information to reflect the current situation at each construction site and help to forecast problem areas. Another key to success was a second computer programme called Promap. Promap provided a probability report on all variable factors to show the most optimistic, most pessimistic, and most probable completion date.

The engineering control group coordinated some 8 500 design drawings and 1 000 specifications and distributed them (helped by a computer) to fabrication sites. Many of the specialist engineers came from Taylor Woodrow's mechanical, electrical, and process division. Although the final assembly of the jacket took place at Graythorp, there were a further twenty-four sub-assembly sites as well. Thirteen other sites were used for assembling the production modules for the platform. The placement of the jacket required fifty-four valves, forty-two ballasting sensing instruments, ten miles of electrical cable, and 100 miles of hydraulic control lines. In the later phases of the project, the accounting team processed more than 2 800 invoices a month, and paid out $1 million a day in up to fourteen currencies. Thistle 'A' was also fairly expensive in people: the peak demand, in the months just before the float-out, was 620 people, of whom 35 were Santa Fé and 220 Taylor Woodrow. As Frank Gibb said later 'A lot of Taylor Woodrow people learned a lot and got a great deal out of the job. In the last few years this has been our major impact in the North Sea. Long after the jacket was placed we had people out there both above and below the water; people like Geoff Hopkinson who spent many weeks in a mini submarine on inspection work.'

Only a very large company or joint venture can afford the risk of being in the North Sea oil game if platforms are its chief business. In between platforms, how do you keep your highly-skilled workforce – sometimes many hundreds strong

-- in employment? If you are specialized, you must diversify; if you are already established across the world with a full order-book, you can probably absorb your team in other contracts.

Taywood-Santa Fé, now a limited company, are convinced that the Thistle approach to building, equipping, and placing fixed-platform oil-rigs is the right one for the immediate future, and they are offering development drilling services to other major North Sea oil companies. Off their own bat, Taylor Woodrow Construction, in an effort to expand British activity in this field, and with the knowledge of the Government's Offshore Supplies Office, have since announced a joint venture with Jebsen U.K. (the British branch of a Norwegian drilling company) to operate and manage the semi-submersible rigs *Sindbad* and *Aladdin* with responsibility for the entire marine, drilling, and supplies operation for the rigs, currently based on Aberdeen. Santa Fé Overseas Inc. will provide the drilling expertise and operate the rigs. *Sindbad* and *Aladdin*, each weighing 18 600 tonnes and accommodating a crew of seventy-seven, can operate in depths down to 650 feet.

So extensive and varied have Taylor Woodrow's activities in this field become that a new company, Taylor Woodrow Energy Ltd., has emerged to look after their interests in subsidiary and associated companies and joint ventures involved in energy-related work. Its brief, on formation in 1979, was to 'monitor the progress, provide appropriate management and support services, prepare long-term plans and help determine the future policy of the various companies. Also, to seek out and evaluate new activities, investment prospects and special projects. . . .'

In January 1978 Taylor Woodrow Construction joined forces with Seaforth Maritime Ltd. to form Seaforth Taywood Ltd., a company based in Aberdeen to provide offshore and onshore inspection, maintenance, repair and commissioning services to the oil and gas industry. Seaforth is a diversified offshore service company with an annual turnover of £16 million and a team of nearly 1 000. Formed in 1972 and with its headquarters in Aberdeen, Seaforth operates through three divisions, all of which provide services to the offshore oil and gas industries.

Six months later Seaforth Maritime became a member of the James Finlay Group concerned on an international scale with merchant banking, international confirming and financing, offshore energy services, overseas agencies, manufacturing and merchanting confectionery, beverage manufacturing, tea growing and international tea trading. As part of that deal Finlay sold 30 per cent of Seaforth to Taylor Woodrow Construction and John Wood Rogers, assistant managing director of T.W.C., became chairman of Seaforth, with Peter Gibson as deputy chairman.

In June 1979 T.W.C. bought a further 15 per cent of the ordinary share capital of Seaforth Maritime from Finlay under the terms of the previous year's agreement, increasing their holding to 45 per cent. A few weeks earlier, Seaforth was awarded a contract by Shell Expro for the design and construction supervision of a multi-functional service vessel (MSV). Under a second contract signed at the same time in London on 22 June, Seaforth will be responsible for the operational management of the vessel for a five-year period with an option for a further five years. The vessel's work will include underwater operations as well as routine maintenance, and emergency fire-fighting/rescue services should the need arise.

The MSV is a dynamically positioned semi-submersible vessel, 100m long by 66m wide, with a displacement of 22 000 tonnes. The contract has been won against major competition from U.S.A., Europe and the United Kingdom. During the course of the tender preparation and subsequent

negotiations Seaforth have been supported by Taylor Woodrow. Support will also be provided during the execution of
the contracts.

A contract for building the vessel has been agreed between
Seaforth Maritime and Rauma Repola with a value of
approximately £40 million. The vessel will be built in Fin-
land and Seaforth, people will be based there to supervise
construction.

Two additional supply vessels, the *Seaforth Victor* and
Seaforth Warrior have recently been acquired by Seaforth.
These 8 000 BHP vessels bring the present fleet to a total of
fourteen, which includes the dive support/fire fighting ship
Seaforth Clansman, presently on charter to the Royal Navy as
their principal diving operations and training vessel.

In the 'watershed year' of 1971, Taylor Woodrow, like
everyone else, were thinking of nuclear power as the way to
the future. The talk was all of AGR (advanced gas-cooled
reactor) versus Magnox (magnesium alloy used to contain the
uranium fuel), with AGR the clear favourite. By the beginning of 1975, the world was talking of an energy crisis.
Suddenly people were wondering uneasily (the OPEC
countries among them) 'Will the Oil Age end in thirty years
from now?' And a spendthrift British Government encouraged an improvident electorate to believe that North
Sea Oil was going to save their economic future. It seemed
sensible to look at alternative sources of energy, and in
Chapter IV we shall see what Taylor Woodrow are doing
in this direction. Meanwhile, whatever happened to the
rest of the power industry? On one side, critics warn of a
'power famine' if the Government does not soon produce a
nuclear policy; on the other, there are suggestions that we
are now over-supplied with power-stations whose cost is
escalating and that 'there may be no more nuclear power-
stations'.

Taylor Woodrow, we know, have been involved in the 'power game' since just after World War II. The first director with experience of power-stations was the late 'A.J.' Hill – and the first complete power-station contract was at West Ham in 1946. (It is interesting to note how many present top men in Taylor Woodrow cut their teeth on that contract: Dick Puttick, chairman of the Group; Frank Gibb, joint managing director of the Group and chairman and managing director of Taylor Woodrow Construction; Len Brooks, director, Taylor Woodrow Construction; Ron Matthews, joint deputy managing director, Taylor Woodrow Construction (Midlands); Peter Hodge, director, Taylor Woodrow International; Sandy Cheyne, director, Taylor Woodrow Construction; and a great veteran of the industry, and ex-director of Taylor Woodrow Construction, now retired, Tom Reeves.)

A number of new power-stations in the Midlands, others in London and the south, and twenty years of the 'power game' during which the company built nearly two dozen thermal, hydro-electric, diesel, and gas turbine stations as far afield as Canada, Trinidad, Nigeria, and Libya. The great landmark, of course, was Calder Hall in 1953 – the world's first full-scale nuclear power-station in Cumbria – a contract managed by a young engineer of twenty-nine named John Ballinger, whose sudden death in 1970 robbed the Group of one of its most brilliant leaders.

Calder Hall, built for the U.K. Atomic Energy Authority, led to the consortium principle for building nuclear power-stations for the Central Electricity Generating Board. By now, being in the big league of nuclear power-stations could mean having to spend £500 000 or more to prepare a tender. One of the first of these consortia, formed in 1955 to carry out the complete design, planning, construction, and equipment of nuclear power-stations, was the Atomic Power

Construction Co. Ltd., consisting of English Electric, Babcock & Wilcox, and Taylor Woodrow. Its name was afterwards changed to British Nuclear Design & Construction Ltd., and it has now become part of British Nuclear Associates. It eventually won a contract in 1957 for Hinkley Point 'A' in Somerset whose planned output was 500 megawatt and another in 1961 for Sizewell in Suffolk (580 megawatt).

The heart of a nuclear reactor is the pressure vessel. At Hinkley and Sizewell the vessels were made of three- and four-inch thick steel, which presented both a transportation and a welding problem. In 1960 a French engineer built an experimental pressure vessel of prestressed concrete. When a new nuclear power-station at Wylfa, Anglesey, was being planned in 1962-4 for an output of 1 180 megawatt, Taylor Woodrow designed for it the world's first spherical prestressed concrete pressure vessels of a minimum thickness of eleven feet. The prestressing operation took almost a year and consumed 3 000 miles of high-tensile steel wire.

Nuclear power-stations at Hartlepool and Heysham (both of 1 250 megawatt capacity) followed, but their operation has been delayed for reasons which will be seen. They have an unusual feature, cylindrical 'podded boiler' pressure vessels which are stressed by winding multiple layers of pre-tensioned steel wire round the curved surface – 'the cotton reel instead of the golf-ball', as one observer described it; the advantage being that, theoretically, the boilers inside can be removed for maintenance. The Hartlepool and Heysham vessels have been developed to their present state against a continuous background of structural and materials research, including model tests of whole vessels, and tests of model end caps only, together with full programmes of investigation into concrete properties. All these reactors are sited near the sea because they need vast quantities of water for cooling

(Sizewell, for example, uses 27 million gallons an hour!) In 1965 came another nuclear contract, the prototype 'fast reactor' at Dounreay, Caithness.

That a massive nuclear power station need not be a blot on the landscape was demonstrated by the commendation given in 1973 by the *Financial Times* Architecture Award, whose report on Wylfa praised 'an unusually sensitive approach in a coastal landscape of great beauty... These huge buildings have a unity and simplicity that somehow relates them to the landscape, aided by the muted use of colour and imaginative form. . . . The project is noteworthy for the heroic scale of its landscaping.'

Taylor Woodrow's nuclear know-how is sometimes exported. Since 1971 they have been retained by Hochtemperatur Reaktorbau GmbH, (H.R.B. German Nuclear Company) as engineering consultants for the design and construction of prestressed concrete pressure vessels for gas-cooled reactors. This work is now carried out by a new (1973) subsidiary, Taywood Engineering Ltd. H.R.B.'s 300-megawatt helium-cooled reactor at Schmehausen in the East Ruhr has a 'pebble bed' using encapsulated fuel about the size of billiard balls. Taywood Engineering is also helping to develop a new kind of reactor, backed by the German Government, using hot helium to drive a gas turbine, thus eliminating the usual steam cycle from the circuit. This involves both the laboratories and the design divisions at Southall, and Taywood Engineering's Dr Malcolm Horner spent a considerable period in residence at H.R.B.'s offices at Mannheim.

In Britain, nuclear energy is now in a situation which has been described as both crisis and stalemate. The general public is uneasy about it, especially about the reprocessing of nuclear waste at Windscale, Cumbria, where Taylor Woodrow has about sixty members of its mechanical, electrical, and process division helping on design. Frank Gibb, chairman and managing director of Taylor Woodrow Construction, sits on both of the principal bodies that spend their lives thinking about the nuclear future – British Nuclear Associates (a consortium of which Taylor Woodrow is a member, on which Frank Gibb represents shareholders) and the National Nuclear Corporation, centred on General Electric (of which he is an independent member in his own right). His predecessor in these posts, the late A. J. Hill, said, 'I think the safety argument is small compared to the environmental problem. We have to consider, too, that the demand for *all* electric power may be decreasing and may go on doing so until about 1982 – even conventional power stations may be included in this trend. Yet nuclear power must play its part somehow, so we have got to be prepared.'

The views of Reg Taylor, director of Taylor Woodrow Construction who has been closely concerned with pressure vessel design, are similar: 'The world needs nuclear energy, but it has got to be made safe. We have designed equipment to *make* it safe.'

For some years there was a controversy about which design of nuclear reactor should be chosen for the next nuclear programme. The British advanced gas-cooled reactor (AGR), installed at five stations, went out of favour and the Central Electricity Generating Board seemed to prefer American designs. Then, early in 1977, it looked as if the AGR was staging a dramatic comeback and with energy supply problems causing increasing concern world-wide, nuclear power now seems back in fashion. In April 1979 Taylor Woodrow Construction took on another contract at Heysham – for the preliminary works of stage 2, another 1 200 MW AGR station to be built beside the first.

Meanwhile there has been much delay at Heysham and Hartlepool. 'We're disappointed, of course,' says Reg Taylor, 'but the plant has to work for twenty to thirty years, so it had better be safe.' Taylor Woodrow changed their original designs in mid-construction to satisfy the increasingly stringent criteria of the Nuclear Inspectorate, a new Government statutory body – for example, the closures of the pressure vessels are of wire-wound concrete instead of steel, utilizing the company's existing technology to add the piece of string to the belt and braces already in use.

While North Sea oil and nuclear power dominate the headlines, we tend to forget the fuel we have known all our lives. It is almost a relief to turn to a fuel we do not have to import, supplies of which may long outlast those of oil. The cheapest coal, obviously, is that which is nearest to the surface. Because construction companies can easily mobilize heavy earth-moving machinery, they are equipped to mine opencast coal. Taylor Woodrow have been doing this since the start of Britain's opencast coal mining programmes in 1942. Pwll-Dhu, near Blaenavon, South Wales, is remembered by many Taylor Woodrow people as one of the roughest and dirtiest introductions to civil engineering it is possible to have, especially in the winter.

Opencast mining seldom attracts publicity beyond its immediate environment, but it goes quietly and profitably on, yielding coal at about half the cost of the pit-mined product – and the equipment and techniques grow more sophisticated year by year. At Rhymney, Glamorgan, 400 000 tons of coal had been won by the end of 1973, and a few miles away, at Dowlais, the Royal Arms Group site had yielded $3\frac{1}{4}$ million tons over a fifteen-year period. Opencast mining, like quarrying for gravel, creates temporary chaos and ugliness, but the National Coal Board is rigorous about the restoration of land after coal removal. The valleys *are* becoming green again. And, just a few miles from Dowlais at Trecatty, Taylor Woodrow are recovering coal, washing it on site and transporting it to the Cwm Bargoed Disposal Point. To get at the coal, a road through the site has had to be diverted and 1·3 miles of new road constructed. Including restoration, the work, which is expected to yield a million tons of coal, will take about five years.

Multiply all this by twelve, and you can visualize the size of what is not only the largest opencast contract, but the largest civil engineering contract of any kind in the United Kingdom. It is at Butterwell, Northumberland, where, as at Trecatty, Sandy Cheyne is the director in charge. In July 1976 two huge 7·65-cubic metre hydraulic excavators appeared with their attendant dump trucks, and began to remove the stiff clay drift which is the first layer covering the coal. In this twelve-year contract, yielding a million tons a year, you have to remove thirty tons of rock and overburden to get at every ton of coal. Those excavators, whose every 'bite' is ten cubic yards, have been imported from America and cost £900 000 each. They were joined, in November 1976, by four Marion electric face shovels with the same bucket capacity – 12½ tons – which can shift 625 tons of rock per hour (rock in this case meaning mostly sandstone). Each machine, it is reckoned, deals with three million tons a year. They work day and night in three eight-hour shifts, and a single eight-hour shift on Sunday. Standing 12·7 metres high and 18·29 metres long, they look like primeval monsters. Excavation continues at all hours, but coal is loaded only in daylight: it is screened, washed, and sent to the National Coal Board for distribution.

Nine of the forty dump trucks are Caterpillar Triple Sevens. These American machines weigh fifty-five tons and carry an eighty-five-ton load. The floor of the driver's cab is ten feet above ground, and its fuel tank holds 265 gallons. Its wheels are twice as high as a man and each tyre costs £5 000. A tyre lasts 3 000 hours, which represents about nine months' work. Biggest animal of all is a 1550 Bucyrus Erie 'walking dragline' known as 'Big Geordie', hired for Taylor Woodrow by the National Coal Board. As distinct from a 'shovel' (which digs the coal face and has only a short reach) it cuts and slews as it strips the overburden. Explosives and rotary drilling machines are also used to get to the coal seams, which vary in thickness from eight inches to one yard and are nearly parallel to the surface.

There is £18 million worth of machinery here, and those machines which are powered by electricity need a 60 000-volt supply. Obviously all this equipment (much of it supplied by Taylor Woodrow Plant Company) needs work-shops for repairs, welding, and general maintenance. The buckets are easily damaged by abrasive rock. Since some of the vehicle engines are worth £20 000 each, it is wise to catch signs of breakdown early: for example, a spectrometer can give early warning of oil contamination. There are special Taymech service vehicles, designed and built for Taylor Woodrow Plant, equipped for high-speed fuelling. Work-shops and stores buildings have been supplied by Arcon, and permanent site offices have been designed and built by Swiftplan: they include a canteen, changing-room, and car-parks.

The impact of all this on a country community can be imagined. The landscape has had to be temporarily rearranged. The construction of a private coal haul road necessitates three bridges and an underpass. A brook has been diverted, and so has a water main. On the credit side, it is reckoned that about 590 local men (in an area of high unemployment) are being kept in work, bringing in an annual cash-flow of some £2½ million, with a further £1 million by way of locally placed orders.

Taylor Woodrow (who after all invented the Pilemaster 'silent piledriver') have done all that is humanly possible about the noise problem. This is why landscaping began long before the coal seams were reached: baffle-mounds, deliberately irregular in shape to simulate rolling meadowland, are seeded with grass and will eventually be planted with trees; and a reservoir is being made at Blubbery Farm, near the local village of Hebron to provide a regular supply of water for dust laying; it will be stocked with fish and, it is hoped, used for canoeing and sailing. The Taylor Woodrow people on site have become an integrated friendly part of the community, identifying themselves with local life through the Butterwell Charity Association, children's homes, old people's centres, and the Women's Institute. And when, in about ten year's time, these twenty-three acres of mining are carefully restored to agricultural land, better drained and possibly more fertile than it was before, the grandchildren of today's young married couples at Hebron may never know that industry was ever here.

IV

Design, Research and Development

PINNED to the wall of Reg Taylor's office in Taywood House, Southall, is a rough sketch which looks like a doodle but is really a system of thought. It shows an inner circle, two outer circles, and a strange fuzzy shape by itself in one corner. The strange shape is the concept, the end-product of an invention. The inner circle represents logical thinking (in which some people are imprisoned all their lives), the area round it is intuition. What this diagram means is that the solution to a problem in civil engineering is not arrived at by logic alone: there has to be imagination, even a streak of madness. . . . This blend of logic and intuition is very much a part of Taylor Woodrow: we have seen it in the mind of Frank Taylor himself, and in the tribute paid to him by Professor Burgess of Salford University – that he had successfully combined 'the brick with the mortarboard'.

'I'm always encouraged,' says Reg Taylor, inventive director of Taylor Woodrow Construction, 'by people who say, of something I've designed, "It'll never work!" Then I know I'm on the right track.'

We began the previous chapter with an account of one of the world's largest and most extraordinary engineering feats, the assembly and uprighting of the Thistle 'A' jacket in the North Sea. However you estimate the cost of it, you are stuck with a figure something like £250 million. This is the sort of fact that sets Reg Taylor thinking: 'There *must* be a simpler and cheaper way of getting oil out of the seabed!'

The first-ever extraction of offshore oil and gas happened in the shallow and benign waters of the Gulf of Mexico. There is believed to be huge reservoirs of oil under the seas, once the continental shelves have been left behind, but it is at much greater – at present un-get-at-able – depths. This may be true of the North Sea, which, however, is *not* benign ('benign' in this context means 'small waves'). 'At present, in the North Sea, we are dealing with depths of up to about 600 feet,' Reg Taylor says. 'And the water is extremely rough. So the cost of structures goes up dramatically; so much so that it could eventually make it uneconomic to drill at all unless we can find cheaper ways.' Cheaper systems could also make it economic to drill in smaller fields – at present the world can afford to recover oil only from the biggest reservoirs. So Reg Taylor sees a burning need for new systems, able to reach greater depths at less expense. Huge steel jackets, very expensive, take too long to assemble.

'It's better, as in life, to *give* a little!' Reg Taylor smiles. Why should not a submarine structure with a platform on top be, at least to some degree, flexible? Why should it not be made of a less expensive material in which Taylor Woodrow are past-masters, concrete? Why should we not use our nuclear power-station experience of spherical concrete vessels, capable of withstanding great pressures, to design a chamber on the seabed in which people could work? How to attach the column to its base so that it remains flexible? The conventional solution to this is a ball-and-socket joint. But joints need maintenance and lubrication. Intuition, with perhaps a dash of brilliance, suggests tendons of an enormously strong synthetic called Parafill, originally developed by I.C.I. for mooring communication buoys in mid-Atlantic comparable to high-tensile steel but much more flexible.

Such a structure is both articulated and flexible, and could be built in either concrete or steel. The undersea chamber could be reached by lift through the column, like 'going down the mine', to inspect it once or twice a month.

The principal economy derives from the *flexibility* more than from the material used, and the whole rig would weigh between 30 000 and 40 000 tonnes.

Taylor Woodrow have been intensively researching the offshore engineering field since 1970. They even bought a site in shallow water off north-east Scotland, and experimented with concrete structures surmounted by a steel deck. In 1974 the E.E.C. advertised its willingness to provide grants for research and development into devices for 'recovering offshore hydrocarbons', provided that research organizations taking part also put up some of the money. Taylor Woodrow, who already had designs for concrete gravity platforms, applied for and were assured of £1 875 000 for the first phase (two years) of a project which would eventually produce structures capable of operating at depths of 500 metres or more.

One result of all this is a structure called Arcolprod, with related creatures whose names are Arcolstar, Arcolflare, Substor, and several varieties of Subprod. Arcolprod can be developed and varied to suit the requirements of different oil companies: it is described as an 'articulating buoyant column production and storage system'. The 'telescoped' form of construction gives stability in towing it out to location, so that the installation is less dependent on good weather: you do not even have to know the water depth accurately until comparatively late in construction. At least 10 000 tons of plant and equipment can be installed on the deck before tow-out. Arcolprod can be adapted so that it can provide a buffer oil store. Among the fascinating ideas Taylor Woodrow are testing is the possibility that the whole column could be detached and floated away for the winter, leaving the chamber on the seabed, and brought back for reconnection in the spring; or that it could be used for recovering oil and gas from ice-infested waters (pack-ice fifty feet thick can travel at about three knots!). In the early days of North Sea oil-rigs, Taylor Woodrow did design some fixed concrete platforms, but so far they have had no takers. Oil companies appear to prefer steel platforms – again, *so far*; but in moments of great optimism Taylor Woodrow people tend to say 'Maybe we tried too hard, but at least we're ahead of our time!'

However, a number of American oil companies are already showing great interest in Arcolprod, which they feel may be the answer to offshore drilling at depths of 1 300 feet and more where the costs of conventional fixed platforms would be prohibitive. On 11 May 1978 'a new generation of deep sea oil and gas production facilities' was announced at the 10th Offshore Technology Conference (O.T.C.) at Houston, Texas, as phase two of the now £3·5 million research and development programme by the Offshore Division of Taylor Woodrow Construction Ltd. Then at the eleventh O.T.C. in 1979 the design study for the Arcolprod won the Petroleum Engineer International special meritorious award for engineering innovation. The Arcolprod programme is supported under Round 2 of the E.E.C. Hydrocarbons Project and also by the U.K. Department of Energy.

Concrete and steel are not mutually exclusive as materials for offshore structures; which you use depends on circumstances; and if Taylor Woodrow state the case for concrete with some emphasis, it is because they have been studying it for about thirty-five years. For offshore structures, it is more economical in deep water. A concrete structure is simpler to install – no seabed piling is required, since its mass enables it to sit firmly on the bottom; and it is extremely stable and easy to tow and to sink. Nevertheless, if steel is required, Taylor Woodrow Construction, by its association with Head

Wrightson Teesdale in the Taywood Wrightson Offshore organization, has all the resources, skills, and manpower necessary.

Reg Taylor was the original nucleus of the research and development department of Taylor Woodrow, back in 1959, when a laboratory was set up at Southall under Professor Kurt Billig, a civil engineer who had specialized in concrete. His assistant, Dr Roger Browne, is now head of research under Reg Taylor's technical direction. He is assisted by Dr Fikry Garas (structures) and Roger Blundell (a model specialist who is now in charge of Concrete Technology and, at thirty-eight, is a world authority on the long-term movement of concrete under load known as 'creep'). Roger Browne (who also has his share of intuition) is a concrete specialist of international reputation, much consulted by universities and Government departments.

In February 1978 it was announced that Taylor Woodrow Research Laboratories had become the first in the construction industry to be accepted under the British Standards Institution's system for the registration of test houses. Under this scheme, test houses which apply for registration are visited by an assessment team of experts who judge laboratories' performance against criteria prepared by the Quality Assurance Council of the BSI. Two of the three certificates of registration granted cover the testing to British Standards of a range of materials including prestressing and reinforcing – steel, concrete, bricks, blocks, asphalt, bitumen, and sealants.

Most significant is the third certificate, for the Measurement of Properties and Specialist Skills, which covers special types of testing and analysis outside the scope of standard BSI testing-fields in which Taylor Woodrow have been working for nearly twenty years. The certificate lists 25 separate skills, in each of which the Research Laboratories' expertise is recognized. BSI registration will benefit the Group as a whole. Not only can existing clients be assured of the wide range of work that can be undertaken, but the BSI Buyers' Guide will recommend the laboratories to many other potentially interested bodies.

Since 1971 the research department has given a central service to the whole Taylor Woodrow group, and also to outside clients. Regularly a technical news service pamphlet goes out to Taylor Woodrow people all over the world. Visiting Dr Browne's laboratory, the uninformed observer notices things like a lump of concrete taken from the site of the old shore railway at Brighton, found while building the new Marina. 'It's not good quality by modern standards,' Roger Browne says. 'But it is eighty years old, and its durability is remarkable.' No concrete is too old to be of interest: part of the old Mulberry harbours, now at Langstone, Dorset, is used as a test bed for steel and concrete research; and, as part of a Government research project on 'concrete in the ocean', Taylor Woodrow are helping with a survey of concrete as it was used in one of the wartime Thames Estuary forts on the Tongue sands opposite Margate.

There are instruments for measuring the corrosion of steel inside concrete: the rate of corrosion is measured by a digital voltmeter. Another experiment is testing the cladding of the American Express building at Brighton for rain and wind penetration; another records an attempt to minimize corrosion by carbon dioxide. A weird sound, as of electronic music, is found to be a vibrating wire gauge which measures strain in concrete, noting and printing any change, in a room kept at a constant temperature. The relationship between concrete and steel in construction poses special problems: for example in some Middle East countries concrete can be less durable than in others, thus reducing the protection which concrete normally gives to steel.

'Instrumentation beats theory every time' is the claim of

those who want laboratory tests to be confirmed by real-life situations. This means using ERG (electrical resistance surface gauges) for steel or reinforced concrete, or VWG (vibrating wire or acoustic strain gauge) for monitoring what is happening on the surface – the latter gauge can actually be embedded in the concrete. A more flexible perspex tube VWG can be used to detect delicate strain in concrete immediately after hardening.

The work of the Materials Research Laboratory became vitally important during the nuclear power research programme of the late 1960s, especially for the design of pressure vessels. There is little about the behaviour of concrete under extreme conditions which the laboratory does not know. Among many unusual test techniques, solid CO_2 has been added to aggregate in a standard concrete mixer to study its behaviour at subnormal temperatures.

Most major structures are model-tested first in the laboratory. Models, varying from scales of 1/128th up to full size, are made in concrete, steel, non-ferrous metals, acrylic plastics or epoxy resins. Obviously this is of great importance in designing marine structures. The laboratory's involvement in hydraulic research is also expanding. Models of harbours, estuaries, and irrigation works have been made, and the performance of concrete offshore structures for the oil industry is the subject of close scrutiny. For Brighton Marina a perspex model enabled Taylor Woodrow to do very rapid research which demonstrated that light concrete caissons with walls only ten inches thick were a better solution than the consultant engineers' recommendation of mass concrete. Research and computer analysis showed in advance how thin concrete would react to battering by waves, bearing in mind that compressed air trapped between water and concrete increases the effective pressure. The breakwater construction contract was thus secured on an alternative design; and from the start of research and design to the final bid was only eight weeks!

Taylor Woodrow's greatest innovation in nuclear power station design was the idea that for pressure vessels concrete should be used instead of steel and that for this purpose it is in most ways superior to steel. Next to this in importance was the wire-winding technique developed to strengthen cylindrical vessels; and among Reg Taylor's earliest inventions closest to the hearts of a grateful public was the Pilemaster 'silent' piledriver. By using a hydraulic jacking system instead of crude hammer blows, this eliminated most of the nerve-racking torment of having piledrivers hammering in the street. The inspiration for this was the result of Frank Taylor's saying, back in 1960, after complaints from a site in Victoria Street, London, 'we've simply got to do something about the noise. For heaven's sake, can't we invent a silent piledriver?' Since then the Pilemaster has been marketed under licence in Japan, Germany, Austria, Switzerland, and America.

It is an old saying that necessity is the mother of invention. The dock gates at Dubai dry dock are a Taylor Woodrow idea developed and designed by T. F. Burns & Partners, consulting engineers, who have an international reputation in the dry dock and harbour field. Conventional dock gates swing open slowly and laboriously like huge doors impeded by water and restrict ship movements when they are open. The 'Promod' system, now world patented, is simple, economical, reliable, and quick, and requires a minimum of maintenance. It opens by, as it were, falling gently forward on its face, resting on pads at the bottom of the dock, and allowing the ship to ride over it into the dock. In its closed position it is retained by props, which also control it as it opens. The gates, manufactured by a consortium of Redpath Dorman Long and Sir William Arrol, are of steel – and a considerably smaller quantity of steel than would be needed for a more orthodox design. Each gate is composed of modules which can be clipped, rather than welded, together on site – and it can be quickly repaired on site by fitting new modules.

One of many outside organizations that use Taylor Woodrow research facilities is the Admiralty. Arising out of their experience of pressure vessels, Taylor Woodrow were asked in 1973 to design a high-pressure test chamber capable of functioning at 10 000 lb per square inch for the Naval Construction Research Establishment. At Rosyth Dockyard, within sight of the Forth Bridge, a cylinder 3·05 metres in diameter and 9·15 metres high, all contained in a prestressed concrete structure 11 metres in diameter and 25 metres high, is creating an engineering 'first'. In this pressure vessel an independent steel cylinder is contained within a prestressed concrete yoke. The first concept was proposed by Taylor Woodrow in 1971. It was the result of an internal competition (no prizes) which was won by John Smith and Don Langan. Years of research and testing followed, involving model tests and computer analysis of the design. Inside the pressure vessel models weighing up to 100 tonnes are hung from the top plate for testing. In explaining to the layman what the chamber (which required 4 500 tonnes of concrete, 400 tonnes of prestressing steel, and 700 kilometres of steel wire to wrap each end) can do, they say: 'The force applied at the ends of the cylinder could just lift H.M.S. *Ark Royal.*'

The study of wave motion is an important element in the design of offshore structures and docks. The behaviour of water and wind in relation to each other and to materials they may damage has been the subject of less integrated investigation than might be supposed. Thus it is sometimes necessary for the TWC design team to simulate North Sea conditions at 100 metres' depth, or to observe what waves actually *do*. This work and experience has enabled the laboratories to make a substantial contribution to the development of floating breakwaters. All coastal or offshore projects tend to be hindered by rough seas. On the coast you can construct a temporary breakwater or cofferdam to protect the work going on within its arms; it means slowly accumulating piles of rock and it is costly; but there are also situations in which you can dissipate the circular wave motion and force it to waste its energy. Where have we seen something like this before? In the allied invasion of Europe in 1944.

Floating breakwaters were developed by Taylor Woodrow from an idea of Professor Alan Harris, of Harris & Sutherland, consulting engineers. In partnership with another firm of consulting engineers, Archibald Shaw & Partners, the two companies formed Floating Breakwaters Ltd. as a subsidiary of Taylor Woodrow International and located in Chichester. In November 1975, Sir Robert McAlpine & Sons Ltd. gave them their first commercial order: a timber breakwater to protect a floating bridge at Ardyne Point, Argyllshire. An unusual bridge, in that it carried not only pedestrians but pipelines to feed a continuous supply of concrete to the Brent 'C' oil platform which was being built about 200 metres offshore. The breakwater was required in four weeks. . . .

There were lessons to be learnt from the 'Bombardon' structure which failed at the Normandy beaches in 1944 because it dragged its anchors in a gale. It was meant to protect Omaha Beach, but nearly ruined the invasion and had to be sunk by artillery fire. Why? It was a massive structure designed to give direct vertical protection. It didn't try to break up and pacify the waves themselves, as a horizontal barrier would have done. An extensive series of laboratory tests was carried out with a horizontal breakwater at Southampton University, at Taylor Woodrow's Southall laboratories (where wave attacks were simulated), at Imperial College, and the National Physical Laboratory, followed by tests in the Solent and finally at Ardyne Point.

Several types of floating breakwaters have been developed to suit different applications. They may be of steel or timber, but prestressed concrete gives the best results for larger structures. A small lattice type is best for yacht marinas in relatively sheltered waters. A large lattice type can be adapted for use in open sea; and a delta-wing type, used in conjunction with a normal buoy mooring, could be used in North Sea operations such as loading and unloading of oil, or as an offshore haven for service boats and small ships. Being mobile, variable in size and quick to assemble, it could also be used in a 'beach-head' operation such as the start of a deep-water port or the addition of new works to an existing harbour. The Ardyne prototype (fifty-five metres long by eighteen metres wide) was moored between the buoys holding the pontoon bridge and the pontoons themselves by six mooring lines, and the estimated maximum mooring force is less than one tonne. Measurements at the site showed up to 75 per cent reduction in the height of waves passing the breakwater. The amount of reduction depends on such factors as the angle of wave attack and width of the breakwater.

This is what is happening on the surface; but Taylor Woodrow have ways of making the seabed talk too. They have Taywood Seltrust Offshore, a joint venture of Taylor Woodrow and Selection Trust the finance company, and their own Terresearch, a soils engineering specialist company. These two together developed the TSO seabed sampler to provide high-quality information on seabed conditions to a depth of nine metres in 300 metres depth of water. With its six 'feet' it looks rather like the module that first landed on the moon. Successful tests were carried out at the Underwater Engineering Group's trials facility in Lock Linnhe, near Fort William, Inverness-shire. The sampler, hydraulically powered and controlled through a flexible 'umbilical cord', is lowered to the seabed from a rig of rugged steelwork capable of resisting rough weather. It can be erected on standard supply ships for offshore work. It can help you to decide what sort of harbour construction will suit a coastal port or whether conditions are suitable for pipelines, sewer outfalls and anchorages; and it can also be used for mineral prospecting and geological surveying. Terresearch have been in the sampling business since 1957, and since 1966 have been using samplers for pipeline and other surveys in the North Sea. The TSO machine can be fitted with a rotary core barrel to obtain rock cores, and can drill holes up to nine metres in depth to form anchorages.

In civil engineering, the disciplines of design, research, and construction are integral parts of a unified process. Recognizing this fact, Taylor Woodrow in 1973 formed Taywood Engineering Ltd. as a separate subsidiary to provide consultancy and engineering services in a wide range of activities. They begin, inevitably, with feasibility and costing studies, and sometimes site-finding studies. By drawing upon and co-ordinating the resources of Taylor Woodrow Construction's various specialist departments, they offer engineering consultancy for either civil engineering or building works; process engineering, mechanical, electrical, and environmental services; architectural design; construction planning and programming; contract management and resident engineering services; and, as we have seen, research and development projects. Some or all of these services, uniting design and research, have been applied to hospitals, power stations, breweries, food and pharmaceutical factories. The most fruitful and economical combination of talents is often realized in management contracts, in which the civil engineering company either provides an extension to the client's own engineering organization or a fully comprehensive service. Examples are the smelter plant built by Taywood Wrightson Ltd. for the British Aluminium Co. at Invergordon, Scotland; a pharmaceutical plant for Beechams in Singapore; and a headquarters complex for IBM at Cosham, Hampshire.

An integrated design service can be of particular interest to a client for whom time is of the essence. For example, Ferodo gave Taylor Woodrow just sixteen months from the date of their first meeting with them to design, build, and install machinery in a new 240 000 square feet asbestos factory at Caernarvon, North Wales: in fact, the factory was able to start production only twelve months after the first briefing. To design, research, and engineering can be added, if necessary, procurement. Taylor Woodrow's word-wide purchasing power enabled them to design, build, and equip a new multi-million-pound pharmaceutical plant for the production of semi-synthetic penicillin for Beechams, from concept to commissioning, in only eighteen months, on time and within budget. Their reputation as consultants has enabled them to be retained, especially in the field of nuclear power, by the Central Electricity Generating Board, Gulf General Atomics of America, and Hochtemperatur Reaktorbau GmbH of West Germany.

The Taylor Woodrow Construction mechanical, electrical, and process division under the direction of Bill Jenkins has contributed greatly to all this, and particularly to modern factories. For example, a client who has a complex manufacturing process may need further capacity. 'M.E. & P.' can support him by planning an assembly line, and even suggesting modifications or simplification of the process itself. 'M.E. & P.', founded eighteen years ago to reduce the dependence on specialist sub-contractors, covers design, engineering, and installation. It needs a lot of headquarters support, and so there are, at Southall, 250 people working full-time on engineering design, another 150 or so in the field (many have been seconded to other members of the Group), and Taymech Nigeria Ltd., currently fields a team of 700 local and expatriate members.

The work of 'M.E. & P.' ranges from the electrical equipment of the Tower Hotel at St Katharine's to extensive and complex installations at the Heysham and Hartlepool nuclear power stations; from the cooling water system at Sizewell to the domestic power and lighting of offices and houses. Although administratively part of Taylor Woodrow Construction, it also works overseas with Taylor Woodrow International and Arcon Building Exports. It has recently worked on two jute mills, one in Vietnam, the other in Bolivia. It has carried out a study for a new optical equipment factory in Poland.

'M.E. & P.' are also very active in a Taylor Woodrow joint venture with other firms in what is called the 'airports package', to develop and provide hydrants and related services for refuelling of aircraft. Taymech Aviation Equipment Ltd., a subsidiary of Taylor Woodrow Construction, designs and manufactures specialized mobile and static equipment for refuelling civil and military aircraft and also produces fire crash tenders and other airport service vehicles. Their customers include such names as Shell, B.P., Gulf, Fina, Chevron and the Ministry of Defence. A Taymech hydrant dispenser was sent to Bahrain where it refuels Concorde. The fire-fighting equipment can take to the sea in a fast light fire-boat with a speed in excess of thirty knots.

At Grimethorpe Colliery, Yorkshire, in what is called a 'multi-discipline job', Taylor Woodrow are managing a project to help the National Coal Board to develop a pilot plant for 'fluidizing' pulverized coal – using coal as if it were oil to increase its combustion efficiency by an estimated 8 per cent. This is being done in association with German and American interests, and the scheme is shortly coming up to the commissioning stage.

'M.E. & P.' did the design work for mechanical and electrical services at the Dubai dry dock; and sometimes they work for other main contractors too (for example, for Costain at Terminal 2, Heathrow Airport, London).

In research and design, computer programmes are at work all the time. They deal mathematically with statistics, variance, matrices, graphing, and contouring. The 'drum plotter' is used for automatic graph and contour drawing, for producing 'critical path' network in planning very complex schedules, for road-alignment drawings, and detailed drawings for reinforced concrete multi-storey columns. Computers work out slope stability, foundation settlement, programmes for sheet-piling; they analyse the behaviour of structures, co-ordinate the surveying of motorways and canals, analyse the stress, movement, and load of pressure vessels.

Taylor Woodrow believe that 'complex engineering problems are often best solved by using mathematical analysis to reproduce the real behaviours observed in physical experiment'. And with a certain whimsical humility, they make their point, on the cover of one of their design-and-research booklets, by showing an enormous iron weight resting on an egg. This is to illustrate 'the strength and modes of failure of one of the most beautiful, most simple, and yet, at the same time, most complex structures of nature – an egg. The shell material is found to be stronger than concrete, and its shape quickly redistributes concentrated loads to give almost uniform membrane stresses.' For an egg is a pressure vessel.

The exchange of knowledge between Taylor Woodrow,

Part of the elevated prestressed concrete structure at Staples Corner Interchange.

Interior of the Channel–7 Edgley Entertainment Centre in Perth, Western Australia, which has seating capacity for more than 8000 spectators.

Early view of Brighton Marina showing the reclaimed land where the caisson casting yard originally stood.

The portal crane places the 110th and last caisson in the breakwaters.

The reclaimed land has been excavated and flooded again to form the inner basin.

A 230-acre wooded conservation area, containing lakes, nature trails, bridle and cycling paths, is part of the recreational amenities provided in The Meadows development at Sarasota, Florida.

A new convent, chapel, and car park in Singapore for the Franciscan Missionaries of the Divine Motherhood.

Bedford Gardens, Brooklyn, New York – a residential urban renewal development.

Semi-detached and town houses built by Heron's Hill Homes, a division of Monarch Construction Ltd.

Chartwell Shopping Centre, Scarborough, Ontario, Canada.

Greenham Concrete delivering ready-mixed concrete at Buckingham Palace.

One of Greenham Plant Hire's fleet of crawler cranes, a Manitowoc 4600 Series 4, working on the assembly of the 26 000 tonne steel jacket destined for the Thistle field in the North Sea.

Sand and gravel raising.

The Adam-style Boardroom at Southgate House retains the beauty of a bygone age.

Not one but two group companies were involved in the construction and fitting out of these stores in Newcastle.

universities, technical laboratories of Government departments, and other civil engineering firms is continuous. Taylor Woodrow, for example, were hosts at a two-day seminar of the Concrete Society in July 1976 at which universities and industry met informally to study and comment on research in civil engineering. The versatile Reg Taylor is also a member of the Offshore Energy Technology Board which advises the Secretary of State for Energy on research and development designed to ensure the safety and efficiency of offshore operations, and on improving the competitive position of British industry in the offshore field.

How much research is speculative? You could answer this by saying either 'all' or 'none'. For problems lead to unexpected discoveries, and the apparently useless discovery is suddenly found to have an application which renders whole systems obsolete. (At the annual dinner of the Cavendish Laboratory in 1932, Professor Sir Ernest Rutherford, having recently split the atom, proposed a toast 'To the electron – may it never be of any use to anyone'.)

Reg Taylor and Roger Browne are more realistic than Rutherford. We live in an impoverished Britain which, pinning its hopes on North Sea oil for the immediate future, is also looking around at other new sources of energy, and energy storage. Solar energy, windmills, the sea – all are being examined, and all are likely to concern civil engineering. The sun, a thermonuclear reactor ninety-three million miles away which has about another five billion years to run, provides more energy in ten days than all the known reserves of coal and oil. But it needs concentrating. How? The Americans want to shoot a solar planet out into space so that its power to absorb sunshine is not interrupted by clouds and nightfall (it would, we are told, need to be fifty square miles in area). Or a 'space shuttle', orbiting at 22 000 miles above the earth and converting energy into microwaves beamed down to the ground (this might have to be about twenty square miles in area). We know that solar energy can be used for home-heating, but nobody has yet found a way of reducing its cost for larger applications. Thousands of heliostats or mirrors could reflect the sun's rays to the top of a tower full of water, which would produce steam, which would drive turbines for electricity (this is already happening in Tokyo and Denver, Colorado).

The sea is believed to be a huge reservoir for solar energy. Could all that North Sea turbulence, untamed by Floating Breakwaters, be converted into a steady flow of electricity? In the tropics the OTEC (Ocean Thermal Energy Conversion) system is trying to use the difference in temperature between the sea's surface and deep water, linking them by vaporized ammonia. Another method proposes a string of huge 'nodding ducks' on the ocean surface converting their variable movements into electricity. And somebody has worked it out that a tidal station on the River Severn would cost over £4 000 million. . . .

When Taylor Woodrow's 'R. & D.' think-tank is ready to make an announcement, it will certainly do so. For the moment, we can look to the work in hand to produce energy from another of nature's traditional sources – wind. One particular project in which Taylor Woodrow is working with such names as Hawker Siddeley Dynamics, Cleveland Bridge and Engineering, the Electrical Research Association, the North of Scotland Hydro Electric Board and the South of Scotland Electricity Board has produced a study entitled 'Development of Large Wind Turbine Generators'. The design feasibility and cost study talks of a turbine with two fixed-pitch blades of rigid steel construction, 60 metres in diameter, rotating at 34 r.p.m. about a horizontal axis and driving a 3·7MW induction generator through a fixed ratio gearbox . . . all of this mounted 45 metres above ground on a nacelle which is turned to follow wind direction, and supported on a reinforced concrete or steel lattice tower.

There are many remote and sparsely populated areas where the cost of distribution of electricity from the main centres of power and the national grid is such as to make locally generated power attractive. If that local generating capacity is wholly dependent on oil or coal, which has to be transported, it is still expensive. But in the Highlands and Islands of Scotland, for example, the North Atlantic air is seldom still.

It is not difficult to picture the benefits of such development, but the study group was quick to acknowledge that high winds are often encountered in areas of high scenic beauty, where the effects on amenities need careful consideration.

Taylor Woodrow have lent support to other ventures to harness the wind, involving single blade windmills, twin bladed ones using helicopter rotor technology, and various methods of converting the energy. One system didn't even bother to produce electricity – the rotor drove an hydraulic pump to force oil through a deliberately inefficient circulating system, thus generating a large amount of heat. The heat was transferred to water in a conventional heat exchanger, supplying a normal central heating system.

So much of what Reg Taylor and his team have worked on over the years has been related to energy in one way or another, that it is particularly fitting that, when the various teams were at last brought together under one roof in July 1979, it was the Prime Minister, the Rt. Hon. Margaret Thatcher, M.P., who came along to perform the opening ceremony. Mrs. Thatcher's government was barely formed when she made known her very firm support for development of what we now call 'alternative energy sources', and while her visit to the new Southall laboratories was planned when she was still Leader of the Opposition, it was particularly gratifying to Reg Taylor and his team that the visit was retained in the very busy Prime Ministerial programme.

They took the opportunity to set up a display illustrating the variety and depth of their research activity over the years, majoring on the three areas of energy – nuclear, offshore and alternative sources – which have demanded so much of their time. It was an impressive display – even to some of those involved.

V

Oman

'IT was like D-Day-plus-3 on the Normandy beaches –
I've never seen men work like it! We had accountants
driving cranes, quantity surveyors driving bulldozers. . . .'
So John Cox, now general manager of Taylor Woodrow-
Towell, remembers early days in Salalah, in the southern
coastal strip of the Sultanate of Oman, some time in 1970.
The pioneer team who were to build a modern harbour and
many other things in this area were striving to get stores off
the beach in time to set up a camp before the monsoon came,
and everyone had been given a crash course in plant management. 'We slept on the beach for a week. Even tents were a
luxury.' Like Alan Winfield, now area manager in Salalah,
John Cox – who lives in an elegant villa in the new residential
district of Medinat Qaboos just outside Muscat – can wax
poetic about stars like diamonds in a velvet night sky when
you're exhausted after a fourteen-hour day.

The monsoon arrives in June and departs in September.
During those summer months nothing could be brought in
by sea – it is a dangerous coast for dhows, the monsoon brings
fog with it and for two and a half months the sun is seldom
seen; and even in the dry season you have to work to the
tides, often at night. For supplies, you are very dependent on
air freight. . . . At least, you were in 1970, when there were no
roads, only camel tracks, but now the monsoon is a largely
defeated enemy, and no longer interrupts work. Enemy? But

it brings fertility, and one of the things you learn to appreciate is the sudden change from brown to green as the mountains take on their summer dress.

Salalah is only seventy miles from the border of South Yemen, 170 from the ill-defined border of Saudi Arabia, and about 500 from the Yemen. From the viewpoint of the young Sultan, thirty-nine-year-old Qaboos bin Said, this is a danger area for the infiltration of Communist guerrillas, and he is determined to keep it strong. Sultan means king, and you address him as Your Majesty. His is the oldest dynasty in the Gulf; his family have been ruling in Oman since 1741, and his ancestors ruled in Zanzibar for some five centuries before that. He is the fourteenth of his dynasty. Educated at Oxford and Sandhurst, he has close ties with Britain and a circle of British advisers. He does not belong to the 'Sheikhs' Club', the rulers of the neighbouring Arab Emirates (known, up to 1970, as the 'Trucial States'), and holds himself aloof from what he regards as excessive speed in modernization: his respect for tradition can be seen in his concern for good design which preserves something of Omani heritage. Nevertheless, since he took over from his father in 1970, he has elected to bring his country into the twentieth century in one generation.

Taylor Woodrow-Towell are doing so many things in the Salalah and Muscat areas that we can select only a few (I was shown a list of 159 'main building orders' and about 100 'small works' currently being undertaken). They have made a film about their activities around Salalah, where the largest contract was to build a new port at Risut, eleven miles from the old town. The film, *A Thousand Days*, shows how, in this remote area, two thousand years of progress have been bridged in a thousand days or just under three years.

Salalah, provincial capital of Dhofar, has only one frontier – the Indian Ocean. Beyond the mountains at its back, Jebel

Qara, lie almost uncharted vastnesses of pure desert, grimly known as 'the Empty Quarter'. There is a doubtful local legend that the Queen of Sheba once had a palace here. It was always a trading country, famous for its valuable incense trees, and for centuries depended for food on fish. You can still see the traditional Omani fishing-boats, made of reeds tied together, cunningly designed so that they 'give' with the waves in rough weather, and rowing-boats with triangular, spatulate oars.

Central to every major development in Dhofar Province is the port at Risut. Before it was built, all cargo had to be carried out on a man's back through the surf and over the beach. Roads followed, then housing, a hospital, a telephone exchange, Government buildings, an airstrip, television and radio studios, and – perhaps most important of all – an irrigation system, so that fresh food could be grown again. What water means to Dhofaris can best be judged from the delight on the face of a Dhofari workman enjoying the sheer luxury of a shower. Guided partly by local lore and partly by geology, water has been found and channelled to where it is most needed. Taylor Woodrow-Towell have trained their own Omani labour force in mechanical skills, instructed them in principles of safety and health (including the use of protective creams against chemicals), and provided a medical team and a dispensary in an area where doctors were almost unknown.

One day, perhaps, the majority of Omanis will be able to afford television sets. But for the time being, TV is part of the Sultan's 'hearts and minds' programme for explaining to the people what is being done for them: there are free public TV screens on posts in towns and open places, and all you have to do is stand and stare.

In its first year of operation, the harbour at Risut, built in the shelter of a rocky headland and completed in 1973, handled over 120 000 tons of freight, six times the amount originally envisaged. Immediately road-building began with some fifteen kilometres of asphaltic concrete surfaced road-way from Ma'murah, at the eastern side of Salalah, to Taqah, a small township on the eastern extremity of the Salalah plain at the foothills of the Jebel Qara. This contract also included about seven kilometres of ring-road around Salalah itself.

By now, too, all the facilities needed by a port were springing up – customs and immigration buildings, adminis-tration block, stores, a police station, accommodation for customs officers, houses for the harbour master and harbour engineer, and barracks for labourers and security forces. To these were added flats for school teachers, a six-mile water pipe-line and reinforced concrete reservoirs, electrical distri-bution, and drainage.

The Taylor Woodrow team, living in comparative com-fort after the initial 'holes in the ground' stage, were allowed to bring out families from Britain, and a small village school was started for their children. It began in the Taywood Club with a nucleus of six British children and one whose parents worked for the Dhofar Development Department. Books were lent by parents, shells and pebbles from the beach were used for counting, mothers took it in turns to teach. At Christmas the children put on a Nativity play in which the 'king' was able to bring a gift of *real* frankincense. By January 1972 the school had moved into a house with proper equip-ment, with nine pupils, enough recorders to form a band, and a full-time teacher.

The Sultan, who knows that Oman's most important resource is oil (found in commercial quantities in 1964) also knows that oil does not last for ever. Ninety per cent of his Government's income comes from oil revenue, and he is using it to build up resources for self-sufficiency in the future. The majority of the country's $1\frac{1}{2}$ million population still depend on agriculture for their livelihood, the main crops being dates, limes, lucerne, onions, wheat, mango, tobacco, and coconuts. About 60 per cent of Oman's budget is allocated to development and building the infrastructure of the country. Hence the supreme importance of irrigation. Among many projects, Taylor Woodrow-Towell have provided a model dairy farm (to which Queen Elizabeth gave some of her dairy cows from Windsor as a personal gift to the Sultan), an abattoir and a veterinary clinic. With their talent for making themselves at home, the Taylor Woodrow team in Salalah have made themselves a 9-hole golf-course between a lagoon and the sea on a piece of land lent by the Sultan.

It is about 550 miles by air from Salalah to Muscat, the capital of Oman, which lies to the north on the lower Gulf coast opposite southern Iran – and it has to be by air, unless you have the time to go by camel, for there has never been a railway although there is a reasonable – unsurfaced – road across the desert. Hence TWINGS, Taylor Woodrow-Towell's own airline in Oman. None of the Taylor Woodrow team today can imagine how they ever got on without it. Some of their contracts are now in Musandam, a remote and mountainous peninsula in the far north of the country, cut off, by historical accident, by a strip of land which belongs to some of the Arab Emirates. Roads are few and difficult, and if you do not fly there, your only alternative is a very slow voyage round the coast in a dhow. In the early days of Taylor Woodrow's work in Dhofar Province, it was possible to ship materials and plant direct to this area. But all imported labour (usually from India and Pakistan) has to be brought into the country via Muscat, the only point of immigration. Those immigrants destined for Salalah had to be housed until flights could be arranged. Since there were very few commercial flights operating, the cost of maintaining personnel in Muscat proved extremely high. A private aircraft would guarantee the movement of men and materials between Muscat and Salalah at an economic cost.

In February 1975 a Piper PA31 Chieftain and crew were hired from Fairflight Charters of Biggin Hill, Kent, which could use improvised airstrips (seldom more than 500 metres long) and operate in summer temperatures of well over 40 degrees centigrade. A De Havilland Twin Otter (hitherto more accustomed to flying for the British Antarctic Survey in very much lower temperatures, wearing skis instead of wheels) was found surprisingly suitable, and Piper and Otter between them carry people and equipment for about 100 flying hours a month. So difficult is transport in the Musandam peninsula that if the pilot has one spare seat, the project manager at Bayah, a seaside terminal of one of the new water supply schemes, is accustomed to receiving requests like this from the doctor in charge of the local health centre:

'My very dear Mr Dent! – Hello! – One of our staff members has to proceed to Muscat very urgently. I shall be extremely grateful to you, in case your pilot could take him along. Thanks ever. Asif Ali Maudin.'

Only ten years ago, in the reign of the present Sultan's father, Muscat was almost a forbidden city. It is locked in a small habour surrounded by black rocks, and its ancient buildings are dominated by a sixteenth-century castellated fort, a relic of the days when the city was a trading post for the Portuguese empire. As recently as 1970 its gates used to close at 9 p.m. and most of the lights went out. The old Sultan personally issued all visas, and nobody was allowed to move from his home without permission. In a sudden permissiveness, to which the Omanis have taken very quickly with no noticeable ill-effects, the new Sultan allowed dancing, smoking, and Western dress; today you see very few veiled women, and only an occasional camel (Omanis ride *behind* the hump) or donkey in streets that are congested with

Japanese and American cars (Britain is represented almost exclusively by Land and Range Rovers and Jaguars).

The Muscat to which Taylor Woodrow first came was the capital of a country which had only three primary schools, each with about 100 pupils and one American missionary hospital at Mutrah, a couple of miles outside Muscat, with about twenty dispensaries to cope with cerebral malaria, leprosy, TB, and trachoma. There were only five European women in the whole country and, by special permission of the old Sultan, John Cox's wife Susi made six.

How does a large civil engineering and construction firm arrive in a country like this, and having arrived, how does it set about getting business? In most big firms operating, or wishing to operate, in the Middle East there are personalities who are generally nicknamed 'Lawrences of Arabia'. Such a one is Ron Whitehouse, managing director of Taylor Woodrow International, a director of the parent company and director of several other interests within the Group. It is he who is primarily responsible for the company's activities in Oman, even though his work field extends through Iraq and Kuwait and Saudi Arabia, as far east as Sarawak and Malaysia, and his time is frequently spent more in the air than on the ground, so much so that jet-lag is for him so perpetual as to be almost unnoticed. It was he who first perceived the full possibilities of working in Oman.

Early in 1969 Taylor Woodrow, like many another firm, was looking at the oil-rich countries. They were by no means first in the field. They sent out a small mission to Oman – a contracts promotion man, an estimator, and Dick Coppock, a director of Taylor Woodrow International (now retired) known to the older generation of Taylor Woodrow people as 'Emil'. Everywhere else along the Gulf seemed to be booming, but Oman wasn't yet. Why not, and could it be made to boom?

Dick Coppock is a past-master at what is called 'establishing a presence' in the Middle East – those early days of sitting in a country with a small team tendering for contracts, often in consortium. It needs strong nerves – and patience, as you wait all day for either payment or an interview, outside the office of a sheikh or his staff whose priorities for use of their available time may not be the same as yours. Do not worry: the sheikh is studying your character, and once he likes and trusts you, you're in. Dick's baptism of fire, if you can call it that, was in Libya in the 1960s with his friend and partner Ali Daqqaq, the U.N. representative in Libya, a Palestinian Arab married to an American girl. Their adventures would make a separate book. In Libya there was a power station for English Electric, the prospect of an oil-jetty for BP near Tobruk, and the mysterious rehabilitation of an old airfield 'to rescue astronauts if a moon-shot went wrong'. It all culminated in the near-disaster of Marsa el Bregha, a harbour job of which Walter Hogbin, John Calkin, and others (some of whom are now in Dubai) can tell tales. The Israel–Arab war broke out just as the huge concrete caissons were floating in from Sicily, where they had been cast, and, as usual, the office team had crash courses in plant operation.

By now Dick Coppock was in Abu Dhabi, on the Gulf, supervising a tiny contract for the Sheikh to build a dozen houses at Al Ain, near the famous Buraimi Oasis (over which small wars have been fought). The Middle East was, for a few weeks, no place for an Englishman, and Dick Coppock escaped by way of Bahrain and the good offices of Ali Daqqaq, flying Tehran–Istanbul–Rome to avoid using Israeli air-space.

Arriving in Muscat in 1969, Dick Coppock's tiny team spent two weeks 'studying the ground' and establishing a base. They happened to know a former general manager of the Oman Oil Company who gave them an introduction to

Haji Ali Sultan. The British Consul also thought well of Ali Sultan, and gladly provided another introduction. Today Ali Sultan says: 'When I met Mr Coppock, I knew this was a firm I can trust.' The first token of his trust was his offer of a flat in his headquarters building to Dick Coppock.

What Taylor Woodrow were looking for was a well-established local firm to form a partnership. Haji Ali Sultan is managing director of W. J. Towell & Co. in Mutrah, which at that time was a mere suburb of the ancient walled city of Muscat. W. J. Towell started as an American company in 1866, and Ali's grandfather in the 1870s was U.S. Vice-Consul in Muscat. Sometime in the 1880s the original Mr Towell was widowed, and he wanted to return to the States. So he handed over everything to Ali Sultan's grandfather who became sole proprietor.

W. J. Towell for the next eighty years or so exported fruit (especially dates) to America and pomegranates to India; imported oil from Standard Oil of New Jersey; were agents for Unilever for fifty-two years; and until recently were distributors for British American Tobacco and Huntley & Palmer biscuits. Ali Sultan and his family have business interests all along the Gulf as far as Kuwait, and he himself is President of the Omani Chamber of Commerce. Towells own 50 per cent of Mutrah's much needed cold store, and also the Mutrah Hotel, one of the two first-class hotels in the town.

Haji Ali Sultan had once had a partnership with another construction firm which went into liquidation (by an odd coincidence, John Cox's first construction job was with the same firm in Gibraltar and he was originally sent to Oman by Taylor Woodrow partly because he had worked in Aden and had experience of Arabia). Ali Sultan had long been pondering a tie-up with a foreign, preferably British, construction firm. For both himself and Taylor Woodrow, therefore, the meeting with Dick Coppock's team was providential.

There was no immediate rush of orders for Taylor Woodrow-Towell. The first pipeline from the Oman oilfield to the sea had gone to another firm; so had a camp wanted by Shell for oil workers. Then Taylor Woodrow and Ali together put in a tender for the first modern hospital in Oman – a £600 000 building to be erected in Ruwi, then a so-called 'barasti' village of huts roofed with palm leaves, but now a flourishing town in its own right. They got the job. By now they urgently needed a new headquarters, and so the 'Towell complex' came into being, overlooking the rough airstrip where the monthly visiting DC3s used somehow to put themselves down before the grand International Airport at Seeb was built. The 'Towell complex', completed early in 1974, contains not only Taylor Woodrow-Towell's headquarters offices but eight shops, a supermarket, and a showroom.

In October 1975 Sir Frank Taylor made a six-day tour of the country accompanied by George Hazell, deputy chairman of Taylor Woodrow International and chairman of Taylor Woodrow-Towell. His first visit was to Medinat Qaboos, the new township being developed in two parts by Oman International Development Co., a new member of the Taylor Woodrow Group. This development provides about 1 000 villas and apartments of various types and sizes, together with a communal area of supermarkets, shops, offices, and other amenities, and will eventually house over 5 000 people. It is about twelve miles equidistant from Muscat and Seeb Airport, and is divided into roughly equal parts, east and west, with a shallow *wadi* running between them. The western half is being developed by OIDC, and the remainder by W. J. Towell & Co. Both east and west are managed by Taylor Woodrow-Towell.

Officially opened by the Sultan on Oman's National Day, 18 November 1973, Medinat Qaboos is described by John Cox as 'my bath-tub inspiration'. He and his family now live in No. 1, Road Four, where, in spite of the water shortage (the district is dependent on a desalination plant), he has managed in two years to achieve a mature-looking garden coloured with bougainvillaea, mauve camel's foot, scented frangipani, and casuarina trees. The British Ambassador is a near neighbour. All roads in Medinat Qaboos are numbered, not named (but there is no Road 13).

It is a curvilinear estate, carefully landscaped, and the houses, mostly of a 'citadel-turret and roof-garden' design, reflect the Sultan's desire to combine the traditional and the modern. (It is significant that one of the first things he did on assuming the throne was to establish a Department of Conservation, and one of the many talents of Taylor Woodrow being deployed in Oman is the delicate refurbishing of historic buildings.) What is wholly modern is the speed of building. Labour, much of it Asian, mainly from India and Pakistan, is expensive. A three-bedroom-house, from foundations to handing over, can be built in sixteen weeks; a two-bedroom-house in fourteen weeks.

The Taylor Woodrow talent for making a home-from-home even in the wilderness is seen all over Oman. In Muscat, Mutrah, and Ruwi, you can point to almost anything and say: 'That wasn't here two years ago.' There are cars and trucks, and soon – ultimate symbol of the twentieth century – there will be parking meters. There is a sense of bustling community. You can join a number of clubs and amenities, such as the Yacht Club formed by Taylor Woodrow and other construction firms and Omanis from the new Ministry of Youth. But in the timeless rock and thin soil where camels and goats nibble the thorn-bushes for food, and there is no Taywood Club to go to, life can be very solitary.

Near the Arab town of Nizwa, to the south-west of Muscat, an oasis where a stream runs through a bunch of date palms and little boys run up to shake your hand and invite you to play football with them, Taylor Woodrow-Towell are building the Qaboos Boarding School. It is 1976. In northern Oman many people live in the hills, and it is national policy to encourage them to come down to the *wadis*. Thus, although the Qaboos School was originally planned to be 6 000 feet up on top of the Jebel, it is now on the open plain: it would anyway have been too expensive to take all the building materials up the mountain by air.

The project manager, Derek Harris, lives alone on the site. At fifty, he came out, leaving his family in the Lake District of England, to live in a tent for the first three months in a summer temperature which sometimes reached 60 degrees Centigrade. He has never been abroad in his life before, and seems to like it. Now comfortably housed by Swiftplan, with air-conditioning, he keeps in touch with the outside world by radio, writes home every day, and is looked after by an Indian chef who once worked at the Bombay Sheraton. Derek doesn't feel isolated: how can you, when you can follow all the sport at home through that invaluable institution, the B.B.C. World Service?

Northern Oman does not get a proper monsoon, and the 'wet' season in fact brings little rain. There are occasional cloudbursts that suddenly swell the stream and fill the dry *wadis*; but mostly the northern Omanis are dependent on wells, for much of the rock is porous enough to absorb water. And if wells run dry, villages die as the villagers drift away to the prosperous neighbouring Arab Emirates.

This situation led to the famous '1 a.m. phone call' from the Sultan's Palace to John Cox, just ten days before National Day in 1975. It was almost a SOS. Could Taylor Woodrow-Towell please immediately do something about the water supply in the Ras Musandam district at the mountainous northern tip of Oman? The local wells, overpumped, had gone saline: many of them were now below sea-level. Never were the advantages of having men, materials, and equipment on the spot, or sufficiently near, better demonstrated: materials from Dubai (eight hours away by road), men from Muscat. In fourteen days an astonishing amount could be, and was, done. Drills were on site in four days. There was no time to ask for design help from London. In a Dubai hotel room, most of the scheme was worked out by a young chief engineer, Rod Northway, after studies by a hydro-geologist flown out from Britain. There was no reliable map, and so the whole area had to be photographed from the air. Land convoys could get as far as Bayah village on the Indian Ocean side, but this was not easy, as they had to go through the strip of Emirate territory about sixty miles wide that separates Ras Musandam from the rest of Oman. The only other access was round the coast by dhow: Taylor Woodrow rent a motorized dhow (normally lateen-sailed) with a full-time Indian 'captain'. The TWINGS aircraft speeded everything up wonderfully.

Seen from the air, the Musandam peninsula is, in Alan Winfield's words, 'science-fiction country ... the sheer mountains rising to over 6 800 feet, are like Conan Doyle's *Lost World* – you can't imagine that people live there until the Piper swoops down to an air-strip in a *wadi*.' Some communities are so isolated that they can only be seen from the air. But where the sparse rain has left a little silt, in a depression 6 000 feet up, there something can be cultivated and people can survive. The headman of a village, thousands of feet below, can summon them if you have work for them; and in the evening, the Jebalis (hill-people) disappear mysteriously up the mountainside to their invisible fastnesses.

The population of Bukha area, on the Gulf side, had

shrunk from 5 000 to 1 000 in the last few years because of water shortage. In a matter of days after the '1 a.m. phone call' there were nine public distribution points with 'non-concussive' taps to prevent waste. Soon there was a 14 000 gallon storage tank at Al Jadi nearby, with a generator and chlorinator house. The next phase was to bring water from the wells at Ghrumdah and carry it by pipeline over the ridge of the Jebel at eighty metres above sea-level (because the rock here is too hard for tunnelling). All equipment above a certain height (where even Jeeps cannot go) has to be manhandled. To carry a pipeline over the higher ridges, Rod Northway (an exceptionally fit young engineer who can climb anything that is not actually vertical) believes that they will have to train men to scale the cliffs with crampons.

The best well produces 7 000 gallons of water an hour which is pumped up to a 20 000-gallon storage tank. Biggest of all is a 1000 000-gallon tank which feeds the Bayah ring main. The next step is an 'export water station' for sending water round the coast by sea to very remote villages. At every water point, or wherever a bowser stops, there are queues of people with water-skins, jars, even dustbins to collect the precious liquid. In charge of all this is another cheerfully isolated Taylor Woodrow community led by project manager Steve Callaghan, production supervisor Ian McClymont, and site engineer Colin Brady, who have converted a tumbledown Arab house into a commodious club with every mod. con.

Taylor Woodrow-Towell did all this at remarkable speed, but they were by no means unprepared when the '1 a.m. phone call' came. In August 1975 Rod Northway had explored the Musandam district around Bukha and Bayah and written a significant report beginning with a survey of the garden of a local Sheikh, Ahmed Abdulla Mohammed, at Al Jadi near Bukha. His was the only sweet water left in the district. He had mentioned the matter to Col. McNeil, of the

Sultan's Civil Aid (a rescue organization for outlying areas). There were between sixty and seventy wells in the Jadi gardens; nearly all were brackish, and bedrock was barely one metre below the bottom. One thing was clear from the start: all vehicles must have 4-wheel drive in a roadless landscape of sand and rock.

At Bayah, Taylor Woodrow have never said 'no' to any task demanded of them, whether it is building a few miles of road or diverting a stream so that it irrigates somebody's garden. Here the first water scheme was for eighteen distribution points (there are now twice as many): again, most of it comes from wells now that the Wadi Khaab catchment area has proved unable to yield enough water. A merchant, Mr Mohamed Raschid, supplies the Taylor Woodrow team and labour force with basic food and materials, and the Wali of Bayah negotiates the supply of local workers who are delighted with forty rials a month plus twelve rials food allowance. The Wali, a man of learning and humour, is mayor, magistrate, and governor of an area of about 10 000 people, and has been heard to say: 'Taylor Woodrow very good. Everybody should have one.'

VI

Dubai

DUBAI, 260 miles north-west of Muscat, on the 'Gulf' side of the Musandam peninsula, was once known as 'the Venice of the Gulf.' Standing at the end of a nine-mile *khor* or creek, it is still beautiful, though the Ruler, Sheikh Rashid ibn Said, is less keen on conservation than the Sultan of Oman. Here there is still an oriental market where Arabs and Persians sit cross-legged, gold-braided turbans mingle with Pakistani astrakhan caps, and traders come from Baluchistan, Africa, and every country around the Gulf that has something to sell. In the clear blue-green water, gaily painted dhows ride peacefully at anchor.

Like other ports along the Gulf, Dubai used to live on gold-smuggling. It emerged as the main port for the Trucial Coast in the early 1900s, when it handled an average of thirty-four ships a year. (Three times as many waited every day to dock in the early 1970s.) In 1937 the present ruler's father, Sheikh Said ibn Maktoum, allowed Imperial Airways a flying-boat base beside the creek. In the 1950s Jacques Cousteau and others did underwater surveys off Dubai and Abu Dhabi in the shallow continental shelf of the Gulf which is never deeper than sixty feet. A seabed concession was granted in 1954 to the Superior Oil Co., but in 1963 the Ruler gave drilling rights to Continental Oil, forming a fifty-fifty partnership called the Dubai Petroleum Co.

Soon afterwards, led by Dubai and Abu Dhabi, a Trucial

States Council was formed (the germ of the United Arab Emirates) and appointed Sir William Halcrow & Partners as their consultant engineers: one of the first things Halcrow did was to carry out a £330 000 survey of water resources. An agricultural school, electrification, a telephone service, an airfield, a trade school – by 1961 Dubai had all these things. In 1967 Costain secured a £9 million contract to build the first stage of an eight-berth deep-water harbour which was extended in 1968 to provide a £24 million fifteen-berth harbour. This is the harbour now known as Port Rashid. The addition of an entirely new dry dock (£232 million) and an extension to Port Rashid (£120 million), for which a joint venture was formed between Taylor Woodrow and Costain, brought the two contracts to £352 million, one of the biggest civil engineering undertakings in the world.

It is difficult to convey an accurate idea of the size of this undertaking. Standing in the middle of it, as I did in 1976, next to the slip-forming gantry where the huge concrete caissons were made (it was ninety-seven feet high), you felt as an ant might feel in the United Nations building. The Dubai dry dock area actually covers only 200 hectares (just over three-quarters of a square mile), but behind it, and bigger than the dock itself, was a vast 'temporary works area' which marked the original shore line: everything in front of it was on reclaimed land, filled in by dredging from the harbour, so that the total area was 270 000 square metres. 'The temporary works area alone,' people tell you, 'would have constituted a major contract!'

Opened by Her Majesty the Queen during her Middle East tour in February 1979, it provides ship repair and maintenance services for tankers plying from the Gulf. There are three dry docks for vessels of 1 million, 0·5 million and 0·35 million tons deadweight respectively, together with eight berths and the buildings and specialized equipment

required for the maintenance and repair of the current range
of tankers as well as the 'ULCCs' (ultra large crude carriers)
of the future.

All the design work, approved by Sir William Halcrow,
the consulting engineers, was by Taylor Woodrow, and involved several special skills of the Group – Taylor Woodrow
International civil design and shipyard equipment design
departments; Taylor Woodrow Construction mechanical,
electrical, and process division and materials and research
laboratories, and Phillips Consultants Ltd. Octavius Atkinson,
Taylor Woodrow's structural steel subsidiary at Harrogate,
supplied 5 500 tons of steelwork for dockside buildings
alone.

The walls of the dry docks are formed by lines of precast
concrete caissons each 30 × 17 × 17 metres, each weighing
3 500 tons. The docks are 525 × 100 metres, 415 × 80 metres,
and 370 × 66 metres respectively. The administration and
temporary works area comprises maintenance and engineering workshops, a club, offices, paint and other stores (including one for 9 metre-diameter ship propellers), a fitting-out
berth, a machine and fitting-out shop 30 metres wide (the
size of an airship hangar), and a gantry crane of 100 ton
capacity, plant storage and labour camps. In the middle
of all this, the planners were careful to leave an old fertility
shrine which is sacred to the many Hindu workers here.

By the beginning of 1974 much preparatory work had
been done, such as the placing of rock fill in the sea to form
nearly three miles of 'bunds' to retain dredged sand; and in
the interim period between the preliminary agreement
between the Joint Venture and the Ruler and the actual
signing of the contract, site investigations (including seismo-
graphic surveys and trial borings) had been carried out to
determine the ground strata beneath the dock site. Dredging
was done by Costain's Dutch subsidiary Blankevoort, known

as COBLA, whose vessel *Global Bay* has a peak capacity of
1 000 cubic metres of spoil per hour.

The shape of the breakwater was evolved after model
studies at the Southall laboratories which simulated the effect
of waves on the breakwater. (The terminology is fascinating
to non-engineers: the 'expected height' of a '100-year wave'
is thirty-two feet; 'significant wave height' means the top
third of it. These expressions are believed to have been coined
by U.S. Army engineers. Other phrases of linguistic interest
which this reporter noticed were 'We're over the learning
curve now', 'you can't do a job like this with a Dinky toy',
and the word *stabit* – a Henry-Moore-like concrete shape,
which, interlocking with others, provides a stable coffer-dam.
They are using 28 000 stabits at Port Rashid; each weighs
fifteen tons and costs £400 by the time it is in place.)

By May 1975 it was known that the dock gates were to be
of an entirely new type, officially described as a 'modular
multiple propped flap gate' in which the moving bearing
surfaces are not loaded when the gate is closed. As we recall
from the more detailed description in Chapter IV, the three
gates are fifteen metres high and together weigh 2 300 tons.

In December 1975 the Ruler of Dubai appointed the
Costain–Taylor Woodrow Joint Venture as contractors for
the construction of the £120 million extension to Port Rashid,
next to the dry dock. Port Rashid, already the largest man-
made deep-water harbour in the Middle East, had in the
three years of its existence already proved a tremendous
success. Another twenty-two berths were to be built, with
provision to handle the most modern 'roll-on/roll-off' container ships. The first five berths – complete with transit sheds
and other associated facilities – were handed over ahead of
schedule early in 1978 and completion of the whole project is
planned for 1979. Thus the Ruler will achieve his ambition of
making Dubai once again 'the entrepôt of the Gulf' (and by

using this phrase he makes it clear that Dubai, by no means as oil-rich as Abu Dhabi, looks to trade and industry as its main source of wealth: hence the new industrial zone with its own port, nineteen miles west of Dubai at Jebal Ali). And if anyone doubts whether so many berths are needed, let him go up in an aircraft and see the patient queue of ships waiting to dock and unload their cargo in a strict order of priority which begins: passengers, food, cement . . . (there were 180 when I was there, and some of them had been waiting two months). And when the jumbo tankers arrive, they will need (and they will have) a turning circle in the dry dock of one kilometre.

In the dry dock 162 caissons were needed to form the walls of the three docks and eight berths. The casting yard where they were made contained ten beds in two rows of five. Underneath were rails on which bogies travelled to move the huge mass of concrete to the water's edge. At a certain stage 54 four-wheeled bogies, each carrying a 100-ton jack, were moved into position underneath. The 3 500-ton structure was then lifted off the casting bed and rolled sideways to the centre of the yard, where it was transferred to a second set of bogies which ran on more rails (they criss-crossed the sideways rails at right-angles). It was then moved down the yard on a hy-draulic ratchet system to a 4 000-ton capacity Synchrolift which lowered it into the water so that it could be floated out to its prepared position. Here one-metre-deep troughs were drilled in the rock to receive it as, guided by mooring winches, it was filled with water to make it sink precisely into the troughs, to be grouted and made watertight. Caissons were launched at an average rate of two-and-a-half per week.

Christmas 1976 saw the critical stage when 370 million gallons of sea water were pumped out of the two largest dry docks in order to construct the dock floors. It was critical because, although every precaution had been taken against possible seepage of water from the sea through and under the cofferdam bund, there was still an unknown factor – the extent to which water might percolate through the rock *below* the seabed. It was also important to monitor the water held within the bund itself, for the floor of the docks is a good twelve metres below the waters of the Arabian Gulf outside the bund. A dry dock has to be *dry*. Dewatering took two-and-a-half weeks – you can't do it continuously, and one metre's depth in ten or twelve hours is reckoned to be a good, cautious speed. All fears were groundless; everything went according to plan.

'We've had a number of technical worries,' admitted Walter Hogbin, Taylor Woodrow's project manager in the Joint Venture when I met him at that time. 'Although they're only half the size of the Mulberry caissons, they're still the biggest ones ever slip-formed in the Middle East. The method of launching them was new to some of us and the launching of the first caisson was probably our biggest worry.' How does it feel to be second-in-command of the biggest civil engineering project in the world? 'I'm absolutely thrilled. We have an élite team here. It's a civil engineer's dream!' What is so satisfying about it? 'We're all grown-up children playing with a giant Meccano set. It's the fun of watching things grow.'

As John Cox in Oman hand-picked some of his team from 'good blokes' he had worked with in West Africa, so Walter Hogbin, still only forty, a veteran of Wylfa nuclear power station and two harbours, Marsa el Bregha and Singapore container wharf, brought with him 'good blokes' such as John Calkin, chief engineer, and Roy Dimond, plant manager, with whom he had worked in Singapore. A planning team spent ten months at Western House, with a nucleus of six or seven engineers gathered around Walter Hogbin and John Calkin – staff organization, supply lines, plant lists, everything – and by New Year's Eve 1973 all was ready.

'Basic planning and supply organization is much more
necessary out here than in Europe,' Hogbin says. The supply
system has been speeded up by Costain-Taylor Woodrow
(hereinafter referred to as 'Costay') who now have their own
berth: at one time there were twenty-five ships full of Joint
Venture supplies queueing up to unload.

'Joint Venture' – 'JV' – you hardly ever hear anyone in
Dubai talk about Costain or Taylor Woodrow, and most of
the time you do not know to which group the person you are
talking to belongs. Collectively, they call themselves 'JV
people'. The JV employs 5 per cent of all the people in Dubai,
with nearly 200 Europeans and some 6 000 Asians, mostly
Indians and Pakistanis. The corresponding Oman figures are
over 200 Europeans and 3 500 to 4 000 Asians. The Joint
Venture is wholly responsible for the Asians, who are housed
in buildings as well as tents. Hindus and Moslems, united
by the task in hand, get on well together but have separate
camps and kitchens to cook the food prescribed for each
by custom and religion. They are recruited by special agents
in India, and flown from Bombay to the Gulf and back
again on leave; fares are paid by the Joint Venture, which
will have the responsibility of returning them home when
the contract eventually finishes.

How does a British community live in this sub-tropical
place where the brand-new roads disappear into the solid
heat-haze of the desert? Despite the apparent sophistication of
the surroundings – the International Conference Centre, the
tall hotels, and a Rank Leisure Centre soon to be born – most
pleasures are home-made and social. Strangely, Taylor
Woodrow have not yet found a suitable place for improvizing
a golf-course – 'it's the greenness of England you miss out
here', Walter Hogbin says, and this is why he goes home for
summer leave to his native Kent. Deprived of golf, he is a
keen member of the Offshore Sailing Club, formed for all

companies engaged on the dry-dock contract, whose commo-
dore is Roger Hayward, resident engineer for Halcrow.
With his Hunter-Europa nineteen-foot fixed keel racing
cruiser (four berths, and the crew is his family) Walter
competes for the Sir Frank Taylor Cup in a series of races
held during the seven months of the ocean-racing season.
When he isn't sailing he is playing squash, often with a
Pakistani statistician named Sajad Vine who just happens to
be a world-class amateur.

How anyone finds time for recreation at all is puzzling.
Work goes on non-stop, day and night, the shift changing at
6.30 a.m. and p.m. The Costay Guest-House, presided over
by Mr Khan who thinks you are seriously ill if you do not eat
a full cooked English breakfast every day, is mercifully a
couple of miles away from the main centre of activity. Here
you are lulled to sleep every night by the music of distant piledrivers, and when you look out of the window you see a
faraway forest of cranes some of which, you are told, are
'higher than Salisbury Cathedral'.

As for holidays, it depends what you mean by them. In
Oman and Dubai certain religious holidays have to be built
into all planning (on office walls in Western House, in
London, there are copies of a long list of them running into
two columns). In Moslem countries Friday is Sunday, so
Christians must perforce work on Sundays. In addition to
official Christian holidays, there are, to name but a few, the
Moslem New Year (3 January), the Prophet's Birthday (13
March), the Prophet's Ascension (28 July), Id-al-Fitr (the
end of Ramadan, four days in either September or October),
Id-al-Adha (three days in December), and National Day (18
November in Oman and 2 December in Dubai). The two Ids
are the ones to look out for – do not attempt to travel during
this time: nearly all aircraft are requisitioned for pilgrims to
Mecca and you will simply be stranded at a plane-less airport.

A few Taylor Woodrow people go home for Christmas leave, but the majority send to England for Christmas trees and puddings which will be eaten with the usual ceremony in a temperature of about blood-heat during what is politely called 'the cool season'. If you want to have a holiday the hard way you can, like Fred and Liz Loadwick on their honeymoon, drive an MG Midget out from U.K. with no maps and no local knowledge of intervening countries, through parts of Turkey where there are no roads, no towns, and certainly no garages for a hundred miles, ending up at Bandar Abbas in Southern Iran, from which the short voyage across the Gulf to Dubai is a comparative luxury.

As always the wives are indispensable. They run schools, they work in offices, they entertain. Walter Hogbin's wife Gerry runs an infant school in their garage. Several other wives do the same. There are about eighty JV children of school age (i.e. 4½ upwards). Liz, wife of Fred Loadwick (he runs a crusher concrete production laboratory), is a trained teacher who in less than two years has become bilingual in Arabic, and now teaches English in an Arab school. There is also an English-speaking school run by Shell, Costain, Taylor Woodrow, and other firms working in Dubai – about a quarter of its pupils are JV children. The Arab school, which is co-educational, is for children of mixed marriages and expatriates who may be here as long as twenty years. One of the Costain wives runs a kennel for pets and also a car-hire service. Carolyn, wife of chief engineer Brian Miller (another veteran of the Singapore container wharf and now at Port Rashid), has two jobs, one as a secretary at the Danchelesco Trading Co. (8 a.m. to 1 p.m.), the other at a local radio station where she reads the news in English at 2.30 and 8 p.m. The Miller children will eventually go to boarding schools in England (there is an air service with 'nanny' stewardesses between London and Dubai known as the Lollipop Special).

What can you do in Dubai when you have a few hours to spare? You can go to the expensive Country Club, or to the Costay Club (of which everybody in the JV is automatically a member, including children), which has a film show twice a week and a games night once a week (anything from squash to tiddleywinks). You can get a little rough shooting (desert rabbits, mostly) at Wadi Hatta, the quarry from which all aggregate comes: to get to it, you follow the Joint Venture's desert road eastwards for about ninety miles, through bits of the neighbouring states of Sharjah Fujira, and Oman until you get to where the mountains begin, in an enclave belonging to Dubai. You would be well advised to do this under the guidance of David Snell, the ex-R.A.F. radio officer, who is in charge of the control-room for the seventy-six radios by which vehicles, offices, cranes, and the Wadi Hatta people keep in touch with each other. But perhaps the pleasantest way of spending a day off is to drive to Khor Fakkan, a beach due east on the Indian Ocean side of the peninsula where there are trees and grass and coral, and the swimming is safe.

We have said that the two corporate personalities of Richard Costain and Taylor Woodrow have been united in the marriage of a joint venture. Why did this happen, how does it work, and what is its future? They are two of the top five international civil engineering firms, and it was known that if ever there were major construction works in Dubai, the Ruler was likely to choose a British firm or firms. The Joint Venture is a marriage of equals, but it was not a shotgun wedding: it is however a practical one. Some local observers have spoken of Taylor Woodrow 'breaking into Costain territory'. Neither partner regards the matter in this light.

The management board of 'Costay' in London is headed by David Newell, managing director of Costain International, and George Hazell, deputy chairman of Taylor Woodrow

International. The joint London managers are Fred Tarrant (from Costain) and Mike Angwin (from Taylor Woodrow). The project office is at Costain's London headquarters, the design department at Taylor Woodrow's Times House Ruislip. In Dubai, the contracts manager is Costain's David Chetwin, usually described in the press as a 'rugged New Zealander', and the project manager is Walter Hogbin. People have to have titles, but all are agreed on one thing: what, either separately or together, they have to offer their clients is human resources. If you have better people, you do a better job. 'As contractors,' says David Chetwin, 'we have one product and that is men.'

All would no doubt agree on another point: that the greatest risk, which dictates the need for complete integration to cut costs, is inflation. Back in 1972 a labourer's pay was eight dirhams (£1.33) a day. Today it is twenty-three dirhams, which is nearly 200 per cent inflation. Since 1974 there has been about 30 per cent inflation on materials. Currency variations have also raised costs. Some of this inflation can be protected, but about 35 per cent of it – for example, salary increases of expatriates – cannot. No wonder David Newell has been quoted as saying: 'Unless you co-ordinate your management policy, commercial policy and financial policy, you are going to waste money.'

This means using what you have got and buying as little abroad as you can. In the workshop area behind the dry dock, the JV makes some of its own furniture (to avoid importing wood), builds some of its own vehicles, spares, equipment, even some machinery. They have their own computers on site. They print their own stationery. Maintenance is obviously of first importance: some of the dump trucks that bring aggregate from the quarries are reckoned to have travelled 330 000 miles. Summing up the whole operation, Mike Angwin says: 'It is a very difficult, demanding job, but we

shall do it by good housekeeping, zeal and efficiency.'
Whether Costain and Taylor Woodrow will come together
in other joint ventures in the future is 'a question of horses for
courses'. Both groups have about half their contracts overseas,
and about a third of this is in the Middle East. They have
resources in the same area, but they also compete in the same
area.

In a recent interview, David Chetwin stressed the enormous importance of back-up resources in the United Kingdom. 'The managements of the two companies decided to
divide the work between them because the human resources
needed to complete in the time and to the standard required
would not only stretch the resources of both organizations
but could also restrict each company's opportunity to enter
other markets. So the job was undertaken by Costain and
Taylor Woodrow as a joint venture, with Taylor Woodrow
handling the design. Fortunately both companies have vast
resources overseas and are providing very competent back-up
facilities in London for such key functions as buying, recruiting personnel, obtaining plant, providing expertise and so on,
and on site one always has recourse to the resources of
London for any particular problems that might arise.'

A civil engineering company that lacked this kind of
experience could find itself in very expensive difficulties,
which is why certain overseas contracts, at first sight very
lucrative, are sometimes turned down. 'Without the experience of overseas contracting and the resources that both
joint venture partners provide, neither contract could have
been undertaken to the price and programme we have
offered.'

In a Middle East country you cannot just telephone someone if you need an extra heavy-duty crane. You should have
foreseen, nine months ago, that you would need it and
ordered it then; you should also have foreseen that there

might be delays due to any number of reasons, and that this notional loss of time must be built into the expected time of arrival. For getting the overall job done, you have to gather round you men who can take charge of whole sections of the work which are middle-sized contracts in themselves – preferably men who have managed entire projects themselves in other parts of the world. You also have to centralize your accounting: the JV spends about a million pounds a week and receives vast payments too, so it makes sense that it should have built its own bank next to the site office – the British Bank of the Middle East, which is part of the Hong Kong & Shanghai Bank.

The Taylor Woodrow viewpoint on all this was summed up by George Hazell, deputy chairman of Taylor Woodrow International, back in 1976. He certainly sees a trend towards joint ventures overseas, especially for the 'jumbo' kind such as Dubai, and especially between British civil engineering groups: 'Let us not lose sight of the fact that British contractors are second to none – thus together they present a formidable force.' While paying the usual tributes to 'capable and efficient team members' and the increasing effort to secure overseas work which caused Taylor Woodrow International, almost incredibly, to double its turnover every year between 1972 and 1975, he is down to earth about the need for profitability. 'Obviously we cannot continue at this rate indefinitely.' For 1976 he anticipated only an 80 per cent increase of turnover on the 1975 figure, 'and then in 1977 we hope to repeat the 1976 figure with a small increase'.

Thus, for profitability, there has to be a wary attitude towards some contracts, especially the 'fixed price' kind which can be a booby-trap in this age of inflation. What are the reasons for *not* bidding for a big contract? 'The factors that could influence our decision are the client's requirements set out in the conditions of contract with regard to the terms

The Regent's Canal makes an attractive setting for the Lisson Green housing development.

Ornamental plasterwork by Jonathan James Ltd.

The St. Katharine-by-the-Tower development in London.

During the Silver Jubilee River Progress on 9 June 1977, Her Majesty Queen Elizabeth visited the St. Katharine development where she was presented with a bouquet of flowers by 12-year-old Ellen Drew.

The attractive award-winning "Rochester" home on the Normandy estate near Guildford.

A two-bedroomed bungalow designed and manufactured by Swiftplan Ltd. for the overseas market.

Fernside Neighbourhood Centre, Alameda, near Oakland on San Francisco Bay.

Work under way in Ghana on the Tono project to irrigate some 2400 hectares of land.

On 5 August 1976 in perfect weather the Thistle 'A' steel jacket was successfully floated out of the Graythorp yard and towed along the Seaton Channel to the open sea.

Production modules under construction at Dragados y Construcciones S.A. yard, Almeria, Spain.

Close-up of a 9·14 m diameter flotation leg assembly.

Industrial premises on the island of Penang.

The first coal seams being exposed near the surface at the Butterwell opencast site.

of payment, penal bonds, arbitration ruling, no escalation
clauses, etc. . . . I suggest that no competent contractor can
afford *not* to pick and choose.'

Often it is the joint venture with a local firm that promises
greater long-term rewards, because its growth begins more
slowly and is based on personal relationship as well as on
diversified work. Huge as the Dubai projects are, George
Hazell has a soft spot for Oman. 'Some people may describe
our joint venture there as a text-book example of how to set
up a joint venture overseas. In the early days of 1970–71 we
went through a period of getting to know each other whilst
we, as Taylor Woodrow International, completed our first
project in Muscat with mutual confidence developing
between both parties; we then entered the next stage where
the Towell organization became our appointed agent. Then,
with an ever-growing order book, it was considered appropriate to set up a JV company.'

Which, as Frank Taylor always says is having a success that
can be described as 'not unsatisfactory'.

VII

Agro-Industry

NEARLY thirty years ago the paper-rationed news-papers of Britain were full of demands for 'a national plan for water'. There were all sorts of ideas, condemned at the time as 'Heath Robinson', for achieving this, including one for pumping sea water from the English Channel through pipelines to the upper reaches of the Thames, so that the volume of water flowing over Teddington Weir could be increased and controlled (nobody said anything about desalinating it).

There had been, in the summer of 1949, a small drought; and it always takes a drought to make people think about conserving water. As soon as rain falls again, the matter is forgotten by all but a few scientific voices crying in the wilderness. One of those voices, a quarter of a century ago, was Taylor Woodrow. Pigeon-holed somewhere in Whitehall is their design to dam the Wash. Interviewed during the great drought of 1976, George Hazell, director of Taylor Woodrow Ltd. and deputy chairman of Taylor Woodrow International said: 'Our considerable irrigation experience is available and could be used by agro-industry and farms throughout the country to overcome drought conditions and irrigate crops, but first of all our country has to overcome the present lack of water available.' Had the Wash Dam been implemented, and 'if this had been the first of many such forward-thinking schemes, I suggest we would not have our present water problem'.

The expression 'agro-industry' has not yet made its way into the *Oxford English Dictionary*, and it is to be hoped that a more precise and less cumbersome word will be found. But it represents a good deal of pretty deep thinking about a huge area of technology where farming, food-storing, energy, water conservation, industry, and ecology all meet together. It requires, in the long run, very large-scale, sometimes national planning. Like the futurology of Herman Kahn, of the Hudson Institute 'think-tank', it gives long-term reason for hope. And it imposes the duty, typical of Taylor Woodrow thought over the past fifty years, of thinking ahead, far beyond the task in hand. If we build a dam for a government, should we not also be helping them with relevant technology – agronomics, soil-testing, livestock if necessary, anything they need which can be easily supplied by our diversified skills or buying organization?

Much of agro-industry is necessarily concerned with food. About 120 babies are born every minute, and the world's population is increasing. It is 4 100 million now, and, barring accidents, it is expected to be 15 000 million in A.D. 2207. The land available for cultivation, however, will remain constant unless new techniques are applied. The first of these is to ensure water supplies for irrigation. Irrigation raises the economic status of rural areas, earnings rise, purchasing power increases to levels comparable with industrialized urban areas.

Vast sums of money are often involved in this, and so it is essential to make a careful distinction between 'planning' and 'implementation'. Planning activities have to be directed towards the reality of possible achievement. You can be over-ambitious. You can start with too few reliable data. It may be far better to plan a limited 'pilot' operation to make sure that the larger one will work. It may be that feasibility studies will reveal that the whole scheme is impracticable in that particular area, or that the cost, under inflationary conditions, will escalate beyond the client's means (though it may be possible to help him to raise the finance).

Taylor Woodrow's background and experience is first in construction, and second in a very full range of engineering and management disciplines. In agro-industrial projects, they are strengthened by their association with companies who are actively engaged in agricultural production and processing, and so can offer a comprehensive planning service. They can undertake the construction and operation of pilot farms or limited areas of implementation and integrate the findings into planning studies which will reveal exactly how to go on to full-scale development, so that the scheme can start paying its way and justifying its investment as soon as possible. While the development is still under construction, resources can be mobilized and technicians trained to begin operating it as soon as construction, or the first phase of construction, is complete (we shall see how this was done in the Romanian irrigation scheme). Much depends, too, on the type of contract, especially when operating abroad. Assuming that a contract for planning will lead to participation in implementation, participation can range from a management contract in which maximum use is made of locally available construction resources involving the client's own personnel, to a complete 'turnkey' package for design, supply of materials and equipment, construction and operation of the whole project.

In north Ghana close to the Upper Volta border about eight kilometres from the nearest town, Navrongo, an important irrigation project is being carried out on the Tono River. It involves an earth dam on the river, land clearing and development, and the construction of gravity irrigation and drainage systems over 2 400 hectares of land for the production of rice and horticultural crops.

The first sod was cut by General Acheampong, the then

Head of State, on 27 March 1975. After a township and a workshop and office complexes had been built, permanent works began in September. They consisted of two main sections, an earth dam to create a reservoir, and the land to be irrigated down-stream from the dam. The original design was carried out by Taylor Woodrow's design assistance team. The dam, 3½ kilometres long with a maximum heigh of 18 metres consists of an impermeable clay core, faced downstream with filter layers of sand and crushed stone, and upstream with further filters faced with heavy rock 'rip rap' to protect it from wave action. In the dam embankment is an offtake culvert and valve tower of concrete, designed to control the supply of water into the main irrigation canal. A concrete 'scour pipe' to minimize silting runs through the bottom of the dam: this has a double function – to empty the reservoir for maintenance purposes, and to enable some water to be drawn off to supply the town of Navrongo. The high water level in the reservoir is controlled by a concrete spillway crest and spillway or overflow channels: the spillway is designed to resist what engineers call a '1 in 200 year flood' which is reckoned to be a flow of 315 cubic metres per second.

The whole of the 1860-hectare area of the reservoir was cleared of trees by heavy excavating equipment: some idea of this task can be gained from the fact that many of the baobab trees were six metres in girth. In creating a reservoir it is sometimes possible to leave trees where they are, but in this case the Ghanaians want to establish a local fishing industry, and submerged trees would endanger boats and nets. The water is fed to the irrigated land by a system of canals – laterals and sublaterals. Upland soils are used mainly for furrow irrigation, good for growing tomatoes and a variety of vegetables; lowland soils are used for the paddy cultivation of rice, which needs controlled flooding. A second main canal, higher up the side of the valley, is fed from the first canal by two pumping stations which lift the water forty-six feet at a rate of 10 000 gallons a minute.

Land preparation in the irrigated area comprises more clearing of trees, and shaping the land to its required levels and gradients by harrowing, levelling, and planing, so that water fed from the twenty miles of canals to fields and paddies reaches every part of the area. Ground considered unsuitable for irrigation will be used for some seventy-five hectares of fish-ponds, fed from the main canal, for the intensive farming of fish.

There is nothing particularly new in this kind of irrigation. The Tono scheme was devised during the 1960s by a Greek firm of consulting engineers on the basis of an idea from the United Nations Food and Agricultural Organization. It was intended to make local farmers' livelihood more secure by ensuring at least one crop a year, and perhaps two. Owing to financial difficulties and political instability, the scheme was shelved for a number of years and then revived in 1974. What Taylor Woodrow have been able to bring to this project is the ability to implement it on a much larger scale and in a shorter time than a smaller contractor could have done. And their long experience of working in Ghana has been invaluable: of the 600-strong team assembled for the project, many tradesmen and plant operators had learnt their jobs with Taylor Woodrow many years before.

One of the toughest tasks was to get the machinery to the site, which is 400 miles from the coast. Much of it was ferried 250 miles along another man-made lake, that giant expanse of water impounded behind the Volta Dam in the 1960s. It is very much an earth-moving job. Now the Tono Valley is the changing its colour from withered brown to lush green as the whole project nears completion and farmers are already drawing benefit from it.

Teamwork in action was dramatically demonstrated on

Sunday morning, 16 September 1976, when the banks of the nearby Doba reservoir burst, imperilling the water supply for both the town of Navrongo and local farmers. The rainy season was just ending and the reservoir was full to capacity. Taylor Woodrow, under project manager Keith Rose and the Tono divisional director Barry Ing-Simmons, who happened to be there on a routine visit, and the Ghanaian authorities quickly got the team together to plug the leak with loads of large stones. Then everybody's Sunday peace was disturbed as machines were mobilized and controlled by radio, a temporary access road to the breach was improvised, and within four hours the flow had been reduced to a trickle, ready for a more permanent repair to begin. In thanking the Taylor Woodrow team for their prompt action, Mr Kwabena Wiafe of the Ghanaian Irrigation Department remarked that had they not been on the spot at the time, the reservoir could have been a total loss, as no other contractor could have mobilized so much heavy plant in time.

The biggest irrigation project so far undertaken by Taylor Woodrow was completed in 1973. Much of the Tono irrigation scheme will be achieved by allowing water from a reservoir to find its own level; but in the Sadova–Corabia province of Romania, the problem was to fetch water out of the river Danube and pump it up to a height of 118 metres, whence it is distributed by grids of pipelines over an area of 300 square miles (twice the size of the Isle of Wight) so that 'artificial rain' can be sprinkled over crops at the turning of a hydrant. The pipes and 'antennae' are supplied by 134 automatically controlled pressure pumping stations, each serving a plot of about two square miles.

It all happened in five years. The Taylor Woodrow Irrigation Group (TWIG) was a consortium of Taylor Woodrow International, G.E.C. Electrical Projects, Sigmund Pulsometer Pumps, and Vickers, headed by Taylor Woodrow

International. Every time a hydrant is turned on, a sequence of pumps and weirs begins automatically to replace the water used, and the 'head regulator' gate at the Danube bank opens slightly to let more water into the system. The system enables this once derelict flood plain and the terraces to the north to yield two crops of fruit and grain a year from soil which used to be so dry that the vines had to grow extra long roots as they desperately sought moisture.

This was only the first development in an ambitious Romanian Government programme of irrigation along the banks of the Danube (it is reckoned that another 16 000 square miles *could* be irrigated). The soils in this area are deep and sandy and respond well to sprinklers. In the bad old days before 1970 the area was stricken by severe droughts and crop yields were unpredictable. Now, the long summer season allows the double cropping of wheat and maize; grapes, peaches, rice, sunflower seeds, tobacco, and alfalfa also thrive here. All this in a country where you can still see *shaduf* wells which date back to Biblical times.

An essential part of Taylor Woodrow's contract with Romania was the handing-over stage. Andrew Leslie (now co-ordinator in Muscat, Oman) was handover manager in the last stages of the operation, having spent three years in the TWIG planning department at Western House. 'We had to train Romanians to work the system,' he says; with a limited command of each other's language this was not easy, 'but we had a 300-page manual to be implemented.' Andrew Leslie was one of the thirteen TWIG members who, although it took a year to get Government permission, married a Romanian girl.

Phase One of the project was brought into use, right on schedule, in June 1972, and the rest became fully operational in the summer of 1974, monitored and automated by computer. Some fifteen miles of main canals, five miles of steel conduits, 230 miles of secondary canals, and 1 037 acres of polythene sheeting to line them, 1 109 miles of P.V.C. pipes, 1 206 miles of aluminium pipes; 100 British personnel and 1 830 Romanians making a new environment – which in the summer of 1974 was featured by Raymond Baxter in the B.B.C. TV programme *Tomorrow's World*. Taylor Woodrow themselves made an award-winning film of the whole operation which Bob Aldred, introducing it to an international audience at a London showing, described as 'a story of a practical and hard-headed act of co-operation between two different ways of life in which a people's socialist republic worked with a consortium of great British firms. It's a good story in which men of different ideas come together to achieve something of human value.'

Long before people started talking about Agro-Industry, Taylor Woodrow had provided, in 1965, a package deal for a poultry farm at Cluthen, Hungary. This was also their second major penetration of Eastern Europe (they had already built a textile mill in Hungary), and it was set up by Arcon (Building Exports), who not only erected Arcon structures but supplied (by air) 54 000 day-old chicks, trained staff to run the farm, and guaranteed the number of eggs.

There was also another TWIG in Brazil – a consortium which included Taylor Woodrow International and Booker McConnell. TWIG Brasil prepared a master-plan for the Petrolina-Juaziero Agro-Industrial Development, a project to irrigate 50 000 hectares (nearly 200 square miles) on the banks of the San Francisco river in north-east Brazil. This again is a drought zone, and the TWIG Brasil study was the latest of several international examinations of the problem of improving the economies of the area, which is known locally as 'The Valley of Hope'. TWIG Brasil has not yet been able to implement its recommendations, for which finance has not yet been raised, but – well, it *is* called The Valley of Hope.

While the Tono Valley irrigation scheme was under construction, another area of Ghana nearby was being investigated for what may be another large agricultural project which goes under the general name of Avu Keta. At Havi, in the Volta region, Taylor Woodrow International are engaged with Tate & Lyle in a joint venture to create a forty-hectare pilot farm which is the first phase of the development of 40 000 hectares for sugar and general agriculture. This involves a detailed feasibility study which includes design and costing of major flood relief works, land clearing, sprinkler and flood irrigation, and other agro-industrial systems. Eventually there will also be a sugar mill.

A similar study has been carried out, also in partnership with Tate & Lyle, at Sunti in north-west Nigeria. This is for the engineering and infrastructural planning and design of an area of 14 000 hectares in a region subject to perennial flooding and waterlogging along the Niger River. This work has been incorporated in a feasibility study for the possible development of an integrated sugar estate and factory geared to an output of 50 000 tonnes a year. It is not yet known whether the Sunti Project will be implemented.

There may very well be other agro-industrial schemes in both West Africa and the Arab world. Taylor Woodrow certainly seem to think so: who else would call a subsidiary company 'Teamwork Agronomics'? This is a company formed for the provision of technical services in connection with an experimental rice-growing project in Liberia. It is worth study simply for its possibilities and the scope of the thinking behind it. Here Taylor Woodrow International were in joint venture with Dalgety Agricultural Development International Ltd., combining their expertise in construction and agricultural planning in the first phase of a multi-million dollar scheme to make Liberia self-sufficient in rice production. It involved the setting-up of a 100-acre pilot farm for growing rice under the mechanically-irrigated conditions envisaged for the main development, hacking down the jungle and pumping water from the Cestos River. A survey of about 30 000 acres of tropical rain forests was also carried out to locate 15 000 acres suitable for the cultivation of paddy rice. The Liberian Government estimated that a yield of 40 000 tons per annum would be needed to make the country independent of imported rice. For Agrimeco, the Liberian Government's agency for all matters concerned with improving agricultural resources, Taylor Woodrow International now have a contract to manage a mechanized land clearance programme aimed at adding 6 000 acres a year to the country's crop-bearing land.

In the Sultanate of Oman, agro-industry is already part of the huge programme of change and innovation envisaged by H.M. The Sultan. Here, among many other projects, Taylor Woodrow have constructed an irrigation system at Garzaiz by which 154 hectares are being supplied with water from tube-wells and irrigated by Farrow 'Dolphin' travelling rain-gun machines. They have also carried out a contract for the 'turnkey' design and construction of a cattle farm which includes 150 hectares of irrigation (again with water from wells), in addition to all the farm facilities – dairy, milk, butter, cheese, and yogurt production, and housing and farm services.

In Malaysia, in 1974, a company called Teamwork Malaysia Sendirian Berhad was formed between Taylor Woodrow International and Malaysian interests. Although a full range of building and civil engineering contracts is contemplated in this area, where Taylor Woodrow have been active for many years, there is some significance in the fact that the chairman and principal shareholder is Tengku Arif Bendahara, who is also chairman of the United Asian Bank and is known throughout Malaysia as 'the timber prince'. The managing director of the new company is Ron Whitehouse, who also master-minds the Oman contracts. The timber operation has since been extended to the vast resources of timber in Sarawak.

It is in a rapidly changing or 'emergent' country that the broadest agro-industrial planning is often possible. The interdependence of industries is clearly revealed when one considers that, for example, brewing and wine-making depend on successful barley and fruit crops; that these in turn depend on irrigation, drainage, machinery, labour, pesticides, chemical fertilizer; that everything depends on communications, power, roads, houses and schools for workers. If cattle are to be reared, they need oilseed and cottonseed in addition to pasture; cottonseed means growing cotton which must either be exported or used in textile mills; the cattle themselves create the need for both a dairy and a meat industry (one of Taylor Woodrow's earliest contracts in Oman was for an abattoir) and tanneries. If you grow food in large quantities you need canning and frozen food factories. If you have a lumber industry, you need pulpmills, for paper, board, packaging and cellulose products. . . . So it goes on.

In a sense, Taylor Woodrow have been in agro-industry since long before the expression was coined. An automated coffee-plant in Ethiopia; sugar mills in British Honduras, Nigeria, and Guyana; a tea factory in Uganda; shoe factories in three different countries; flour mills in Nigeria, Guyana, and Nicaragua; six breweries in Nigeria and Ghana and several more in Britain; a cold store on Ascension Island; a citrus packing station in Libya; six textile factories in West Africa; and irrigation and water supply systems in several continents.

We return again to water, and the world's need of it. We need not be unduly alarmed at current talk about the world's water supplies being 'exhausted by A.D. 2000'. The solution lies close to hand. Taylor Woodrow regard agro-industry as one of their growth areas for the future, and this above all requires water conservation and distribution.

VIII

Homes and Gardens

I N the beginning, as is generally known, there were two houses in Blackpool. The fact that the Taylor Woodrow Group today is a world-wide organization undertaking vast projects of civil engineering is never allowed to obscure that fact. Most builders begin by building houses, and as we shall show, there is a great difference between a house and a home. Taylor Woodrow Homes Ltd. is the company that carries on the founder's first aim – to build homes for people who want to *own* their homes. This, to achieve the ultimate aim – a satisfied customer – requires research and imagination as well as bricks and mortar.

Don Slough, chairman and managing director of Taylor Woodrow Homes, says: 'About 52 per cent of people in the United Kingdom own their own houses, and most of the rest want to as soon as they can afford it.' A chartered surveyor who learnt surveying by correspondence course, he got his practical experience in the Surveyor's Department of Bexhill-on-Sea Borough Council, and joined Taylor Woodrow in 1953. For a man who today says that 'from the earliest age I always wanted to build houses' it was exactly the right time to join: post-war restrictions had at last been lifted, a Tory government was allowing free enterprise its head, and 'speculative building' could be resumed.

That expression needs cleaning up: in the 1920s, 'speculative building' meant rushing up gimcrack houses at cheap prices for quick profits. Unless we can rehabilitate the expression we should probably drop it altogether and use some such phrase as 'free enterprise building'. A speculative builder today is a man who studies the market, finds out the kind of houses people really want, tries to give the buyers something his competitors haven't thought of, and then designs and builds houses with as much individuality as possible in the pleasantest possible surroundings at realistic prices. The interior fittings and layout are of great importance, and a feminine viewpoint must be consulted at all times; one of Taylor Woodrow's greatest assets is having Lady Taylor on the board – first as a director and now as deputy chairman. They also welcome constructive suggestions of other director's wives.

Taylor Woodrow have built their share of council houses, and 'contract houses' (many of them on a 'design-and-build' basis) by competitive tender, and to criticize local authorities' housing policies might seem to be quarrelling with their bread-and-butter. But they do sometimes feel there is room for improvement, in both design and cost. Another phrase which needs a new image is 'council house'. There is even a small social stigma at work – (remember the words of 'My Old Man's a Dustman'). In districts where they have been building close to a council estate, Taylor Woodrow have been surprised by the number of council house tenants who have inquired about the new 'speculative' houses going up. Despite political schemes to enable council house tenants to buy their houses, it almost looks as if many people regard a council house as 'somewhere to live until you can afford something better'. (Myton's refurbishment of council houses may be one answer to this.)

Today, Taylor Woodrow Homes are building mostly in the southern counties, with offshoots to Norfolk (King's Lynn) and Yorkshire. Dick Mooney has recently been made deputy managing director for U.K. operations with Arthur

Driver as assistant deputy managing director. Since 1968 they
have had a branch in Scotland under Bill Goodhew. In 1978
this became a fully fledged company – Taylor Woodrow
Homes (Scotland) Ltd. with Don Slough as chairman and
Bill Goodhew managing director. House-buying is a fairly
recent development in Scotland where for many years people
seemed to prefer to pay rent.

A demand for homes often follows other big contracts,
such as power stations: the people who work there need
homes nearby, and so a new community is born. For some
buyers, customer-satisfaction leads to a repeat order if there
are Taylor Woodrow houses in the right district: just
under one-third of buyers go for another Taylor Woodrow
home when the family increases or they have to move because
of the husband's job. Some families are in their third Taylor
Woodrow home. A first-time buyer usually wants a two-bed-
room 'starter' house. Most Taylor Woodrow homes are in the
£16000 to £30 000 price bracket, but a luxury detached four-
bedroomed house with double garage goes up to £40 000.

In Scotland, work has been in progress since 1972 at
Craigends, near Glasgow, on 2 000 three- and four-bedroom
houses. Craigends, once the home of the Cunninghames,
Lairds of Craigends, of whose house only a ruined tall tower
overlooking the River Gryfe remains, is one of those typical
dignified woodland settings favoured by Taylor Woodrow.
In Basingstoke, Hampshire, nine-tenths of a 1 085-house
development at Brighton Hill, and another 221 slightly more
expensive houses at Kempshott Hill are nearing completion.
In Kent, there is a new large development at Vintners Park,
Maidstone, which includes a shopping centre run by Taylor
Woodrow Property; and at Ashford, Kent, work started in
1976 on a 500-house estate in the grounds of a former stately
home, Godinton Park, in the Weald of Kent. At Warren
Wood, High Wycombe, the 'Belgravia', a split-level design

for a four-bedroom detached house, may be seen to advantage in a natural woodland setting. As in many Taylor Woodrow developments, environment here was one of the key factors in buying land. At King's Lynn, Norfolk, 600 houses are being built, and there are new Taylor Woodrow developments at Foxhills, Aylesbury; Flitwick, Bedfordshire; Newport Pagnell, Buckinghamshire; Haxby, Yorkshire; Bournemouth, Hants; Maidenhead, Berks; and more new sites are coming on stream as new land is acquired.

Taylor Woodrow Homes, the oldest member company of the Group, is in touch with every other home-building part of the Group, and so can provide a valuable service to overseas companies, processing sales inquiries for Taylor Woodrow's resources in Canada, Perth (Western Australia), Gibraltar, Mallorca, and of course the new American developments described in Chapter IX.

All buyers of Taylor Woodrow's homes are offered good mortgage facilities, and each home is inspected by the National House Building Council, an independent, non-profit-making body, approved by successive Governments, and having among its members representatives from building societies, building employers' organizations, the Royal Institution of Chartered Surveyors, the Royal Institute of British Architects, building trade unions, and consumer bodies. Taylor Woodrow are founder members of the N.H.B.C. (as they are also of the American Home Owners' Warranty). The N.H.B.C. publishes booklets advising people on what to look for in buying a new house, and offers a ten-year structural protection plan.

The demand for homes is always with us and continues to grow. Many buyers see house-ownership as one of the few reliable forms of investment in inflationary times. From the builder's viewpoint, much depends on changes in Government policy on releasing land for building, and the ability of prospective buyers to increase their personal savings. Land prices have been unstable since 1971, and the skill and experience of Taylor Woodrow Homes in buying land has stood them in good stead. In 1973, for example, the building land market underwent a considerable change as labour and materials costs rose sharply, and many builders were left holding expensive land which they had bought on the expectation that house selling prices would rise ahead of costs. The Community Land Act, introduced in 1975, which siphons off the development value of land to the Government instead of the landowner, has not made things easier.

Many old prejudices went by the board when, a year or two ago, the biggest, newest (and possibly last) of the New Towns laid its plans for housing its people. At Milton Keynes, Buckinghamshire, Taylor Woodrow are building 160 homes for sale on a 10½-acre development. For the enlightened Corporation is providing for a large measure of home-ownership in Milton Keynes. There are detached, semi-detached, and terraced dwellings, all with garages and in the £20 000, to £25 000 price range. Building began in the spring of 1977, and the first owners were in residence by the beginning of 1978. Detached houses have central heating installed, and central heating is an optional extra for all other units. Lord Campbell of Eskan, chairman of the Development Corporation, said in an interview in Febuary 1977: 'We are naturally delighted with this substantial investment in Milton Keynes by Taylor Woodrow Homes. We have been greatly encouraged by the number and quality of private developers coming forward with proposals for homes here. They are helping us to get back to our policy target of 50 per cent home-ownership – a target which the economic circumstances of the past few years have made it hard to attain.'

The estate, called Golden Valley, is in the Eaglestone

quarter of Milton Keynes. There is to be substantial landscaping and tree planting, a park, children's playing facilities, and many other amenities, including two hospitals
and a Health Centre for Eaglestone.

Meanwhile, Taylor Woodrow Homes continues to expand
abroad. When did it take the basic decision to look overseas again? ('Again', because of course the Group had been
in the eastern States of America since 1935. In Mallorca,
where Sir Frank and Lady Taylor have a holiday house of
their own, Taylor Woodrow homes are built by local labour
under Señor Jaime Ballester.) Probably soon after they made
£1 million profit. We shall see in the next chapter the daring
venture in Florida at The Meadows, Sarasota. Though well
researched Florida was, at that time, new territory to Taylor
Woodrow. On the other hand, the Group had had one foot
in California for a number of years, and not only in the
property sphere. There is also 'Taycal' (Taylor Woodrow of
California Inc.) in San Francisco, headed by Ted Marsh in
London with Roger Machin in charge locally: it is owned
50-50 by Taylor Woodrow and I.C.I. Pension Fund. There
were, therefore, on-the-spot ears to the ground. The actual
command to advance farther into California seems to have
been given during Frank Taylor's visit to Sarasota in November 1976. Could there be a repeat of the Sarasota success story
in California, 3 000 miles away? On 2 January 1977, a land
investigation team comprising Bob Stephens and Gordon
Tippell flew out to study, not only land, but the whole
market – the kinds of houses preferred, income brackets, price
ranges, mortgage facilities, the speed of building and selling
to be expected. They were closely pursued by Don Slough
and his co-director Dick Mooney, who were there for three
weeks, and (on 18 January) by Frank and Christine Taylor. In
the name of Taylor Woodrow Homes Ltd. they bought 300
acres of land at Bear Brand Ranch West, Laguna Beach, about

sixty miles south of Los Angeles. Construction will start in 1979. It will not be a 'P.U.D.' (Planned Unit Development) like The Meadows at Sarasota, nor will there be any need to group everything round a golf-course, since there is already one nearby. At the same time, they also decided to buy land for 260 housing plots at Visalia, between Los Angeles and San Francisco, where Taycal already have a shopping mall. There Taylor Woodrow are laying out the site for themselves and Taycal on a joint venture basis, and selling off serviced lots to other builders.

Later they bought land at Rancho Mirage, near Palm Springs in southern California, where work began in March 1978 on the Casas de Seville development of seventy-two luxurious detached homes in carefully landscaped surroundings.

Laguna, Palm Springs and Sarasota, apart from the sunshine and the sea, are very different. It may not be quite true that 'no part of Florida is more than 50 feet above sea level', but most of it *is* pretty flat. California has perhaps the greatest variety of scenery of any land in the world, and around Laguna it is hilly and will need a different type of planning.

The opening up of Arabia points to a new market for new types of house specially designed for sub-tropical countries. Shortly after World War II, an old subsidiary called Builders Supply Co. was renamed Swiftplan and given new tasks. For many years it has specialized in industrialized timber buildings and demountable partitions, paying special attention to noise reduction. (*How* swift Swiftplan can be was seen in 1960, when they built a pub in a day – 'The Rising Sun' at Clanfield, Hampshire.) They have provided many short-term houses for construction sites, and in 1966 they put up eighty-eight Multiflex houses for the Corby Development Corporation. The 'system', 'method' or 'modular' buildings in which they specialize have placed them among Europe's largest firms in this field, in which they have been established for more than twenty years. They have a highly mechanized modern factory at Southall producing thousands of components. Aided by Swiftplan's team of qualified architects, engineers, and drawing office staff, the client can practically design his own building, whether it is 100 or 10 000 square metres.

Such a system of variable components obviously lends itself to offices, laboratories, schools, hospital extensions, canteens, social clubs, computer centres, factories for light industry, shops, and even churches. Many of these buildings (which are *not* regarded as temporary) can be put up in from ten to sixteen weeks. In the early 1970s, boroughs implementing the reorganization of infant and junior schools into first and middle schools (which meant that primary school-children had to be accommodated for an extra year) found that they needed buildings which could be provided in a single financial year. (In 1974, with rapid inflation complicated by a 3-day working week, this need was especially acute.) To overcome these difficulties, the Borough of Ealing, in West London, was glad to be able to turn to Swiftplan's systems. Moreover, demountable classrooms can be relocated in any subsequent reorganization or expansion. In nursery schools, the flexibility of this type of structure is particularly valuable for groups of different sizes.

At St Thomas Comprehensive School, Exeter, the problem was to convert a girls' school to a mixed school, modifying existing buildings without a clash of styles, doubling the size of changing-rooms and kitchens – all without seriously interrupting school activities – and adding a sports hall and activity centre.

Lest it should be thought that Swiftplan are wedded to comprehensive education, let it be recorded that several public schools have reason to be grateful to them, notably

Rugby, whose Bursar, Lt.-Col. Ingram (himself an architect) worked with Swiftplan's design team to produce the school's handsome art centre.

In 1971 Swiftplan formed Cymru Buildings Ltd., formerly Cases Industrialized Buildings Ltd., a South Wales firm providing similar structures in a different style which is now maintaining much-needed employment in a special area centred on Neath. Cymru has for years specialized in a system they call RAPID (the initials stand for Re-locatable Accommodation Providing Instant Development), and rapid it certainly is. It brought into Swiftplan something they had hitherto lacked – a rigid relocatable timber-framed system of prefabricated units. To test it, in November 1974, the design, manufacture, and erection of a prototype was completed in four weeks. But Cymru can be even swifter than that. A recent contract was for an office complex of 325 square metres for the West Glamorgan County Council in Swansea. It has an H-shaped outline and is made up of twenty-five basic units. The office was built and handed over in a fortnight.

We have seen how useful the Swiftplan range of structures can be for construction camps anywhere in the world (including those of the Taylor Woodrow Group who have faith in their own products); and probably their biggest-ever contract (over £1 million) was for Matthew Hall, as main contractors, to build a camp north of Peterhead for the labour force which was bringing in North Sea gas to the mainland. It was what is called a complete 'turnkey' – supplying units and equipment down to the last spoon and fork.

Swiftplan units are light, airy, and warm. Sometimes they have been used by hospitals as 'decant units' while the main hospital buildings are being modernized or extended, only to find that the patients don't want to be moved back into the main building!

Vernon Beck, chairman of both Swiftplan and Cymru – they are now known as Swiftplan Ltd. (incorporating Cymru Buildings Ltd.) – knows a lot about timber (he was for many years in charge of all Taylor Woodrow joinery in West Africa). 'But we have got to move in new directions,' he says. 'Government cut-backs and the general financial climate mean that we must look abroad. It looks as if the school buildings market in Britain will be almost static until the 1980s.'

It makes sense to look towards the Middle East, where Taylor Woodrow are increasingly strong. In Saudi Arabia temperatures may reach 60 degrees centigrade in the summer, and so new designs and different materials are needed: heavier timber, made resistant to termites; less glass, smaller windows (and they must all have flyscreens); overhanging roofs to give shade, thermal insulation, and of course highly efficient air-conditioning. Show houses have been built for inspection in Riyadh and Jeddah in Saudi Arabia, and others in the Sultanate of Oman (and there are prototypes behind the Swiftplan factory at Southall). Such a house can be erected by four men in fifteen days.

Designs range from 2- and 3-bedroom bungalows to 2-storey houses, detached or semi-detached, and usually arranged so that there is a sheltered patio or courtyard. It is not easy selling houses in Saudi Arabia: many prospective customers expect a developer to take the whole financial risk, and land is extremely expensive: much land around cities has been bought in expectation of rapidly rising prices (in one district someone was asking £1 million per acre!). This in the end could be self-defeating, for there is a ready market for houses from about £40 000, which is what an Arab with a middle-class clerical job can easily afford.

'Modular' houses can be transported all the way from Southall in crates or containers, or stacked in lorries, and the components are easy to manhandle. There may come a time when Teamwork Saudi Arabia Ltd., located at Dammam, near Riyadh, will recommend a factory nearer at hand, but for the present it is not needed. Every component and room is tested for dry-heat and humidity, and relatively maintenance-free decorative finish materials are essential.

The actual rooms are basically the same as a house in Britain would contain – bedrooms, bathroom, separate cloakroom, kitchen, L-shaped dining room – but (studying the market) they are often arranged in such a way that a male visitor can enter the front door and go straight into the main reception-room (usually called the *majlis* and furnished chiefly with cushions) without encountering any of the host's womenfolk. An Arab acquaintance, explaining this to Vernon Beck, said of a friend and neighbour: 'He's an awfully nice chap, I've known him for years, but we've never seen each other's wives.'

IX

Transatlantic

THE sub-tropical city of Sarasota, Florida, on a bay of palm-fringed gleaming white sand containing cays or keys and lagoons, overlooking the Gulf of Mexico, was born in Edinburgh, Scotland, in 1884. A British firm called the Florida Mortgage & Investment Co. had bought 50 000 acres and was selling them cheap to would-be emigrants. In 1885 a colony of sixty-eight men, women, and children, mostly from Scotland, went out there. By 1910 Sarasota had a population of 840. In the same momentous year sixty-one-year-old Mrs Potter Palmer, millionairess leader of Chicago society, felt she could not stand Chicago winters any longer and came south. She said that Sarasota Bay was 'more beautiful than the Bay of Naples', and bought 140 000 acres of it. The Florida Boom, which reached a climax in the 1920s, was already beginning on the east coast of the peninsula, but few people at that time knew about the west coast except Mrs Potter Palmer and the descendants of the immigrant Scots.

Circus magnate John Ringling and his formidable wife Mabel took over in the 1920s. He bought St Armands Key, planned a shopping circle, organized land zoning, built a huge museum to house his collection of Old Masters, and a vast house modelled on the Doge's Palace in Venice at a cost of $1½ million. When he died, he left the lot to the State of Florida.

Today, Sarasota is a cosmopolitan city of retired million-aires with impressive houses along the beaches and canals; of writers and artists; farmers and ranchers on the rich soil behind the city; and retired workers from all parts of the U.S.A. and Canada living in modest but comfortable houses or apartments for which they have been saving for years. Here, on lagoons and long narrow keys (some man-made) connected by bridges, they can find the tropical-island fantasy of their dreams, and spend the rest of their lives fishing and golfing or just watching wildlife. No wonder Sarasota has the second-fastest population growth of any city in America.

Enter, in 1973, Frank Taylor's old friend and American associate Jack Kony, one of many thousands of people who, after the rough and tumble of business life in New York, have elected to seek the Sunshine State. Not that Jack and his wife Rhoda could be described as 'retired' – they are far too active, and Jack, in his late sixties, still has many fingers in many pies. It was a memorandum from Jack Kony that first started Frank Taylor thinking about Florida. Jack has known Florida since 1925. At first he recommended Longboat Key where he himself lives; but Frank Taylor said 'No. Too many old people. People who are retired need to live in a community of mixed age groups.' And in that moment, the seed of The Meadows estate was sown – a multi-million-dollar community development to provide nearly 4 000 houses with related urban facilities.

Some weeks later, David Nash, a director of Taylor Woodrow homes and an urban planning expert, flew out to look for a likely piece of land – not on the crowded coast, but a few miles inland. He had a tough time at first, and pays tribute to the help and experience of Jack Kony, of his attorney George Dietz, and of course the tremendous support from the Taylor Woodrow Homes team in London, headed by Don Slough, as chairman and managing director. Taylor Woodrow were up against stiff competition and local environmental lobbies, one of which eventually was persuaded that the development would actually enhance the rural amenities. After over twenty public hearings, Florida was satisfied that Taylor Woodrow meant no harm, although they were planning to develop agricultural land; and in the end, a lady who had consistently voted against it turned round suddenly and said: 'I guess I like it. I've already decided which house I want!'

The Group acquired 1 300 acres of land near a proposed interstate highway. The contract negotiations took six weeks' dealing with the owners in Miami, and Taylor Woodrow were nearly 'gazumped' by a higher bidder. There was a maze of regulations to be satisfied – noise pollution, air pollution, schools, hospitals, medical services, traffic generation, and even protection of endangered animal species. Drainage and water supply tested the Group's engineering skill, for Florida is wetter than is generally known: it has fifty inches of rainfall annually, most of which falls between June and September, and drought in January.

Taylor Woodrow Homes – supported by Frank Taylor – had taken a big but carefully calculated risk: in a year of recession, they had bought land without planning permission. When at last, in November 1974, final approval came, they found themselves responsible for the improvement of highways, traffic signals, help in building schools, providing extra patrol cars for the police, and assistance in providing the County water supply – hence the one million gallons a day wastewater plant to be dedicated to the County of Sarasota, and the central irrigation system – the first development in the area to store and re-use rainfall.

A central feature of The Meadows is an 18-hole golf-course, which requires a lot of water, but can also be ruined by too much of it. Because Florida building regulations insist that at least 50 per cent of such a site must be open space, the whole complex development has been planned *around* the golf-course, which blends well with the 'cluster-housing' amid trees and the 'curvilinear' roads which Taylor Woodrow had introduced to America as long ago as the 1930s.

When The Meadows is completed, in the late 1980s, it will have over seventy-two acres of lakes (some big enough to sail on, others stocked with fish): naturally, the houses and apartments fronting the lakes cost a little more. There will be churches, swimming pools, a tennis centre, riding and walking trails, nature reserves and horticultural farms where residents can have their own market gardens and grow their own food if they wish. The Meadows is planned for a population of 10 000 including 1 500 children for whom two schools are provided. A ten-acre village centre and an office complex (for lawyers, doctors, and other professional people), a shopping centre, roads closed to through traffic so that children can play safely, other roads so they can get to school without crossing a main highway – no detail has been forgotten. Much of the design and landscaping has been done or co-ordinated by Roger Postlethwaite, who went out to Sarasota from Taylor Woodrow Homes in 1974.

If you live in The Meadows you have the choice between various types of ownership, from single family housing on a comfortably sized lot, to a *condominium* where you shuffle off many of the worries of maintenance. This is a system similar to that under which blocks of flats are often run in Britain, and Frank Taylor believes it may eventually come to British housing developments too. It repays study, and we shall meet it again in Canada. In a condominium, residents jointly own certain 'common elements' – parkland, pools, recreational facilities, the outer structure of the building – all of which are maintained and insured by the condominium association to which residents must belong, and to which each home-owner contributes a small monthly maintenance fee. At present, Taylor Woodrow run the whole project through their non-profit-making Meadowood Management Company. Eventually they will hand the entire development over to the residents themselves.

Who buys condominiums? The population of Florida is increasing by 6 000 *a month*, and 'retirees' certainly lead the field, followed by 'empty-nesters' – couples in their late forties or early fifties whose children have grown up and left home. 'Retirees' usually buy their houses ten years before they retire, using them as holiday homes in the meantime. Estate brokers make much of the selling points that Florida has no income tax, no inheritance tax, and no estate tax.

You can join the golf-club or The Meadows Country Club if you like, but there is no obligation. By British standards, the golf comes fairly expensive – $15 a round, at which price 30 000 to 35 000 rounds a year are needed to make a profit. But then, it costs $200 000 a year to maintain the greens, and $20 000 a year for fertilizer and insecticides to keep down the destructive 'webworms'. You travel around the course in an electric golf-cart made for two with a 'Surrey fringe' on top; it deprives you of exercise, but it speeds up the throughput.

Taylor Woodrow are the developers, but do not build all the houses, some of which have been built by other developers, including the Group's own Monarch Investments of Canada, and their associates Blitman Construction. Many homes are at the upper-end of the market – say $50 000 to $80 000 plus the cost of the land. Designs vary widely, but all have the effect of blending unobtrusively with the background. The model homes – the 'Chartwell', 'Wentworth', 'Burnham' and 'Oakdale' – cater for the needs of different-sized families. They have had to study the Florida market intensively. Florida is full of destructive insects, so nobody wants a big garden: people use shredded bark to keep down weeds. All insects are referred to comprehensively as 'bugs'; one of them is the famous 'love bug' which flies south to find a mate; some are so small as to have earned the name of 'no-see-ums'. Against all these, Floridans have patios covered in with fine wire mesh, sometimes in the middle of the house, known by the Hawaiian name *lanais*. The kitchen is often in the middle, connected with living-rooms – this is possible because American systems of air- and smell-extraction are more efficient than in Europe; and kitchens seem to have been designed for ready-to-use packaged ingredients – no need to chop onions or grate cheese.

Florida has snakes, too: surveyors are obliged by law to wear leather snake-boots that rise above knee-level and carry a first-aid kit (a knife and serum) for snake-bite. Raccoons sometimes raid your dustbin. As for alligators, well, they are now 'protected reptiles', not as fierce as their reputation. You get used to your 'friendly neighbourhood alligator': there is one which lives in a pool beside The Meadows golf-course, and passing golfers feed him marshmallows. The trouble is, he thinks golf-balls are marshmallows too.

'The Meadows', said the *Sarasota Herald-Tribune* in October 1976, 'is more than just a name.' The paper's sports reporter praised Frank Duane, designer of the golf-course, for giving it 'that back-to-nature feeling' and 'forcing the golfer to become a thinker'. And, in an interview, Larry Weber, director of golf operations (Taylor Woodrow captured him from the famous course at Fort Lauderdale), makes no secret of the fact that it is designed to become a championship course with, naturally, ringside seats for the lucky residents of 'one of the world's most ambitious and idealistic village communities ever planned'.

Nearly 2 500 miles away, in California, Taylor Woodrow's

interests have been mainly in the field of property, which we shall look at in Chapter X. In February 1977 came the news that they were also going to build homes at Palm Springs and Laguna, south of Los Angeles.

On 1 March 1978 a ground-breaking ceremony (with gilded shovels) was performed by Sir Frank and Lady Taylor and Mr Harold Jones, Vice-Mayor of the town, on a 25-acre site at Rancho Mirage, Southern California. Here, conveniently near two country clubs, Mission Hills (with an 18-hole championship golf course) and Tamarisk, a 72-home community, offering residents the ultimate in elegant seclusion, is rising: it will be known as Casas de Seville. Houses (priced from $150 000 upwards) have been designed to blend with the contrasting severity of the surrounding desert and the 'resort lifestyle' of date-palm-fringed Rancho Mirage, a luxurious oasis in its midst. Casas de Seville is Taylor Woodrow's first Southern California residential development (to be followed by 750 houses at Laguna Niguel). Residents are offered a choice of six distinctive Spanish-style exteriors and three different interior floor plans, all with patios. Like The Meadows at Sarasota, it has been designed to conserve natural resources and yet provide such amenities as tennis courts and swimming pools.

All homes (some reserved before they have been built) will be single-storey, with concrete driveways, thermostatically-controlled central and air conditioning, and insulated walls and ceilings for energy conservation. The entire community will be enclosed by a perimeter wall with an electronic security system for 24-hour protection.

In charge of activity locally are two vice presidents, Gordon Tippell and Richard Walmsley.

The third area of America in which the Group is firmly established is, of course, the eastern States, where they have been in partnership with Blitman for fifteen years. Their sphere of activities here could hardly be more different from the fantasy world of Florida. Taylor Woodrow have 49 per cent interest in both Blitman Construction and Taylor Woodrow Blitman Inc. 1971 found Blitman with an order book of $60 million, developing a parking garage, a department store, and a shopping centre at Rockville, Maryland, and several apartment developments in New York, Massachusetts, and Rhode Island; and soon they were active in New York City, Virginia, and Washington D.C. as well, while also keeping a watching brief on whatever might soon be happening in Florida, and seeking new business in the eastern States, with the amount of caution needed: in 1974 and 1975 there was the ever-present risk of cancelled contracts due to economic recession.

In Bourne and Brewster, two housing projects were completed in 1975. The Canalside project is by the Cape Cod Canal in Bourne, and consists of 112 family apartments and a community building on a rolling wooded site. The King's Landing estate, also on Cape Cod, is a similar development of 108 apartments. Blitman Construction were meanwhile doing a Myton-type refurbishing job at Peabody, Mass., where an old tannery was ingeniously converted into Crowninshield Apartments – 284 flats for elderly people – using old artifacts in a decorative way: the scheme won an award from the New England Regional Council of the American Institute of Architects. In the same year Blitman did a beautiful renovation job on Lederer's famous fine leather goods store on Madison Avenue, New York City. Another notable renovation was that of the Third Avenue offices of Blue Cross Blue-Shield, the largest voluntary hospital and medical-surgical care programme in the United States.

One of the things Blitmans and Taylor Woodrow have in common is complete classlessness and racelessness in employee relations. Just as Dick Puttick refers to his Group as 'a team of both sexes, many races, nationalities and religions', so Howard Blitman believes that 'equal opportunity in employment and good business practices go hand in hand with success'. In Britain we have the Race Relations Act: in America they have Executive Order 11246, which provides that contractors engaged in federal projects agree not to discriminate. Neither Taylor Woodrow nor Blitman has ever needed such legislation; nevertheless Blitman, in 1976 were pleased to accept an award from the U.S. Department of Housing and Urban Development for their 'splendid record as an equal opportunity employer'.

We said, in an earlier chapter, that 1971 was a 'watershed year' of change. If that change was reflected in Taylor Woodrow's Canadian interests, it was probably one of policy influenced by local conditions. Back in 1953, when Taylor Woodrow had bought a controlling interest in Monarch Investments, the company had been split into Monarch and Taylor Woodrow (Canada), the latter being concerned mainly with civil engineering contracts. But from about 1971 the emphasis clearly moved to property owning and development, notably of office blocks and shopping centres. At present they are not pursuing general contracting.

Nevertheless the Group has a healthy record of building in Canada, and a drive in Toronto provides evidence of this. The Hydro Research Laboratory in Kipling Avenue; the Customs Building on Front Street overlooking Lake Ontario; the Y.W.C.A. Building on Woodlawn Avenue; the Stables at Greenwood Race Track; a Hockey Equipment factory in Alliance Road; office buildings at 42 and 45 Charles Street, and at 801 Bay Street; and of course Monarch's own elegant headquarters at Willowdale. The Company's activities ranged from the Pacific coast in the west where mine preparations were undertaken in the Queen Charlotte

Islands to the Atlantic seaboard where the Mactaquac Dam was built on the St. John River in New Brunswick.

There are two big universities in Toronto. For Toronto University, Taylor Woodrow built a residence building, a dentistry building, and an atomic laboratory; and for York University, a residence building and a science block. If you travel by underground railway, you have the satisfaction of knowing that three sections of the Toronto East-West Subway were tunnelled and built by Taylor Woodrow. For the Ford Motor Company, a new Head Office at Oakville, and the Ford Spare Parts Depot at Bramalea. Out at Sudbury there is a Taylor Woodrow pelleting plant, and on Alexander Street, Toronto, are the three-block City Park Apartments. Charlie Waggett, recently retired general manager of Taylor Woodrow of Canada, a Northumbrian who is also a veteran of Taylor Woodrow in Kuwait and Nigeria, will tell you, almost with a tear in his eye, that City Park was Taylor Woodrow's very first job in Canada, way back in 1954.

Two of the marks of the 1970s have been scarcity of mortgage money and exceptionally high interest rates, and these slowed down the sale of houses and serviced building lots on developments in Ontario at the beginning of the decade. There was, too, an over-supply of office space. French Canada and British (now increasingly multi-racial) Canada (Quebec and Toronto), are very different; and in Montreal business was slow. By 1972 things were picking up, and the Canadian building industry was producing a record number of homes, many of them on land holdings owned by Monarch. In October 1972 Monarch Investments bought an 80 per cent interest in Terminal Towers (Hamilton) Ltd.

Terminal Towers gets its rather funereal name from the fact that it stands on the site of the old Terminal Building, built in 1897 as the headquarters of the Cataract Power Co. of Hamilton to bring power from St Catharines, forty miles

away. Terminal Towers, when Monarch first became interested in it, was thought to be 'ahead of its time'. The original
developer had been Felix Fenston, one of the British 'property-
boom whizz kids' who made news in the 1960s. He had run
out of finance while Terminal Towers was being constructed,
and Taylor Woodrow, who were building it, had to assist
with a substantial bridge loan in order to keep the property
afloat. Taylor Woodrow were repaid, but the property
continued to suffer from inadequate management, high
vacancies, and high operating costs. How this complex,
which includes such diverse elements as offices (very flexible,
with movable partitions), apartments, an enclosed garage,
a shopping centre, a magistrate's court, and a Holiday Inn
with bars and restaurants, 'came into the family' has been told
by Colin Parsons, who became president of the Monarch
Group when Roy Wykes assumed the chairmanship in October 1976. Colin, a bearded Welshman in his early forties,
joined the Group in Toronto as an accountant, and had shot
to the top in fifteen years.

Of the Terminal Towers deal, which gave the Group one
of its major assets, he says: 'The development got into trouble
in the leasing period in the late 1960s, and the problems were
compounded when Mr Fenston's son, who was in charge of
the development, was unfortunately killed in an air crash.
Shortly after, Fenston himself sold control of all his companies in those halcyon days of the English property boom when
property was at historically high levels.

'The new U.K. owners decided that they did not want to
retain Terminal Towers in their portfolios, in spite of the
fact that Taylor Woodrow, who already owned a minor part
of it, advised them that the property was improving and a
turn-around in its fortunes was imminent. This was of
particular significance, as the owner of the property would
participate in the increased profits because most of the leases,

including the hotel, provided for a percentage of sales to go to the owner.

'The owners of the property listed it for sale with an agent and quickly accepted the first offer they received, which was from a European investor. Taylor Woodrow made a counter-offer, but the vendors decided to allow the European group to continue with its negotiations to acquire the property. The startled agent, hearing that Taylor Woodrow were interested, advised the new intending purchasers of the fact. They took this as an attempt on the part of the U.K. vendors to get them to minimize the amount of checking on the property and the condition of the leases etc., in order to ensure a quick closing.

'The new intending purchasers' reaction was the very opposite: they intensified their efforts to show what problems existed with the building, and it culminated in their turning up at closing time with a 20-page-long offer which was so complex that it defied quick rationalization; and furthermore, they reduced the amount of their bid to below the pre-negotiated level!'

Colin Parsons is modest about his own part in the negotiations, which he conducted on behalf of Taylor Woodrow. Quick to take advantage of the muddle, he resubmitted the Monarch offer in two simple, typewritten pages, which the vendor was equally quick to appreciate and agreed on the spot to accept. 'We in Monarch felt it was a good buy because it had been well built by Taylor Woodrow and we could see that with good management the property could be fully rented at reasonable rates . . . . Adding to the delight of an economically sound purchase', Colin ends his story, 'was the fact that, due to the way in which the purchase was structured, all of the profits from the development in the subsequent years up to the late 1970s have been tax-free, thereby enhancing an already significant cash flow.'

Canada seemed to be skilfully evading recession in 1973; home building continued, the demand for office space rose, construction began on a new shopping centre in Toronto, and Monarch acquired more land in 'strategic' locations in southern Ontario for future development. Meanwhile a newly-formed Industrial Development Division under the stewardship of the urbane Gerry Des Lauriers, vice president, had gained contracts for two new head offices and plants. Even in Quebec business was looking up. In July 1974 Monarch's new Chartwell Shopping Centre in Toronto opened, making four such centres operated by Monarch; and in eastern Canada houses were going up in five areas.

The general strategy of the Monarch Group, which has been in business for fifty-six years (thirty-three of them as a public company with an independent board of directors with shares quoted on the Toronto Stock Exchange) and is one of the oldest Canadian real estate companies, is worth studying. It has established a reputation for good quality construction over the years, and since World War II has specialized in acquiring large tracts of land that are turned into subdivisions. (You have to be careful how you do this, says Roy Wykes, or the Government will accuse you of hoarding land.) The secret is to buy land, equip it with services (drainage, power, etc.) and then sell off plots to builders. This gives a continuity of work over many years, with the additional advantage that once the development has been started, the value is built into the remaining lands due to the quality of the product produced in the early years.

A typical example is the Chartwell subdivision in the Scarborough district of Toronto, which was acquired in the early 1960s and came under development some years later: of 850 acres about 600 are residential, the rest industrial and shops – really a small new town. The project is now just over half-way through. This is where the far-sightedness comes in.

At first the site seemed rather remote; now it is one of the best located subdivisions in the Metropolitan Toronto area, due to the tremendous population growth which has taken place in the Province of Ontario – and indeed in the whole of Canada, whose population has trebled since 1945. In 1956 it was approaching 16 100 000: now it is around 23 million.

Chartwell's houses range from moderate-priced 'condominium' town houses selling at $57 000 to large single family houses at about $100 000: there are also 'semis' (not at all like British semi-detached!) at about $75 000. Building began in 1967. Some of the town houses are rented, some sold (but not freehold, nearly always condominium). In 1968 Monarch began selling plots to other builders too. By an ingenious economy, open spaces are used for more than one purpose: for example, parkland and playing fields are combined. There are two local schools, junior and senior (primary and secondary) to cater for the new community (but parents have no choice of school unless they are French-speaking Catholics, for whom special schools are provided). Chartwell is undoubtedly Monarch's most profitable housing project. It has its own shopping centre with two restaurants about three-quarters of a mile away, and Scarborough town centre is only three miles distant.

Another phase of the Chartwell development, now about five years old, contains more Monarch-built houses, and some of these *are* freehold. Here we come to some specifically Canadian requirements in housing. Many are 'split-level' (called either 'side-split' or 'back-split'). Nearly all have a basement, generally used as a boiler-room, with a 'rec-room' (for games or any other leisure purpose), sometimes (if it is on the right level) with a 'walk-out' through a large sliding window into the back garden. Here there are a few five-bedroomed houses. Most houses of any size at all have at least two bathrooms. This phase has only one school (a 'K to 5' = kindergarten to five years old).

In another phase of Chartwell, the town houses are smaller and closer together, often on a 20-foot frontage, sometimes built as 'semis' which, to satisfy the law, may be linked through their basements.

At Heron's Hill Homes, Scarborough (named after the site of Monarch's own headquarters in Willowdale, seven miles from downtown Toronto), we see Monarch as both developers and as builders steered by the firm hand of the Senior Vice-President of Monarch, Ed Winship, a former war-time RAF fighter pilot whose experiences stood him in good stead in his subsequent career in land development in Canada and Australia. Here sizes and prices ranged from 1 348 square feet, three bedrooms at $62 400 (minimum down-payment $9 600) to 1 652 square feet and four bed-rooms at $67 000 (minimum down-payment $12 400). Some have three toilets, one of them discreetly known as a 'mainfloor powder-room'. Most have single garages (the two- or three-car family is less common in Canada than we might suppose). The down-payment is on the basis of a high-ratio first mortgage. Walkout basements are $1 800 extra. Certain fixtures are included, such as floor coverings, refrigerator and cooker, automatic humidifier and others, but air-conditioning, curtains, etc., are extra.

Notice that Heron's Hill Homes are planned for a different price-range and age group from, say, Chartwell: they are promoted more vigorously, they are more 'modern' for younger people, with earthier colour-schemes. So we here have Monarch mopping up the competition by competing with itself, and appealing to the young with (for example) a leaflet for those who are making up their minds: it carries a toy bumblebee, who is saying 'Be a "Bee Back" – you'll be glad you did!' To help buyers through the difficult first years of home ownership, the Chartwell Homes Division of Monarch Construction has recently introduced CHAMP (Chartwell Homes Assisted Mortgage Program) in which an interest-free loan is available for five years, secured by a five-year interest-free mortgage.

Canadians like (and this is a feature in many houses) a kitchen leading straight out of the 'family room', which is *not* the same as the sitting-room, and is usually L-shaped with a dining area. They expect to find a built-in dishwasher and washing machine, and Monarch offer an 'appliance package' of machinery which is often kept in the basement. The basement is *sine qua non* in Ontario: the lady of the house will have her ironing-board there, and the man his do-it-yourself workshop. Basements must be four feet below the frost-line (to cope with severe winters) and driveways must always go *up* to houses, not down, because there is always a drainage problem when the thaw comes. (Those winters make all construction work difficult: for weeks on end bricklayers cannot work outside, and concrete placing is similarly hindered. Canadian houses are built of materials designed to withstand extremes of heat and cold; thus the 'old English weatherboarding' effect you see on some houses is really aluminium.) Ontario now has a considerable Italian population who like to use the basement as a wine cellar (most of them make their own wine): wine would freeze if it were stored at ground level.

If you are building or selling houses around Ontario, you have to consider such facts as that a higher proportion of all buyers are Chinese (ex-Hong Kong or Shanghai), and that Canada's divorce rate is now one of the highest in the world (one in three). This creates a new market, which is also related to the national trend towards smaller units and smaller families. The average Canadian family moves house five or six times in a lifetime. The house market is very competitive and

Initial sections of the world's first prestressed concrete floating breakwater being towed into the Clyde at Govan in Glasgow.

The TSO seabed sampler undergoing trials at Loch Linnhe.

Air B.P. refuelling Concorde in Bahrain.

Pilot plant for Glaxo Laboratories Ltd., Greenford, Middx.

Bird's eye view of the interior of the reactor hall at Hartlepool nuclear power station, Co. Durham, where the 16 ft thick top cap of the first reactor pressure vessel was concreted in a continuous pour lasting almost 24 hours.

Durability tests on existing concrete structures.

Hydraulic model investigation.

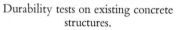

Tenth-scale model of part of the Staples Corner flyover undergoing structural tests.

Group training at Aldermaston Court.

Apprentice training at Southall.

Mrs. Suzanne Quentric, draughtswoman with Phillips Consultants Ltd. at Reading.

The life-size figures personify energy, enthusiasm, and teamwork.

Salalah's Risut Harbour in the Sultanate of Oman is a bustling port. It handled 120 000 tons of freight in its first year of operation.

Housing in Medinat Qaboos.

Government offices in Dhofar.

Work in progress on the three dry docks at Dubai. The largest will be capable of receiving tankers of up to one million tons deadweight.

Exposed – the sea bed within the drydock immediately after dewatering and before construction of the dock floors.

Monarch are doing more and more marketing and research into it – for there are reasons to suspect that the demand may be less in the mid-1980s, and that the condominium idea may be weakening. There is plenty of land in Canada, but most of it is in the wrong place. Of desirable land, reasonably near urban amenities, there is always a shortage.

Meanwhile Monarch are buying land and looking shrewdly to the future. Westminster Park in London, Ontario, 900 acres, is on the Chartwell model and is three-quarters complete – a more moderate price-level subdivision which, over the years, has contributed significantly to the housing market in that area. One of its model houses is called 'The Southall' after the first South of England headquarters of Taylor Woodrow. Soon the Unionville subdivision will open – about 400 acres on the outskirts of Metropolitan Toronto, set in very attractive countryside, which will provide 1 500 homes over a period of years: higher-priced houses in a district with strong historical associations and many antique and craft shops. Incidentally, this land had been purchased in 1969 which demonstrates the length of time it takes even in Canada to process land for development.

Three hundred and twenty miles away, just outside Montreal, John Saunders fresh out from Taylor Woodrow Homes in the U.K., began development during 1976 at the Vaudreuil subdivision – 450 acres of single family bungalows selling at about $33 000 each, right on the shore of the Lake of the Two Mountains and within easy commuting distance of downtown Montreal. It caters specifically for French-speaking Canadians. A major acquisition a few years ago was the Burlington subdivision, about twelve miles from Hamilton, strategically placed near the Queen Elizabeth Way. Thus Burlington is getting under way just as Chartwell is reaching completion.

Monarch and Taylor Woodrow have played a major part

in the development of many shopping centres, so very much a feature of Canadian urban life (and already establishing themselves in Britain) – the Yorkdale, the Bayview-Sheppard, Eglinton Square, Kipling Heights and Chartwell, all in Toronto; another in London, Ontario; and the unique complex of Terminal Towers in Hamilton. Monarch believe that participation in them is as nearly inflation-proof as anyone can get. 'Shopping should be like a carnival!' said the New York property tycoon William Zeckendorf, many years ago. 'We must make housewives say, not "Oh dear, I've go to go shopping today!" but "Whoopee! Let's go shopping!"' Zeckendorf is believed to have invented the modern shopping centre by marrying commerce to exciting architecture. Everything is under the same roof, including a cinema. Thus a day's shopping can be a holiday. Monarch's Bob Wells, a marketing expert who learnt his trade organizing hard-selling bookstores, says of Yorkdale (Taylor Woodrow's first Canadian shopping centre contract): 'Housewives drive in here or come by bus from fifty miles away. They window-shop in the morning, go to a movie – the cinema is built-in of course – then buy their goods, have a meal at the restaurant, and go home happy.' Yorkdale, built by Taylor Woodrow in only fourteen months in 1967, is Canada's most spacious shopping centre and one of the biggest in the North American continent – to use Gordon Selfridge's phrase, a 'cathedral of commerce'. It has a car-park for 7 800 cars. Like many shopping centres, it contains a supermarket and two department stores, Simpsons, who, with Eatons, lead the field in Ontario, You go downstairs to the 'budget level' (Canadian for 'bargain basement'). To a visiting Englishman, the only comfort missing is a public convenience; but it simply isn't a Canadian custom – you are supposed to go to a restaurant or a car-park and use *their* facilities.

You are immediately aware of design at Yorkdale. In the

'Mall' area – the Simpsons section – Taylor Woodrow built the first self-supporting concrete spiral staircase in Canada; and you cannot help observing the almost ecclesiastical vaulting of one ceiling, for which craftsmen from Jonathan James were specially flown out from England. Equally design-conscious, yet very different, is Monarch's Chartwell Shopping Centre in Scarborough, opened in July 1974, and landscaped with trees to obscure the parking lot, whose lights are shielded to prevent the glare intruding into nearby houses. The main tenant is Canadian Safeway Ltd. whose handsome supermarket stocks over 6 000 different lines of grocery and general merchandise.

Whether it is Kipling Heights or Chartwell or Eglinton Square, the Monarch team controls and supervises the marketing tactics and profitability of many stores, working with traders' own publicity efforts. Arthur Leitch, the conservative director in charge of properties, is a little shame-faced about a publicity stunt which involved dropping coloured ping-pong balls containing advertising from a helicopter, which was frowned on by the police.) A more serious approach to marketing certainly pays off – and achieves surprising things. At Eglinton Square shopping centre, a development dating back to the 1950s, the Canada Permanent Savings Bank has a modest unit which used to look like all the other savings banks. With judicious handling of a large extension at the right time, Monarch took it in hand, and soon it had pale green boudoir lighting and décor of the kind usually associated with ladies' hairdressers or perfume boutiques. The number of accounts rose from 4 000 to 11 000 in two years.

X

Men of Property

'WHATEVER happens to the currency, bricks and mortar always keep their value.' Well, yes, so long as there is not a revolution or a take-over by the State. And if we add, to bricks and mortar, concrete and all the other materials that go into construction, we can easily see how this bit of peasant wisdom makes it prudent for a construction group to own and rent property as well as to build it. Only it is not as simple as that. You have to choose your area carefully, study local needs closely, and make sure that you are not building, say, offices, in a place which will be over-supplied with offices by the time they are ready for use. Gone are the boom days of the 1960s when any fool could get a tower block built knowing that he could immediately let every square foot. Taylor Woodrow were able to survive the collapse of the property boom because they were cautious, and saw property as part of the Group, not a quick-profit enterprise in itself: it was an opportunity to develop by the co-operation of the property and the construction companies.

John Topping, chairman of Taylor Woodrow Property Co. Ltd. and a member of the parent board, has had many years' experience in property and real estate. He learnt the nitty-gritty of it with the National Coal Board Pension Fund, which owns a very large amount of property, and afterwards with Goddard & Smith, the West End estate agents, before joining Taylor Woodrow in 1963, when the property subsidiary was formed under the managing director-ship of the late George Dyter. 'We take calculated risks, but we don't speculate,' he says. 'Our thinking is as long-term as possible: we seek to create sound investments in major towns and cities which will show real growth. We diversify within reason, in politically settled countries (and there aren't so many of them left!) where foreign assets are not likely to be seized by a revolutionary government.' Property is also a hedge against inflation, and creates an asset for the Group's shares. The managing director of Taylor Woodrow Property is Peter Hedges who, still only 36, has been involved in all the company's major projects since he joined as a develop-ment surveyor in 1966.

To operate overseas, the Property Company has generally acquired interests in or formed associations with local companies. In 1968 a new company, Taylor Woodrow (Arts/Loi) S.A., was formed to develop a large office block in the centre of Brussels – 170 000 square feet of offices on ten floors, with a private penthouse, fully air-conditioned and double-glazed throughout and including 216 private parking spaces.

In Australia, Taylor Woodrow embarked on a number of projects, the most spectacular of which was City Arcade, Perth, a large shopping and amenity complex in the heart of the city. For this Taylor Woodrow was the design winner in a world-wide urban redevelopment competition. It contains shopping arcades on four levels, a fourteen-storey office block and an 850-seat cinema. After a difficult period in Australia, the Group has now opened a new office in Sydney, and their first major property undertaking is a tower apartment block in the heart of the city.

The 'watershed year' of 1971 found Taylor Woodrow Property with an investment portfolio which could be broken down into 38 per cent shops, 42 per cent offices, 8 per cent industrial, and 12 per cent residential. It was working on freehold shopping centres at Swanley, Kent, and Port-chester, Sussex, most of which had been prelet. A major office development at Southampton, and office scheme, 'County Gates House', at Poole, Dorset, were being started. At Leicester, a £2·8 million central area complex, incorporat-ing a new theatre; at St. Katharine-by-the-Tower, an 830-bedroom hotel, as part of the first phase of a huge scheme which we shall examine in detail later in this chapter. At Stockwell, south-west London, Taylor Woodrow Develop-ments Ltd., the property trading subsidiary, had completed letting of an industrial scheme, to be offered for sale.

More shopping centres were planned at Weymouth, and 'mixed developments' elsewhere in London including one at Great Portland Street. By 1973 the Leicester Haymarket centre, with shopping malls on two levels connected by escalators and lifts, nearly eighty shops and parking for more than 500 cars was fully operative, and the new civic theatre had been opened by Sir Ralph Richardson.

1974 and 1975 were years of difficulty and uncertainty in the property industry, and Taylor Woodrow Property reacted by consolidating. The removal of controls on business rents enabled the company to review rents; and it was in this year that the properties being developed by Myton were acquired in a streamlining operation that included Churchill Square, Brighton, which was nearing completion, and the Anderston Cross centre in Glasgow. This policy prepared the company well for the slightly easier atmosphere of 1976. In this bottom-of-the-market atmosphere Taylor Woodrow Property went ahead in partnership with Standard Life Assurance and the local Teignbridge Council, with the important Market Walk shopping centre at Newton Abbot, Devon, built by Taylor Woodrow Construction and opened in May 1979. It consists of twenty-three shops, a supermarket, two stores, and office and restaurant facilities; and it has involved the refurbishment of two longer-established markets.

In California, Taylor Woodrow had developed two shopping centres in partnership with Sutter Hill Ltd., shopping centre developers of Palo Alto, near San Francisco: one of them, Fernside Neighborhood Centre, is at Alameda, near Oakland; the other, Sequoia Mall, is at Visalia in Tulare County. Visalia is prosperous, with a large 'catchment' of shoppers, and is also the gateway for tourists to the hardwood forests of Sequoia and Kings Canyon National Parks at the foot of the Sierra Nevada mountains. Tenants at Alameda shopping centre include a Pay-Less super drugstore, an Alpha-Beta supermarket and a parade of 'convenience shops'. Sequoia Mall comprises forty-five unit shops set between two big department stores, Sears Roebuck and Mervyns.

In 1977 the Group purchased the Western Plaza Shopping Centre, in downtown Los Angeles, as a going concern. It is considered to have great potential for improvement, and its acquisition will further strengthen the company's portfolio in south-western America.

In 1978 Taylor Woodrow Property opened an office in Atlanta, Georgia, thus establishing a presence in this prosperous growth area. A new neighbourhood shopping centre was acquired in Lexington, South Carolina, and a new shopping development is under construction at Rome, Georgia. At Houston, Texas, a commercial warehouse centre is being built to serve a major industrial area; and at Harbison New Town, South Carolina, an office block is going up which will be 50 per cent pre-let to Harbison Development Corporation. And down at Sarasota, Florida, work has started on a village shopping centre for Taylor

Woodrow's 'Meadows' development.

And at Southampton, England, the Central Station area was being developed, with a major office block, Nelson Gate.

In October 1976, the city pages of national newspapers began to show great interest in 'Tricentre', an ambitious £19 million plan to redevelop the site of a well-known girls' school, immediately adjacent to Bromley South Station in south-east London. Bromley School is a member of the Girls' Public Day School Trust, a group of schools which has opted for independence from the comprehensive movement. Tricentre will provide about 215 000 square feet of offices, making it the largest development envisaged for a London suburb since the so-called 'collapse of the property market' in 1973. Under the agreement between Taylor Woodrow and the Trust, a new school is being built on a site already owned by the Board of Governors at Bickley, Kent. 'This major office development represents one of the most important schemes to be carried out in the Greater London area south of the Thames for some years, and its scale is in line with the type of building erected in Croydon in the early 1960s,' said the *Daily Telegraph* on 5 October 1976. There are other new office developments nearing completion at Swindon and, in association with AGB Research Ltd., at Hanger Lane, Ealing.

The 1973 property slump affected another Taylor Woodrow subsidiary interested in property – Taylor Woodrow Industrial Estates Ltd., formed in the 1950s, which has made a remarkable recovery under the leadership of Len Howard, John Hone and Ray Norris. No view of the Group's future would be complete without a look at what is happening here.

John Hone, who became chairman in the autumn of 1978 on the retirement of Len Howard, trained as a quantity surveyor and, while still in his twenties and early thirties, was running estimating, development and construction companies of his own in Canada and the United States between

1957 and 1967. Moving to Northern Ireland and the Isle of Man, he ran similar enterprises there before joining Taylor Woodrow in 1971 as general manager of Taylor Woodrow Industrial Estates, becoming managing director two years later.

Ray Norris, a chartered surveyor, joined him from Taylor Woodrow International, for whom he had managed developments in the Bahamas and the West Indies. He is now managing director of Taylor Woodrow Industrial Estates. His meeting with John Hone is an example of Frank Taylor's sympathetic interest in the private lives of his team, and his intervention at a time of need. He heard that Ray's wife had just died, leaving him with four young children to bring up. An overseas man all his life so far, Ray now needed a home-based job for the children's sake. With one of his flashes of intuition, Frank Taylor introduced him to John Hone. The two men took a shine to each other, found that they thought alike on many things; and their partnership has been good for the company. They seem to draw additional strength from having moved out of Mayfair into leafy Buckinghamshire. Their headquarters is now a restored eighteenth-century house in Beaconsfield which was once a nunnery, then a home for retired clergymen, and has a ghost which has been seen by several team members.

Both men were alive to the new situation of the early 1970s. It was not enough to buy cheap land wherever you could find it and hope that someone might want an estate built on it. It is of critical importance *where* the land is. 'There's a proverb in our business,' John Hone says. 'The first, second and third rules are location, location, and location!' To this end, he sold off some estates which were never likely to prosper because they were in the wrong places; because, regrettably, industry is not building many new factories, and we are still importing too much, new work tends to be dominated by warehousing. And warehouses today need to be near motorways.

There are of course exceptions. The Irlam Estate near Manchester seemed far from ideal, but resourceful negotiation turned an old soap works site into a plastics factory for a Dutch client who wanted to be in just that place; and an equally unpromising piece of land happened to suit Tesco, who built thereon the 10-acre Irlam Hypermarket, the biggest in the North of England. In Scotland, warehouses were built on forty acres at Rutherglen and twenty-eight acres at Birkenshaw.

The 150-acre Nursling Estate near Southampton, a joint development with the Barker-Mill Trust, is one of the new breed. Situated on the M.271 Motorway, which links the M.27 South Coast Motorway with Southampton's container ships and so with the world, it is quickly accessible from London, Portsmouth, Bournemouth and the West. Taylor Woodrow's development programme has been phased to meet continuing demand over the next ten years, and design standards and landscaping are strictly controlled. For Debenham Stores a distribution centre has been purpose-built. Pye Telecommunications are there too along with such well-known names as Union Castle, B.A.T., Tube Investments, Lex and Scottish & Newcastle Breweries.

Two other new estates have been begun in 1978 – an 18-acre trading estate at Newton Abbot, Devon, and the company's first joint venture with a local authority, Wakefield Metropolitan District Council, Yorkshire. The Wakefield development, within the Whitwood Freight Centre, is at Junction 31 on the M.62 Motorway – a key central position for the whole of the United Kingdom. Taylor Woodrow's 12¾-acre site is being developed to meet the demand for *rented* warehousing as an economical alternative to specially commissioned buildings at a time when building costs are still steeply rising.

Tyneside is another obvious case of 'location, location, location'. Here Taylor Woodrow Industrial Estates is completing a 37-acre trading estate at Dunston, near Gateshead, which they acquired as long ago as 1969. Over 150 000 sq. ft. of industrial and warehouse space has been developed, and a £20 million brewery is in the final stage of construction for the Northern Clubs Federation Brewery. Among many well-known names represented here are Pirelli, Smith's Industries, Ladbrokes, and Calor Gas.

Like Taylor Woodrow Homes, the Industrial Estates company is looking across the Atlantic for future expansion: the two companies may soon find themselves in partnership. California, which boasts some industrial developments which might almost be called 'pretty', mixing factories and workers' houses in cleanly landscaped environments, seems more than a possibility for their combined talents.

Looking at the property market as a whole, the immediate future, commercially, seems to lie at home, in shrewdly identifying opportunities and exploiting them; and overseas, as John Topping says, in penetrating economically stable countries. But there is a broader, more imaginative way of looking at the future than that. Taylor Woodrow Property, like other parts of the Group, are willing to risk a prudent proportion of time and money in another kind of speculation – the speculation of thought and imagination, of asking the eternal question: what is new? What could life be like in ten, twenty, fifty year's time? Of course there are bound to be schemes which, for one reason or another, do not get off the ground, often because they are ahead of their time. But research and experiment are never wasted, and occasional breath-taking boldness pays off.

Back in 1963, Taylor Woodrow spent £25 000 on what they called 'the Fulham Study'. No architect, developer or construction company had ever attempted anything quite like it before. It was the result of an invitation to Frank Taylor by the then Minister of Housing and Local Government to consider the possibilities of large-scale redevelopment of obsolescent residential areas in London, on the basis of partnership between private enterprise and local authorities – a partnership to which Taylor Woodrow are well accustomed.

The supreme example of urban renewal in the south of England is Taylor Woodrow's St. Katharine-by-the-Tower, which has been called 'one of the most ambitious private-enterprise developments since the Great Fire'. London's Dockland, now that the Port of London has moved downstream to Tilbury, and the quaint, late-Victorian Tower Bridge which seldom has any serious reason for raising its creaking bascules, had been the despair of the Greater London Council and, before it, the L.C.C. What is to be done about Dockland? Can we not agree about anything? Must it be given over to rats, must it crumble so that it is only fit to be used as sets for Battle of Britain films? Can it be converted into anything useful so that the Victorian Society won't object? The committees and planners had reckoned without an ebullient man named Peter Drew, now chairman and managing director of St Katharine-by-the-Tower Ltd., chairman of the London World Trade Centre Association (whose significance we shall see in a minute), deputy chairman of Taylor Woodrow Property Co. Ltd. and a director of the parent board. One of the great virtues of the Taylor Woodrow organization, which is rooted in the personality of the Founder himself, is their willingness to listen to a man with a streak of creative madness and back him to the hilt.

St Katharine is the vision of Peter Drew and his helpers. The Docks, covering twenty-five acres (ten of which are water), would become a new community of mixed elements – a large hotel, an export or trade centre, housing, schools, a sports centre, a yacht club, an interdenominational chapel…

We shall see, as we go along, how some of these objectives had to be modified, and other new ideas were added to them. And there have been obstacles all the way.

Early in 1970 the Greater London Council held a competition to find both a suitable design and developers able to carry it out. The matter was to be treated as very urgent, in fact only *three months* could be allowed for preparing entries. Taylor Woodrow had done a river survey some years before, but they had to compete all the same, and among several rivals they were up against a powerful consortium. 'In those days,' Peter Drew says (and he is speaking of only nine years ago), 'the chances of submitting a scheme with any chance of its being accepted were about one in forty. Clients' offices used to be waist-deep in feasibility studies.'

Much of what followed was inspired by what Peter Drew candidly calls 'my rather autocratic style of management'. Working all hours, he and his team produced an explanatory brochure in ten weeks, and broke the back of most of the planning in two months. The plan was presented dead on time, in May 1970, but the G.L.C. took somewhat longer - until November - to make up·their minds. They awarded Taylor Woodrow the project on 25 November, which happens to be the feast-day of St. Catherine of Alexandria.

Peter Drew is generous in his acknowledgement of all the help he received from various sources: their very number is a tribute to his thoroughness - the Master of the Royal Foundation of St. Katharine, the G.L.C., the Borough of Tower Hamlets, the Department of Trade, the Port of London Authority, the Consultative Committee on Thameside Planning, the British Helicopter Advisory Board, Shell-Mex B.P. Ltd., the Metropolitan Police . . . . The result was, in the words of the brochure, 'creative conservation of the potential of the site and buildings in both the national and local interest'. The many uses proposed were complementary, but the one which made the Taylor Woodrow plan different from all others was 'the creation of a British Export Centre linked to a major hotel with conference halls and other facilities. The hotel will attract tourists and special entertainment facilities are provided which will also become a centre for the locality. A wide range of residential accommodation for newcomers and the present residents of Tower Hamlets is provided, all fully integrated in a unified building complex with shops, schools and club facilities.'

National, international and local: all things to all men? It was easy to anticipate all the doubts the critics would voice. Yet the intuitional acclaim was immediate among those who first saw the artist's impressions. The *Architectural Review* praised a daring concept which, while it had no intention of losing money, was obviously not concerned primarily with financial return; and the London correspondent of the *New York Times*, in March 1970, thought that 'it could give ideas to another city with moribund waterfront areas – New York'.

There are legitimate doubts whether St Katharine Docks were ever totally profitable. They were built, to designs by the great Thomas Telford, who engineered the dock works, and Philip Hardwick, who was responsible for the warehouses (which became 'listed buildings' after World War II), at the tail-end of a 'docks boom' between 1789 (the Brunswick Dock at Blackwall) and 1829, when St Katharine Docks were opened. Other docks opened on the south bank of the river. There were, by the late 1880s, ten dock complexes in the Port of London, and the dividends of St. Katharine's were down to one per cent. True, St Katharine's had a romantic history – tea from China (the *Cutty Sark* berthed there, and there, too, the clipper races used to end), ivory from Africa, wine from France and Portugal, carpets and opium

from the Orient, bales of wool from Australia and New
Zealand. Yet the promoters of St Katharine's seem never
to have foreseen an age of larger ships – the limit was only
1 000 tons – and the docks lost out to their competitors.
They certainly could never have adapted themselves to
containerization; and anyway they had been terribly damaged
by bombing in World War II.

The Borough of Tower Hamlets had, for nearly two cen-
turies, been very dependent on the docks for employment. In
February 1977 *The Sunday Times*, in conjunction with the
Gulbenkian Foundation, held a conference on the future of
Britain's cities, backed by a series of articles in the paper.
Peter Wilsher, looking at Tower Hamlets, described it as '7·8
square miles of abandoned dockland, basement sweat shops,
traffic-jammed highways and brooding tower blocks . . . .
By 1900 its population had reached almost 600 000 –
bigger than present-day Liverpool.' This was its high peak;
it had been declining ever since: its population in 1974 was
150 100, and may now be less. This decline has not been
justified by any more parks or gardens or spacious prosperity.
'Between 1961 and 1971,' Wilsher continued, 'the number
working in the borough dropped by 38 000 – almost
one-quarter.' Factories have closed down or moved away. The
closure of the London and St Katharine Docks was primarily responsible for the loss of 10 000 jobs during this decade,
and nearly 2 200 more disappeared in the run-down of the
West India and Millwall Docks. The rate of unemployment
is 14 per cent. Income per head is the third lowest in London.

Into this gloom came a ray of hope when Taylor Woodrow
revealed their plan for St Katharine-by-the-Tower. *The
Sunday Times* did not at first approve of it: in Mr Wilsher's
words, 'it is in Tower Hamlets but almost aggressively not
of it – addressing itself quite unashamedly to the affluent
society which has so patently passed the rest of the area by'.

Yet the young Socialist Chairman of the Borough Council, Paul Beasley, longed to see 'garden-lined avenues leading down to the river' – none of your standard council estates like Dagenham – 'trees and open space' – the kind of things Taylor Woodrow are now providing. Peter Drew has had to cope with demonstrations outside his house, and there was a demonstration outside the Tower Hotel when it was opened. In 1972, *The Sunday Times* even accused Taylor Woodrow of making '£200 million profit out of public land'. Public land? And wherever did they get that figure? Certainly no reporter ever checked with Peter Drew.

The turning point of the row was probably the 1973 G.L.C. elections, in which both Conservatives and Socialists seemed to be claiming credit for St Katharine-by-the-Tower. There was, it is true, still an extreme left-wing who thought the whole scheme ought to be stopped, but the moderates won. There were some surprising reversals of opinion, notably Percy Bell, chairman of the planning committee, and Illtyd Harrington, then Deputy Leader of the G.L.C., of whom Peter Drew says: 'He was awfully rude about me when I first met him, but now he's a firm ally!'

Mr Harrington handsomely acknowledged his conversion in *The Sunday Times* of 25 April 1976, in an article headed 'Don't let Dockland Bleed to Death'. St Katharine's was *not* 'an élitist intrusion into what is primarily a working-class area'. Such a large plan could be more easily undertaken by a private firm willing to take the risk than by a local authority responsible to ratepayers. 'By building a World Trade Centre close to the Tower of London, Taylor Woodrow are providing a modern trade facility of national significance, but more, they have reasserted the contemporary importance of the historic centre of the metropolis.' As for the housing shortage in the East End, 'local authorities need rate revenue, and the comprehensive form of redevelopment at St Katharine's illustrates how it is possible to generate this from commercial sections of a project, to pay for the social demands that citizens have a right to expect'. As for houses, 'there is little point in having houses for people who are jobless. The re-development of the St Katharine Docks will provide employ-ment for about three times the number of workers engaged at the height of the dock activity in 1860.'

St Katharine's, he concluded, was now 'a stimulating place, thanks to the skilful combination of old and new'. Moreover Taylor Woodrow 'have tried to develop genuine relation-ships between local people and the development team. . . . Already the rate of revenue generated by St Katharine's is greater than that ever obtained from the Port of London Authority for all the port installations in Tower Hamlets.'

'Most of the objectors,' says Peter Drew, 'are *not* natives of Tower Hamlets. Often they are trouble makers who have been moved by the Greater London Council and given housing which they don't like. The genuine locals want to clear old rat-infested docks and build decent houses. But to many of them housing is useless if there is nowhere for them to work. I'm all for bringing industry back into Dockland, but some employers fear labour trouble here. Still the dialogue continues. Our own record is pretty good – we have created about 3000 jobs around here.'

St Katharine's had reason to be grateful to Government policy in 1969, for in that year, to encourage tourism, grants for new hotels were introduced (£1 000 per bedroom) with the stipulation that any such hotel must be completed within four years. There was no problem in building it, but at first no hotel group wanted a hotel in dirty old dock-land. It may have been the enthusiasm of Peter Drew ('we're building a new West End in the East End!'), or it may have been that Lyons Strand Hotels, having lost a coveted site in Holland Park to Hilton Hotels, decided to come east after all; anyway, work started on the Tower Hotel in July 1970, the 'first sod' having been cut by Sir Desmond Plummer in a bulldozer: Sir Desmond, then Conservative leader of the G.L.C., had always liked the St Katharine's idea and had been dreaming of a dockland marina for about ten years.

The original plan provided for a 'British Export Centre' which has been renamed 'World Trade Centre'. The Centre, and international World Trade Associations, have developed only slowly. Peter Drew offers various reasons for this, among them a rather too bureaucratic approach by some countries, and he thinks it not impossible that it may have to split up into less cumbersome units – he envisages, for example, a possible return to the old title 'British Export Centre.' Both the World Trade Centre (an idea mooted as long ago as 1965, when it was 'before its time') and the London World Trade Centre Association are the creations of Peter Drew, who is chairman of the latter and also vice-president of the World Trade Centres Association. Peter Drew is emphatic that the World Trade Centre idea is not wholly his own: it was the dream of a famous Japanese politician, Gaku Matsumoto, who, as chairman of the International Ports and Harbours Association, had visited New Orleans and seen for himself what could be achieved by such an institution in what has become America's second largest port.

The London W.T.C. Association now has more than 1 200 members, all directors of companies predominantly concerned with overseas trade and 80 per cent of them direct exporters: they elect their own board. It was only the third such association in the world, but there are now many more. At present Taylor Woodrow run it and the Centre, but eventually the Association will take over all organization.

What does the World Trade Centre offer to a member or a

company? It has educational facilities – the London World Trade Institute has a full programme of short- and long-term courses, one-day conferences and personal language tuition. The 1977 programme included a six-month course for a Certificate in Export Office Practice, Professional Parts 1 and II courses (for which you need four O-levels including maths and English), and half-day seminars on trading opportunities in individual countries of the world, with businessmen and experts from these countries speaking – for example, from such commercial 'blocks' as COMECON, OPEC, the Developing countries, and EEC and EFTA countries. Short-term courses (some of them held in Liverpool and Glasgow as well) in conjunction with the Institute of Export cover documentation, finance, training, licensing, how to lobby your M.P., developing export sales, the commodity markets, import procedures, and presentation skills (however good your product or service, you must study how to demonstrate to your prospective customer that he needs it). Multinational operations, the implications of floating exchange rates, marine cargo insurance – it is well worth going back to school at the World Trade Institute. The 'business game', a 24-hour exercise in which the problems – perhaps export, or industrial relations – of a real or imaginary company are debated and 'solved', is another learning method. As for language courses, they can be 'group', 'private' or 'crash', and it is practically guaranteed that after ten lessons you will be able to book an hotel room, buy a flight ticket, open a bank account, follow street directions, order a meal or talk your way out of a parking ticket in the language of your choice. It goes without saying that traditionally important commercial languages such as French, German, and Spanish are offered; and it is interesting to note that among languages being covered in the present academic year are Romanian, Arabic, Dutch, Italian, and Portuguese.

Members of the World Trade Centre have at their disposal a research and information department and business library. Services for international businessmen, available day and night, include photocopying, shorthand-typing and telex, prestige office suites, a rent-a-desk service. If you belong to the London World Trade Centre Association you can use the World Traders Club, which holds monthly luncheons with guest speakers who are leading figures in trade and industry. There are exhibition halls used by major international companies such as IBM, Rank Xerox, I.C.I., and Plessey. You can hold your A.G.M. or a company promotion here, and take advantage of all the water in and around St Katharine's by hiring a barge or other river craft and literally 'floating' your company. Available for charter is an historic sailing barge, the spritsail *Lady Daphne*; there it is in St Katharine's Yacht Haven by Tower Bridge – it can be hired for twelve people on overnight charters or forty people for a day trip. When in London you can stay either at the 826-bedroomed Tower Hotel or in one of the service apartments in the converted Ivory House, and eat in any of six restaurants (more are planned).

The World Trade Centres Association was once described by U-Thant, Secretary-General of the United Nations, as 'the United Nations of Commerce'. There are ninety members in forty countries so far. World Trade Centres are in operation in Brussels, Tamuning, Kobe, Tokyo, Seoul, Wellington, Madrid, Gothenburg, Dallas, Houston, Indianapolis, Los Angeles, New Orleans, and New York; and others are under construction in Copenhagen, Hong Kong, Bombay, Singapore, Baltimore, Toronto, Kinshasa, and Moscow where a $180 million project is being completed. Well may Peter Drew, looking out of the window at his house in St Katharine's (it is a bow-fronted Regency house with a balcony where the dockmaster used to live), or from his office (con-

verted from the checking department of an old rum warehouse), think: 'We've certainly started something.' No
wonder the *Investors Review*, at the end of 1972, awarded
him the title of 'Perseverer of the Year', and the State of
Louisiana, eighteen months later, made him an honorary
Admiral.

Well, it gives him a professional interest in the Yacht
Haven, whose berths began to fill up in the summer of 1973
(one of the first was taken by Arthur Lowe, 'Captain Main-
waring' of television's *Dad's Army*, for his handsome steam
vessel). Here Taylor Woodrow Construction have provided
240 berths for yachts of overall length up to 100 feet. Many
marinas rely on restraining piles, which were not permitted
to penetrate the soft puddle-clay lining of the docks; so
instead ninety-foot piers 'cantilever' from the main access
pontoon to resist horizontal wind forces. Although the
original mechanical equipment for operating the lock gates
has been retained, a completely new control room was
needed: the architects, Longleys of Crawley, designed the
new control room and Taylor Woodrow designed the
control system.

One of the trickier problems was that of an eighteenth-
century building known as 'G' Warehouse. In their original
recommendations to the developers in 1969 the Greater
London Council had labelled it 'could be demolished'
(the area on which it stood was needed for housing development). By July 1975, when Tom Freakley, then chairman of
Taylor Woodrow Construction ceremonially handed over
the keys of the building, whose ancient timbers and mellow
brickwork had been restored almost to their original
condition, it was known that it was to become a public
house and restaurant. Meanwhile it had been discovered that
'G' warehouse had been a nineteenth-century brick shed
enclosing a wooden structure dating from about 1750 with

some parts possibly much older (some experts suggest 1492, the year in which Columbus discovered the West Indies). It was very well worth preserving; but what about the housing scheme? Clearly the old-new pub must be moved somewhere else. This was done by jacking up the timber frame and moving it bodily to a new site about 150 feet north and turning it through a forty degree angle to a position beside the north wall from which people in the bar on the balcony would be able to enjoy a superb view of the Yacht Haven and Ivory House. Here the restoration was finished.

The move took place on 8 May 1974, and Taylor Woodrow called in Pickfords, the world-famous removal firm, to assist in shifting a 130-ton building. The timber skeleton was braced with a framework of scaffold tubes and timber props, and jacked slowly up four feet above the ground to bring it on to the same level as its future site. This took several hours – 'the really nail-biting part of the operation', said one of the men who did it, 'yet not a crack or groan was heard from the timber frame'. The rest of the move happened during the following week – the very slow journey on rollers, pulled by static diesel winches, over pre-laid steel plates. Having arrived at its destination, the frame was jacked down about a foot so that it rested snugly on its pre-constructed basement. Throughout all this manoeuvring, two sparrows, who had nested in the structure several weeks before, successfully hatched and reared a brood of fledglings.

The building is now a Charrington's Vintage Inn called the 'Dickens Inn'. There is no pretence that Charles Dickens could ever have drunk a pint there, since in his day it seems to have been an army victualling store used mainly for barrels of porter; but it may before that have been a brewery – so at least there is some continuity of use. However, at the official opening in 1976 the guest of honour was Cedric Dickens, great-grandson of the author, who, having arrived in a horse-drawn coach, unveiled a bust of his ancestor, observing that St Katharine's had been mentioned in no fewer than twelve of Dickens's works.

The whole atmosphere of St Katharine's, the Yacht Haven and the Thames lends itself to sailing events. In August 1975 the largest sail training fleet to gather anywhere in the world converged on Tower Bridge for the Port of London Clipper Regatta. They came from Britain, Holland, France, Germany, Denmark, Poland, Sweden, even Russia. Among the many craft moored inside the Haven were the four boats entered in the *Financial Times* Clipper Race around the world, and the crews were welcomed by the then managing director of the Yacht Haven, Robin Knox-Johnston, winner of the first single-handed round-the-world race in 1969. The Regatta was visited by Princess Alexandra and her family who arrived appropriately in the P.L.A. vessel 'Nore'.

Part of St Katharine's Yacht Haven is also an open-air floating maritime museum. Thus the steam ferry s.s. *Yarmouth*, built at Lowestoft in 1895, which used to run as a ferry service between Great Yarmouth and Gorleston carrying thousands of holiday-makers, arrived on 14 May 1976, and was lifted out of the water on to a concrete plinth by a Manitowoc truck crane from Greenham. After restoration it will be opened to the public as a museum of the history of steam.

Here, too, you can see the old *Nore* lightship, built in 1932, which used to guard the Edinburgh Channel off Margate; the steam tug *Challenge*, rescued at the eleventh hour from a scrap merchant, and the last survivor of the 1931 generation of steam tugs; and another old Thames sailing barge, the *Dannebrog*, built in 1901 but still in service as recently as 1973, a rare example of a boom-and-gaff rig vessel. Another familiar vessel which visited St Katharine's in 1974 was the topsail schooner *Charlotte Rhodes*, known to millions of television viewers as the flagship of *The Onedin Line*.

For local people, Taylor Woodrow have built 300 G.L.C. homes in a traffic-free development which makes generous use of landscaped courtyards and children's play areas. They will provide accommodation for 906 people in maisonettes and flats overlooking the Yacht Haven. Most of the family units are in three major 'spines' enclosing large open spaces and allowing maximum private open space for each family with patios or terraces. Parking for 270 cars is on two levels beneath the 'spines'. The major pedestrian level is a deck street, one storey above quay level, with stepped ramps for mothers with prams. Accommodation for one and two persons is provided in a 'cluster block' ranging from four to nine storeys. This is council housing conceived with real imagination.

St Katharine-by-the-Tower has attracted international praise. It has received awards for conservation, design, tree planting, floodlighting. It has been studied by the U.S. Federal Board of Urban Renewal. It may be that Taylor Woodrow have created a new industry as well as a new concept. They have certainly created a new community. 'We were helped, in a negative sort of way,' says Peter Drew, 'by a study of the Barbican development in the City – it's deserted at weekends, which isn't at all what the planners intended.' Nobody who lives at St. Katharine's could ever possibly be bored, and few would want to go away for the weekend.

It is all happening a little more slowly than anyone intended, and all along it has been fraught with difficulty. The target date for completion of the whole St Katharine scheme – 1985 (sixteen years after its inception) now looks optimistic. 'B' Warehouse, for example, with its dignified colonnade, was recommended by the G.L.C. as a listed building – 'retention considered desirable'. Could it really be enclosed with glass and used for exhibition purposes, using the splendid *porte-cochère* as an entrance hall? The retention of 'B' Warehouse (at an estimated cost of £10 million) would call for the exercise of great skill in order to meet the proper requirements of building and fire regulations. Should it be used to house a museum of old machinery? It was originally intended that it should be converted into an export centre, but in fact a modern building called Europe House was acquired from the Port of London Authority to house the World Trade Centre. Could 'B' Warehouse, then, be used as an extension to it? Or should the much-destroyed Warehouse 'C' inherit this role? In 1974 the G.L.C. Planning Committee were thinking on these lines: they recommended that 'C' Warehouse should be demolished on the understanding that suitable materials recovered from it could be used to reconstruct the fire-damaged part of 'B' Warehouse, and that 'C' Warehouse should be laid out as a public amenity area. There would be no objection to including some of the offices in 'B' Warehouse as part of the World Trade Centre, if consent was forthcoming from the Historic Buildings Board of the G.L.C.

In 1974 Taylor Woodrow applied for an office development permit for 217 000 square feet of 'B' Warehouse. They would really like to demolish it and build an independent office block. This was opposed by such bodies as the Victorian Society. 'It's a dangerous building in its present state,' said Peter Drew. 'There have been several fires there and local fire brigades hate it – the timber floors between the cast-iron columns are very inflammable.' Ultimately the decision came: permission was given for the old warehouse to be demolished and the modern replacement will be – from the outside at least – an exact replica of the original.

'We have conserved (and conservation does not necessarily mean total preservation) more than the G.L.C. originally asked, and more than we originally promised,' Peter Drew maintains. You realize how much has been conserved when you sit in the restaurant underneath Ivory House, a beautifully restored Italianate warehouse, and admire the vaulted ceiling; for you are in the old wine vaults whose deep bays lead off into snug areas, each furnished in solid oak and decorated in the style of different periods in Britain's history – House of Hanover, Court of St James, Dick Whittington's Parlour. And outside, old and new have been ingeniously blended: between the Tower Bridge and the Tower Hotel, in a circular pool where a fountain plays, stands a bronze sculpture 'Girl with a Dolphin' commissioned by Taylor Woodrow from David Wynne, the internationally renowned sculptor who carved the famous Taylor Woodrow 'Teamwork' placed outside Western House.

It is not easy to make trees grow amid buildings. Peter Drew claims he has exploded the myth that they always have to be plane trees. £1 000 worth of trees have been planted so far at St Katharine's. The first was a willow by Ivory House, at a ceremony attended by the cast of the musical play *Fiddler on the Roof*. But the willow didn't flower. It took Captain John Bowman, who runs the seamanship school at St Katharine's, to explain the facts of life: trees and plants don't flower without bees. Captain Bowman is also a bee-keeper, and obligingly started a Taylor Woodrow apiary. 'The main achievement of our bees,' he says, 'has been to pollinate all the trees within a radius of about two miles.' Hilary Peters of TV fame contributed to the general effect by going round dockland in a boat planting self-seeding plants wherever there was a patch of soil. Plants attract insects, plants and insects together attract birds; and all this has lured back to the area birds which had deserted dockland in its sadder days. Nothing but brambles and willowherb flourished in dockland before Bowman's bees: now flowers, fruits, and berries grow apace. In 1974 the bees produced over 100 lb of honey and won first and second prizes for their honey at an Essex horticultural show.

The Taylor Woodrow team at St Katharine's are now turning their attention to fish, now that much of the Thames has been purified. They monitor water samples and the fish population (Thames eels are very good) and organize fishing permits and prizes. . . . What, you may ask, has all this to do with property development?

Looking to the future, Peter Drew would reply: 'Everything.' He thanks his stars for three things: a great idea, a lot of luck, and opportunity. For St Katharine's-by-the-Tower is a landmark in the story of urban renewal. It points the way to the future. Only a decentralized Group which gives maximum freedom of enterprise to its constituent companies could have undertaken it. The techniques learnt here have given the company an unique opportunity to secure further major works of this kind. There is now a scheme, about eight times as big as St Katharine's, to revive the whole of Surrey Docks, including road-building and two tunnels under the Thames. This scale of thinking is so large that such projects, needing finance of the order of £400–£500 million, will probably have to be carried out by consortia of two or more firms.

'It is a tremendous vision.' No wonder Peter Drew loves his job so much that he says, 'I really ought to pay Frank Taylor for letting me work here.'

XI

Royal Occasions

S T KATHARINE-BY-THE-TOWER has a special place in the hearts of Taylor Woodrow people, not only because it is an achievement of which they are rightly proud, but because it was for them the climax of the Queen's Silver Jubilee. Her Majesty's Royal progress down the Thames on Thursday, 9 June 1977 was watched on television by more than 200 million people, who saw her step ashore at St Katharine's Pier from her Port of London Authority barge *Nore* escorted by Thames watermen in scarlet uniforms. As she made her way informally around the Yacht Haven and the London World Trade Centre, watched by ten thousand people and a thousand children, it was clear that she was enjoying herself enormously. A mighty cheer of welcome went up from the sailing fraternity as she walked round the central yacht basin. Then 12-year-old Ellen Drew, daughter of Peter Drew, chairman of St Katharine-by-the-Tower Ltd., became a world TV star for a few seconds as she presented a bouquet to Her Majesty.

Sir Frank and Lady Taylor were then presented to the Queen, and Sir Frank gave her loyal greetings from the entire Taylor Woodrow team at home and all over the world. The Queen also met Dr Arthur Fleischmann, who had carved a commemorative sculpture for the occasion, and Sir Frank took her into the specially-built Coronarium to unveil it. This perspex sculpture, commissioned by members of the

London World Trade Centre Association, of which Sir Frank is president, is carved out of the largest acrylic block in the world. Designed as a stylized version of the Imperial Crown, it stands on a stone slab in the centre of a ring of columns which were salvaged from the old warehouses of the docks, and the tops of their capitals are linked by a white concrete ring 3 feet deep and 31 feet in diameter. Situated on the most prominent spit of land in the middle of the old St Katharine Dock, the Coronarium is floodlit at night so that it looks like a giant star with the crown at the centre.

Among the thousands welcoming the Queen were members of the Taylor Woodrow team and their guests from commerce, industry, and the press. To secure the fullest possible record of the occasion, Taylor Woodrow's member company Kadek Vision laid on the biggest-ever commercial video-cabling installation in the country. This relayed the B.B.C. transmission to Taylor Woodrow guests and the press. It meant laying three and a half miles of cable in less than twenty-four hours.

As the Queen and Prince Philip toured the Yacht Haven, there were many who remembered that there had been a previous Royal occasion seventeen months before, when Princess Alexandra, the Hon. Angus Ogilvy, and their children Marina and James arrived on the same PLA vessel *Nore* after reviewing the ships moored in the river for the colourful 1975 Port of London Clipper Regatta. Now, for this Jubilee event, every yacht, indeed the whole of St Katharine's, was en fête with flags of all nations. Another flag, dominating the Silver Jubilee Gardens next to the Royal Festival Hall on the South Bank, had been raised by Sir Frank Taylor to mark the Queen's birthday on 21 April, which he did, at the invitation of the Greater London Council, to a fanfare by trumpeters of the Kneller Hall School of Military Music. The flagpole, a

British Columbian red pine 106 feet high, is a relic of the 1951 Festival of Britain.

It was a time for remembering all that had happened in the world, in Britain, in the Taylor Woodrow Group, since Elizabeth II had ascended the throne on the death of her much-loved father early in 1952, the year when the end of tea rationing was front-page news; when Sir Winston Churchill was still Prime Minister; when Parliament was discussing a White Paper on the outrageous idea of commercial television; when young people were still conscripted for National Service, the first British atomic bomb was detonated on the Monte Bello Islands, General Eisenhower became President of the United States. . . .

Taylor Woodrow's Australian company was building thirty-six miles of oil pipeline for Shell, linking Geelong to Newport; there was much activity in East and West Africa; Arcon tropical structures (one of them for a church in Jamaica) were doing well all over the world; in London Battersea 'B' power station was under way, and at Heathrow the great tunnel connecting Bath Road with the central terminal area was in progress – the first of many London Airport contracts, and the predecessor of many major tunnelling jobs for which Taylor Woodrow have established a well-known expertise.

In 1952, with a young Queen on the throne and the worst of the post-war years behind them, people looked forward hopefully to a 'New Elizabethan Age', a time of freedom from controls, of opportunity for enterprise, technology and the arts. The young Queen and her technologically-minded husband were to identify themselves with many Taylor Woodrow enterprises in the first twenty-five years of her reign, as were other members of the Royal Family. In November 1955 she had visited Myton's Colleges of Technology, Commerce and the Arts in Birmingham, and in the following month she had opened the new Central Terminal Buildings at Heathrow Airport, built by Taylor Woodrow Construction. During Royal tours of Africa the following year, the Federal Law Courts at Lagos, Nigeria, built by Taylor Woodrow's West African company, were inaugurated by the Queen, and the Royal Technical College, Nairobi, built by the Group's East African company, was opened by Princess Margaret. Prince Philip had inspected Calder Hall, Britain's (and the world's) first atomic power station, built by Taylor Woodrow Construction, in 1955, and in October 1956 Her Majesty threw the switch that first sent electricity flowing from it into the national grid.

Five months later she visited the newly-completed Faculty of Letters building at Reading University; and Myton were again honoured by the Queen's presence when, in December 1960, she opened the Ariel Hotel, the world's first completely circular hotel, at London Airport. And when, that same year, Nigeria celebrated its independence, it was with the in-auguration of Taylor Woodrow's wharf extension at Port Harcourt, which was carried out by Princess Alexandra.

Princess Margaret has associated herself several times with Taylor Woodrow projects, opening the Ferodo factory at Caernarvon in 1962 and flying to Singapore ten years later to visit the Jurong industrial estate and open Beecham's new penicillin factory there.

In March 1966 Bob Aldred used a scale model to demon-strate to Princess Margaret some of the features of the Ocean Terminal in Hong Kong, in the British Engineering Exhibi-tion which she officially opened as part of the British Week in the colony.

The first British monarch to arrive by train at London's Euston station some 130 years ago was Queen Victoria. Queen Elizabeth II remembered this when she opened Taylor

Woodrow's completely redeveloped Euston in October 1968. 'My family,' she said, 'has used this station many times.'

In Jubilee Year itself, Taylor Woodrow were honoured by no fewer than seven Royal occasions. Tuesday 22 March 1977 found H.R.H. Prince Charles in the Upper Region of Ghana. After elaborate safety precautions at Paga airstrip, about five miles from Taylor Woodrow International's Tono irrigation project (including floodlighting towers, a crash fire rescue team and a cattle-clearing team to keep the airstrip free of straying cows, sheep and goats), all organized by Taylor Woodrow, Prince Charles's Andover of the Queen's Flight touched down safely. Having inspected a guard of honour, he met and chatted with wives and children of team members from the Tono project, and then drove to Balgatanga, the regional capital, to attend a durbar in his honour, with a display of dancing and drumming.

In the afternoon Prince Charles visited the 4 000-acre Vea irrigation works and the Tono project itself, pursued by villagers who had been waiting outside the Tono Club almost since dawn to catch a glimpse of him. On arrival he was greeted by the Director of Irrigation, Mr E. D. Kemevor, who introduced him to Taylor Woodrow's director-in-charge, Tom Norris, the general manager in Accra, Mike Walker, and the project manager, Keith Rose. Suitably hard-hatted, Prince Charles then toured the dam works, talked to more local team members and their families, and returned to the Tono Club, where the Paramount Chief of the Navrongo area presented him with a traditional smock, trousers and many-coloured headdress which, to the delight of everybody, he wore on the spot.

While all this was happening his cousin, the Duke of Kent, touring the British Industrial Exhibition in Caracas, Venezuela, visited the stand of Floating Breakwaters Ltd., a subsidiary of Taylor Woodrow International. Showing great interest in how they worked, the Duke brought President Perez of Venezuela along to meet Taylor Woodrow members and explained to him the meaning of the 'four men' symbol, assuring him that it was known all over the world. The President, fascinated by the possibility that floating break-waters might be the answer to Venezuela's harbour problems, encouraged his own technicians to study them.

So strenuous were the demands on the Queen's time and energy as she toured Britain in Jubilee Year that she must have been glad of the help she received from other members of the Royal Family who represented her when she could not be in two or more places at once. During her Scottish tour in May 1977 Her Majesty opened the new extension to Aberdeen's Town House, where she unveiled an engraved plaque in the council chamber. The 'granite city', whose welcoming motto *Bon Accord* is said to date back to Robert the Bruce, is capital of Royal Deeside. After the unveiling, Norman Baker, chairman of Taylor Woodrow Construction (Scotland), was presented to Her Majesty, and he in turn introduced other team members to her.

Aberdeen, by tradition a Royal capital, is now also the oil capital of Europe, and both its population and its communications are expanding. In June 1977 Princess Alexandra opened the new terminal building at Aberdeen Airport, to which Taylor Woodrow contributed the car parking and roads.

In London, on 31 May, Princess Anne had opened the Royal Borough of Kensington and Chelsea's new town hall complex, designed by the late Sir Basil Spence and his partners and incorporating a council chamber with individual microphones and a sophisticated electronic vote-counting system. Among many distinguished guests at the ceremony were Sir Frank and Lady Taylor and Tom Freakley,

then chairman of Taylor Woodrow Construction, and Mrs
Freakley. Before leaving, Her Royal Highness unveiled a
commemorative plaque in the civic entrance. It was, she
said, 'a splendid edifice', and she was pleased to note, in one
of the gardens at the southern end, a giant redwood sapling,
carefully retained by the architect, which had been planted
by Baroness Churchill in memory of her husband, who
had been an Honorary Freeman of Kensington.

The Queen visited Nottingham in July 1977 during her
Silver Jubilee tour of the Midlands. On the afternoon of
28 July she arrived at the University Hospital complex to
open the new medical science block which Taylor Woodrow
Construction (Midlands) had built for what is now the Trent
Regional Health Authority. This, one of the City of Nottingham's many 'firsts', is Britain's first wholly new teaching
hospital foundation since 1893. The whole complex will have
a capacity of 1 400 beds and the medical school will accommodate at least 160 students. Appropriately, as was revealed
when the Queen unveiled a plaque, the new block is known
as the Queen's Medical Centre.

The National Association of Boys' Clubs is associated with
Taylor Woodrow in three ways: Roy Spiers, Group per-
sonnel services manager and a director of Taylor Woodrow
Services, is a member of the Association's Council; the
Group sponsors a number of the Association's tug-of-war
activities, and Taylor Woodrow Construction have recently
renovated the Association's headquarters at 24 Highbury
Grove, London, N. This was formally opened by the Duke
of Gloucester on 17 October 1977. An architect himself, the
Duke showed a keen interest in techniques used by Taylor
Woodrow to bring an old building up to completely modern
standards. After touring the building, the Duke was delighted
to meet his 'namesake', television personality Arthur Mullard,
known as 'the Duke of Islington', who lives in the Borough.

Amid many excitements, Jubilee Year gave the Queen another chance to ride in an underground train. On Friday 16 December 1977 she officially opened the final stage of the Piccadilly Line tube extension to Heathrow Airport. Her Majesty travelled in one of London Transport's most modern trains which now carry passengers from Central London to the Airport in forty minutes. (It was, significantly, twenty-two years to the day since she had opened the new Central Terminal buildings there.) The new airport station, the civil engineering work for which was carried out by Taylor Woodrow Construction, has Trav-o-lators connecting it with each of the terminal buildings, and is situated in a triangular area between the airport control tower and two multi-storey car parks.

Jubilee Year, which for the Group had begun auspiciously with a Queen's Award for Export Achievement to Taylor Woodrow International for the second time, officially ended on 3 June 1978 – a date which, by happy coincidence, was linked to two other anniversaries, both marking 150 years: the foundation of the St Katharine Docks, and the foundation of the Institution of Civil Engineers. The latter's annual Conversazione, held at its Great George Street headquarters, included an exhibition of twelve engineering models, of which three were of Taylor Woodrow achievements – the famous wire-winding system for nuclear pressure vessels, the Romanian irrigation scheme, and the redevelopment of St Katharine itself. When the Queen and Prince Philip visited the exhibition, Peter Dawson, Chris Irwin-Childs and, for the second time in the Jubilee year, Peter Drew, met the Royal couple and explained to them the features of the models.

The Queen's Silver Jubilee cheered up the nation, giving back something of a national pride that seemed to be slipping away. For Taylor Woodrow it had a more personal meaning, on that sunny June day below Tower Bridge as the Royal Progress down the River, past a thousand years of history, ended at a rejuvenated dockland, reclaimed from ruined warehouses, symbol of an obstinate hope for the future. To that Royal Progress Taylor Woodrow are proud to have been able to make a modest contribution.

XII

The Old and the New

NOT far from the northern extremity of the Piccadilly Underground Railway is a station called Arnos Grove. It is in the London suburb of New Southgate, where there is also an Arnos Park, which got its name because some Italian workers, in the first few years of the eighteenth century, could not pronounce the name 'Arnolds'. 'Arnolds' was the name of an estate here before James Colebrooke bought it in 1719. Mr Colebrooke wished to build himself a stately home, to plans by Sir Richard Naylor.

Poor man, he never lived to see it completed, and it was his son George (he became a Baronet) who was its first occupant. The next owner was Lord Newhaven, who added extensions to the north and south wings and a porch on the west side, and renamed it 'Arnos Grove'. In 1777 the house was bought by Isaac Walker, whose family and descendants lived there until the beginning of the present century. There were seven Walker brothers, all brilliant cricketers, and if you visit the house today you will see a plaque commemorating them just to the left of the main entrance. The Walker family did great things for the people of Southgate, founding schools and raising money for the building of a local church. The present Walker Primary School is named after them.

What, you will be asking, has all this to do with the Taylor Woodrow Group? Be patient a little longer and all will be revealed. The sixth of the cricketing brothers, V. E. Walker, in 1896 modernized the house and installed electric light – the first house in Southgate to have it. V.E. also added another porch on the north door. Meanwhile the family had been increasing the estate so that it consisted of 300 acres when Lord Inverforth bought it in 1918. This was a new post-war and highly taxed age in which landowning peers could no longer sit back and enjoy their estates, and in 1928 Lord Inverforth began developing his land, except for forty-four acres of parkland, which he sold to Southgate Urban District Council who turned it into Arnos Park. The rest was sold off for housing, and the house itself was sold to the North Metropolitan Power Company. It had been the first house in the district to have electric light, and now, not inappropriately, it was the headquarters of a body which eventually merged with the Eastern Electricity Board when power was nationalized after World War II.

Known until recently as Northmet House, and extended by the electricity people, the building changed hands in 1975. The new owners were the Legal & General Assurance Society Ltd. who, finding that the interior, with its superb murals and period fittings, had been neglected for many years, decided that something must be done about it. They therefore called in Myton Ltd., whose Special Works Department was asked to refurbish the whole building, which was renamed 'Southgate House'.

We have so far seen Myton mainly as a performer of unusually swift refurbishment and co-ordinated detail work. But the versatility of this Taylor Woodrow subsidiary goes far beyond this. If you ask Myton people why their company is different from Taylor Woodrow Construction or any other part of the Group, they generally murmur something about 'parallel working'. Well, other parts of Taylor Woodrow could make the same claim, but there is something about the size of contract Myton choose, and the way they tackle it, that shows the concept at its best. 'Parallel working' is especially important in the present financial climate. It means tight cost control, the earliest possible start of building, rapid completion, and minimum maintenance. It also means appointing the main contractors *at the design stage*, so that they can work alongside the design team in developing the outline conception into working drawings: this will result in a building that can be constructed quickly and economically and still be of the finest quality. Whether the project is an office block, an hotel, a shop interior or the complete refurbishment of an old building, the system is applicable. The client knows exactly when he can take over and carry on his business. 'Parallel working', generally with a fixed fee contract can be fairly claimed to beat inflation, since the work can be started so much sooner and, indeed, is often complete by the time a traditional building contract could be set up and work begun.

There are people at Myton – and one of them is Barton Higgs, chairman and managing director – who really love old buildings and have a special feeling for them. 'I don't think a building is worth saving just *because* it is old,' Barton Higgs says. 'But if it is a fine example of its period, and hasn't been spoilt, no trouble is too much in restoring it.'

When you enter Southgate House, you see at once what he means. It is, of course, a 'listed building' of architectural and historic interest, but this fact alone hardly prepares you for what you are going to see. The upper walls and ceilings of the entrance hall are decorated with fine murals painted in 1723 by the Belgian artist G. Lanscroon. From the ceiling hangs a 36-lamp three-tier Flemish chandelier in polished brass. The lofty reception-room and the antechamber, both on the ground floor facing west, are in the Adam style, with fine plasterwork and classical friezes by Sir Robert Taylor (1714–1788). As part of their work Myton redecorated these rooms and installed new heating, ventilation, and electrical equipment throughout the building.

Lanscroon had been a pupil of Antonio Verrio, whom he had helped with the decoration of the State Apartments at Windsor Castle for Charles II and at Hampton Court for William III. The murals had been restored in 1968 by the generosity of the Borough of Enfield, but were in a cracked and fragile condition when Myton had to deal with them. Barton Higgs has 'before and after' photographs of them: 'the cracks in some of the murals are clearly visible in the photographs taken before restoration,' he says. 'You can imagine what a delicate task it was to alter and renovate the surrounding structure without damaging the precious ceiling.'

The Grand Manner in mural decoration is out of fashion today, and as you ascend the main staircase you may reflect that the Triumph and Apotheosis of Julius Caesar is not the most comfortable subject to live with. He enters Rome in triumph from foreign wars, surrounded by slaves, flower sellers, and winged cherubs, and it is a pity that one of the previous owners of the house put in a new doorway which cut off part of Caesar's chariot. The procession continues along the landing to the left, with Diana, Goddess of Hunting, and the spoils of war borne on a litter by men burning incense. Among the marchers are women (probably modelled on ladies of the Colebrooke family) carrying musical instruments and baskets of fruit. On another wall are the nine Muses, extolling in music the virtues of Caesar, who is sitting on a cloud; and Caesar is finally seen, dressed as a soldier, ascending to heaven where he is welcomed by Jupiter and Juno. In this last scene he is only a little obscured by the addition of the central light fitting.

The painted ceiling was the worst problem. It was discovered that, immediately above it, the main wooden beam carrying the floor had fractured, and another two beams had large cracks, so that the ceiling was actually sagging and the painting was threatened with worse damage. How could the structure be repaired without disturbing the ceiling? Myton called in Phillips Consultants Ltd. (Taylor Woodrow's own consultant engineers who have a sixty-strong design team) who worked out a scheme for inserting a steel beam in the roof space with steel rods hanging from it, right through the next floor to give additional support. These rods were cunningly concealed, some of them being incorporated in an attractive bookcase installed in the manager's office (bearing in mind that, despite Caesar's Apotheosis, this was, in its more prosaic function, an office building). Cork was laid on the floor above, to deaden noise and vibration which might cause further cracking. The structure having been repaired and the ceiling stabilized, the painting was restored by Paul Fodor.

Myton carried out purely practical alterations to provide open plan offices and new suspended ceilings in fissured tile. Outside, the whole façade was redecorated and the stonework cleaned, and most of the 300 sash windows needed new cords. Below, the basement was dark and dingy and for years had only been used for storage. The Legal & General wanted to have a restaurant, kitchen, bar and coffee lounge here, and so Myton divided the basement into rooms, knocking walls down to give an open-plan effect (one was two feet thick, and had to be broken through to make a service hatch).

As so often happens, Myton had to work so that neither the outgoing tenants (the Electricity Board) nor the incoming tenants (Legal & General) lost any work-time. The first phase began in May 1975 while the Electricity Board were still using the building; they left it in December, and the second phase, begun in January 1976, was completed in June as the Legal & General moved in.

Myton Ltd., a building and civil engineering company originally based on Hull, joined the Taylor Woodrow Group in 1955. While it has always made an important contribution to the Group, it took a long time and the weathering of many difficulties to reach its present identity. While not the first Taylor Woodrow subsidiary to go in for property development as well as construction (Taylor Woodrow Construction had a substantial interest in the 20 Albert Embankment project in 1955–56), Myton was to move into this activity in a big way. In the 1950s, says Oliver Marriott in *The Property Boom*, 'contractors came more and more to the conclusion that anything their clients could do, they could do as well if not better'. So we find Wates, Trollope & Colls, and Myton trying their hands at it, and, a few years later, going in for a new trend (new to Britain, though not to America), that of 'town centre renewal', with mixed developments comprising shops, offices, residences, and recreational facilities in various combinations. The great developers of those years were Lord Samuel, Felix Fenston, Harry Hyams, and Ravenseft.

This coincided with a south-east England office boom and a movement, as City rents rose and more and more City offices became cramped and obsolete, towards decentralization, especially of anything (such as computers) which can be used by remote communication.

In 1970 Myton, in association with local authorities, were working on two large 'town centre' type developments – residential-shopping-office complexes – one on fifteen acres overlooking the sea at Brighton (Churchill Square), the other on seventeen acres near the Clyde in Glasgow (Anderston Cross), both begun in the mid-1960s, in partnership with Standard Life Assurance. Churchill Square included besides entertainments and car-parking, one of the most successful shopping schemes in the south of England, including many household names like Sainsbury, British Home Stores, Tesco and also Selfridge.

There was a good example of 'parallel working' in 1970, when Myton converted 100 000 square feet of old Victorian warehousing into modern offices for Babcock & Wilcox Ltd. in only fifteen weeks – an eighteen-month job under traditional procedures. And an equally good example of quality 'refurbishment' was that of Glasgow Stock Exchange, whose old 'Franco-Venetian' facade (dating back to the 1840s) with its slender stone pediments rising seventeen feet above the roof, and the upper part of the Bell Tower, were carefully preserved while the rest of the building was demolished and replaced with a complete new Stock Exchange, modern offices, shops, and – very necessary for jobbers and brokers – a built-in public house. A system of interlocking steel supports was designed to support the fragile façades. The Stock Exchange was promised that it could be back in business within two years, and indeed it was. Myton by now had a Glasgow Regional Office, opened in 1967, which in the following seven years helped provide the Group with a fine reputation north of the border, now being pursued and developed from the same address by Taylor Woodrow Construction (Scotland) Ltd.

At York Gate, Regent's Park, London, Myton (again in conjunction with Standard Life) began in 1967 a large residential and office development which demonstrated contrasting skills – a modern apartment block next to two conversions behind carefully preserved Nash façades (one into offices which were occupied by International Distillers and Vintners, the other into one of the most gracious terraces in London and now housing many famous names).

Myton know a lot about hotels, which they have built all

over the United Kingdom, and 1973 was a good year for them. The 200-bedroom Elizabethan Hotel at Shepperton, Middlesex, scarcely looked Elizabethan from the outside (though there is a richly coloured Elizabethan mural in ceramic tiles in the reception area). It stands in eleven acres of landscaped grounds overlooking the Thames near Walton Bridge – a country hotel within easy reach of everywhere, including several golf-courses. The Elizabethan (three stories) could hardly be more different from the 25-bedroom Albany in Glasgow, opened in the same year – it is fourteen floors high. Work on the Glasgow project began in August 1970 and the structural work was completed in only eleven months, so that the 'topping out' ceremony in July 1971 was nineteen weeks ahead of schedule. The long national builders' strike in the following summer seriously disrupted the finishing work; yet, by 'parallel working', Myton rearranged the programme so that the client (Strand Hotels) could open the public areas, banqueting and conference suites on time. A connecting bridge over Waterloo Street links the hotel to the other Myton development, the Anderston Cross Centre.

The year 1973 also saw the completion of the new 230-bedroom Portland Hotel in Manchester – a typical Myton job involving the preservation of the stone façade of a Victorian warehouse while constructing a twentieth-century hotel and an office block inside it.

Myton have, over the years, done a prodigious amount of work for British Home Stores. Their Worthing store, including an attractively appointed restaurant for 350 people, was completed in only twenty-eight weeks: B.H.S. had never before finished the fitting out of a new department store in less than thirty-six weeks. And in the following year, 1974, B.H.S. stores at Newcastle and Lewisham were ready for trading, the former, despite a late start, being open in time for the Christmas trade.

British Home Stores, maintaining the principle enunciated long ago by Gordon Selfridge that the buying mood is often revived by having a restaurant on the premises, have recently reconverted the brilliant but unsuccessful Biba store in Kensington. So Barbara Hulaniki's Art Deco dream world of the 1920s and 1930s, with its 156 tons of marble and seven miles of carpets, and its two twenty-foot escalators (which project manager Dave Skelley and his team had to roll into position on a bridge of railway sleepers and lines to avoid straining the floor) became another, more conventional, Myton contract which however still demands the Myton speciality of co-ordinating a myriad different fittings and the work of specialist sub-contractors within a very tight-time-schedule.

Myton are also well known in the Isle of Man, where they have had several contracts since the early 1970s. One of these was Derby House, in Douglas, a five-storey office and banking hall built for the Julian S. Hodge Bank (Isle of Man) Ltd. The Taylor Woodrow Group, famous for introducing apologetic notices on sites during the construction to express their regret at the noise and disturbance they inevitably cause, paid tribute at the opening to a special guest of honour – eighty-seven-year-old Mrs Bell, who lives in a cottage adjoining the new building and who had 'smiled cheerfully' at the team all the time they were working.

There was a considerable public outcry when, in 1974, Covent Garden fruit, vegetable, and flower market was moved to Nine Elms, south of the Thames, and there were fears for the historic buildings that were left empty. Replete with old associations (from Nell Gwyn to *My Fair Lady* by way of David Garrick at the 'actors' church' of St Paul's), the old market, whose central building was opened in 1830, had existed on this site for 300 years, by right of a Charter granted to William, Earl of Bedford, by Charles II. It is now being restored by Myton, to whom the Greater London Council have awarded the biggest refurbishing contract ever given by a local authority, and will be used as a shopping area with offices and leisure facilities. Three parallel rows of market shops are joined at the east end by a colonnade surmounted by a terrace which was once an ornamental promenade with conservatories and a fountain. There are other colonnades on the north and south sides whose stonework, defaced by iron sheds and cement repairs, is being restored to its original silver-grey granite: the rest of the stonework is sandstone. All the work is due for completion in 1980, and is part of a still larger scheme to 'revitalize' the whole area.

When money is tight and housing budgets are cut back, the Myton talent for refurbishment is a useful money-earner in hard times; and as an investment, the big property owners (who are often insurance companies and pension funds) sometimes find they can get a better return from up-dating spacious old buildings than from demolition followed by new construction. (Also it is much easier to get planning permission.) Old buildings often have large rooms and high ceilings which lend themselves to the incorporation of a mezzanine floor and partitions, or to great economies of space by resiting grandiose staircases. Two examples, widely differing, can be quoted: the complete refurbishment of an old depository in Davigdor Road, Hove, to provide 70 000 square feet of air-conditioned office space; and the careful, almost loving, conversion of 4–12 Queen Anne's Gate, London, into offices for Amalgamated Investment & Property Co. (*not* to be confused with Queen Anne's Mansions). It was a mini-Southgate House type of job in which an historic building was converted to a totally different use while fine old ceilings and façades were carefully preserved or reproduced.

The plastering work at Queen Anne's Gate was carried out

by Jonathan James Ltd., one of Taylor Woodrow's specialist companies, who are much concerned with the restoration of old buildings (but equally capable of adding decoration to new ones). Master craftsmen in plastering, suspended ceiling work and mouldings, they are frequently sub-contracted by other construction companies for tasks which only they can do so well. For their work at Queen Anne's Gate, they were awarded the Plaisterers' Trophy for 1973 by the City of London's Worshipful Company of Plaisterers.

Jonathan James have done other work in the City. In the early 1970s, the Corporation of London was renewing, in the form of a piazza, most of the buildings surrounding the historic Guildhall. The Guildhall Library of 200 000 volumes, 60 000 prints, and many thousands of manuscripts (including a bit of Shakespeare's handwriting and an original copy of Magna Carta), was being moved from a Victorian–Gothic building to a well-lighted block which it shares with Corporation offices. Jonathan James, under main contractors Trollope & Colls, contributed the new library's coffered ceilings and other high-quality plasterwork in the Reading Room, with mouldings from their workshops at Rainham, Essex.

They were sub-contracted again by Sir Robert McAlpine & Sons for their biggest-ever contract at the ambitious Brent Cross shopping centre which opened in March 1976. Brent Cross (not far from Staples Corner) is the largest enclosed shopping complex in Britain: only the Victoria Centre, Nottingham, built by Taylor Woodrow Construction (Midlands), can be compared with it. Jonathan James contributed ceilings in all the nine malls (the longest is 100 metres), and a fibrous plaster dome which bears a striking resemblance to some of the Taylor Woodrow–Monarch shopping centres around Toronto which we noted in Chapter IX. For this, Jonathan James again won the Plaisterers' Trophy.

There is yet another kind of refurbishment, just as much of the seventies, which Myton have been carrying out recently. This is the 'revitalization' of local authority housing. This is likely to suffer some recession as the struggle to combat rising rates proceeds, but it is interesting to note the standard of housing which is now regarded as basic. Most of Myton's 'revitalizing' has been done on a number of different contracts in the North East, between Tynemouth and Hull, and the work has generally included the installation of new services (electricity, central heating, and hot water), the provision of a new kitchen and bathroom, the renovation or replacement of windows (sometimes with double glazing), and roofing, and internally any necessary alterations to the plans by new partitions, together with the repair or replacement of joinery and redecoration. Outside, new lawns, paths, and garden fencing are generally provided, with play areas for children. It may lack the glamour of Southgate House or Queen Anne's Gate, but it is still well worth having.

XIII

The Greenham Group

PLANT, sand and ballast, concrete, electrical equipment, tools, tyres – the activities of the Greenham Group are multifarious, and we cannot in a short survey cover them all. Up to the late 1950s Greenham Tool Company operated from headquarters at 618 London Road Isleworth. The range of products it offered the construction industry and local amenities was small, and most of its business was done within about five miles of its offices. In 1954 another branch was opened at Aldridge, Staffordshire, to serve the Midlands. It was slow to get off the ground, and not until the 1960s did the Tool Company as a whole take the 'great leap forward' that transformed it from one of the smallest contractors' tools and protective clothing merchants in the country to possibly the largest in the field today.

The manager of the Tool Company in the 1950s was George Borwell (he is now chairman): and to him much of the credit must go for pressing hard for growth, efficiency and change in a highly competitive world. 'We've grown from one branch with voice-pipe communication system to a national network of branches', says managing director Ken Lampit, 'and we are now considering developments with the third generation of computers including word processors, visual display units and a big push forward into the world of micro-processors and silica chips.'

After setting up Aldridge in the Midlands, Greenham

acquired S. V. Newbold Ltd. to form the Southampton Branch in 1961. At this time the Company became involved in sales to industrial users, away from its traditional markets, a development which was to have far-reaching effects in the years to come.

At about the same time there was considerable dealing in Government surplus material and the profits from this were used to develop an efficient direct mail department at Aldridge where records are kept of the some 35 000 customers that make up the clientele of the world of Greenham Tool.

During the remainder of the 1960s branches were built at Tottenham, Newcastle, Crawley, Thornaby-on-Tees and Exeter but during the last year of the decade, the Aldridge Warehouse was reduced to a smouldering ruin by fire which was brought under control early in the morning; however, by 4 o'clock in the afternoon of the same day customers in the Midlands were being supplied with their requirements from other branches in the North and South.

Expansion continued, with modern warehouses in Manchester and Glasgow. In 1971 they acquired, from George Cohen Machinery Ltd., that part of their business which sold non-mechanical contractors' tools and protective clothing following which the branch at Taff's Well, near Cardiff, was opened.

S. R. Walsh Ltd., which had developed from a family firm of haberdashers and outfitters with five shops in Bolton, had gradually specialized in such lines as donkey jackets, boiler suits, safety shoes, helmets, rubber boots, and safety eyewear aimed particularly at local authorities. Since 1941 the company had been run by the founder's daughter Phyllis, who, under her married name of Mrs Phyllis Taylor, continued for two years as a director of S. R. Walsh and regularly attended board meetings of Greenham Tool Company. New branches of Greenham Tool in Leeds and

Newbury followed and in 1972 the new ICI product of Cambrelle was introduced to the market. The first major venture by the company into material supply as opposed to tools and clothing, it has become an integral part of the product line and, now known as Terram, is a material for temporary access roads, land drainage and other stabilization problems.

Greenham people always use the word *customer* in bold type because they believe in quality with price and service with courtesy. As Nick Greenham, the founder, used to say, the customer pays our wages'. One arm of their comprehensive marketing is direct mail. 'Our last mailing,' said their director in charge of publicity, Brendon Reynolds, recently, 'weighed over six tons and filled 250 mail bags, all in colour booklet form.' He also defines the company policy as 'providing quality goods that *don't* come back to customers who *do* come back.'

The latest departure is that the company will now accept Access and Barclaycards at all branches and is aiming for business from the people who work for customers as well as from the trade customers themselves. The slogan will be:

If you work in the trade why not buy at trade prices.

Lines now handled by the company total more than 6 000. For one market alone – factories – they supply everything from industrial floor cleansers, paint removers, and detergents to specialized soaps, disinfectants, paper towels, and toilet rolls.

The hire shops which operated fairly successfully in the early 1970s were phased out in favour of limited small hire operations from Callerton near Newcastle; from Glasgow and Southampton chain saws, flood lights, dehumidifiers, heaters, etc. are available to the trade and private buyers.

All Greenham companies have stories of derring-do in emergencies. Here is one from Greenham Tool. In 1976 exposed grain stores at Hasaka, a province of Northern Syria, were threatened with ruin when early rainstorms swept the area. To save the harvest (75 000 tonnes) the Syrian Government appealed for help. Greenham Tool received a rush order for 100 tonnes of heavy-duty polythene sheeting to cover the grain. Even Greenham do not keep that amount in stock, but they mobilized other sources in record time. The material was delivered to Luton, Manston, and Heathrow airports, where specially chartered aircraft were waiting to 'airlift' it to Syria. One of them, a Boeing 707, had to have its passenger seats stripped out to accommodate the polythene. The harvest was saved!

At this time, director Brian Abrahams, responsible for purchasing, was stretched to the limit but he applied his basic philosophy which is to get goods at the right price and ensure that the customer gets what he wants, when he wants it. The buyers now range world-wide looking for products and to keep abreast with modern technology in a still expanding service industry.

In the area of export this has been expanding progressively over the years and received a great fillip in 1977 with an order in excess of £1 m for dustbins for Saudi Arabia. This was as a result of great work by Bill Bonneywell, marketing director, in the face of international competition.

Since 1975 S.R. Walsh have maintained their connection with Bolton through one retail shop selling leisure wear and protective clothing to the general public, but a new warehouse has been opened in Abingdon, Berkshire where, under general manager Len Poulton, a large wholesale business is developing in overall clothing and gloves. At the same time the 10 000 sq. ft. warehouse at Lostock near Bolton is being expanded by an additional 20 000 sq. ft. to provide bulk storage for much of the protective clothing for distribution either direct to customers or to branches; an extension of this to handle safety and fashion footwear has been operating in Bradford since 1976.

To cater for additional expansion associated with industrial and credit card business, a new 10 000 sq. ft. warehouse is being built at Tottenham; extensions are under way at Manchester and Crawley; plans are in hand for additional space at Exeter – in addition to the new warehouse obtained in recent years to replace the small one in the centre of the City; and possibly most important of all, total occupation of the Isleworth premises for eventual development into a large warehousing and distribution complex for Greenham Tool, Tyre and Electric Companies.

Like many other companies in the Greenham Group, Greenham Tyre Co. was an offshoot of Greenham Plant Hire. In the post-war years its main customers were transport contractors, local garages, and the construction industry; but the big tyre manufacturers were finding and controlling their own distributors and Greenham had to find other means of competing. Between 1965 and 1968 new branches were opened, but aimed basically at the passenger tyre market.

Greenham Tyre Co. used heavy press advertising and millions of door-to-door leaflets to promote their wares. Special discounts were offered to members of sports and social clubs and motoring organizations. The business continued to expand and sales representatives called on industrial users, and the company maintained a small fleet of service vans for breakdown and site use. Everything possible was done to take the physical labour out of tyre changing, using such equipment as the Collman press, which can remove a giant tyre from its rim and put on a new one faster than any other known method.

Among major Greenham Tyre customers is the British Airports Authority, and Greenham maintains a 24-hour service to London Heathrow and other airports. British Oxygen is another customer needing top speed service when emergency supplies of oxygen have to be rushed to hospitals.

With longer life tyres, improved vehicle suspension, and roads, the tyre industry has been changing rapidly and with it Greenham Tyre Company have adapted to the new conditions. They are now involved in their own tyre remoulding operation, the importing of tyres and the provision of specialist services to the larger industrial users in the truck and earthmover area. Still able to provide a passenger tyre service but on a reduced geographical area, the company is moving into the 1980s with a realistic approach to the problems facing the industry as a whole.

Greenham Electric Ltd, formed in 1965, sells a wide variety of electrical equipment to the industrial user and especially the electrical contractor. At its main warehouse in Isleworth more than 8 000 items are stocked, ranging from the smallest fuse that exists to giant 800-amp switch-fuses. The company specializes in the complete package deal, particularly for cables, switchgear and light fittings for use on every kind of construction site.

Although London and the home counties are its principal U.K. market, its tentacles are stretching out over thousands of miles. Cables and switchgear for a car-factory computer system in Moscow, switchgear for Taylor Woodrow's vast irrigation project in Romania, electrical equipment for the new TV studios at Kano, Northern Nigeria. A council house in London, a sheikh's palace in Saudi Arabia, the electrical fittings for a hotel in Malaysia complete installations for a large contract in South America – Greenham Electric deal with them all in the course of a day.

In naval terms the 'flag company' of the Greenham Group is Greenham Plant Hire which has grown dramatically in recent years and now has the largest fleet of giant Manitowoc cranes, which helped it to get in early on the North Sea oil boom. (There may be another, if smaller, oil boom off South Wales in what is already being called the Celtic Sea.) In 1971 it began diversifying to clients outside mainstream building and civil engineering markets, which (if you exclude the petro-chemical industries) account for about 45 per cent of its turnover. In recent years the Greenham forklift fleet has expanded to nearly 1 000 trucks.

The future – and bigger profits – seem to lie in larger, more specialized equipment, and this is where Greenham Plant Hire seem to be going – hydraulic excavators, traxcavators and telescopic lorry-mounted cranes from 6 to 116 tons. There is a Crawler Crane Division, whose largest machine can lift up to 600 tons – these can be mounted on oil-rigs in the North Sea.

A good example of how Greenham Plant Hire operate happened in November 1975, when a tentative inquiry was received from a company of consultant engineers, Rig Design Services of London. Their requirements might have daunted a less flexible and well-prepared hire service. They wanted some Manitowoc 4100W ringer cranes for offshore work. Bob Widger, general manager of the Heavy Crane Division, had a meeting with the consultant engineers, who at the time were retained by Occidental Oil Company for the Piper 'A' Jacket which had recently been positioned in the North Sea.

The jacket had been positioned, but it had not yet been anchored to the seabed. Because of bad weather, the main contractors had been unable to land the twenty 120-ton piles needed to secure it. Their own 2 000-ton-capacity floating crane could not cope with the job because of adverse weather conditions. Rig Design thought that using an H3 semi-submersible drilling-rig was the only answer. Accordingly Greenham Plant Hire were asked to supply two Manitowoc 4100 W's which would be mounted on the specially-converted semi-submersible rig. The rig thus became a temporary construction vessel with accommodation for 300 men and two 280-ton capacity cranes which could complete the piling, and this was possible in bad weather because the new rig allowed far greater stability in heavy seas.

After conversion in the Aker shipyards in Oslo, it was agreed that the cranes would be limited to 130 tons capacity each at a maximum boom length of 120 feet to allow for the pitch and roll of the rig and high wind speeds. The construction vessel continued to work throughout the winter of 1975, and proved so successful that since then Greenham Plant Hire have provided five more Manitowoc cranes for similar operations, all mounted on semi-submersible rigs.

Another 'rescue operation' was carried out by Greenham Plant Hire's South African company in 1975. A 250 000-ton oil tanker, the *Chrysanthy 'M' Lemos*, registered in Monrovia, en route to the Gulf, developed serious engine trouble and had to put into Cape Town for emergency repairs. Being an oil tanker it carried no derricks on board. How could damaged major components in the transmission train be lifted up from the bottom of the ship, which was as high as a 14-storey building?

The solution was to hire two mobile hydraulic boom cranes from Greenham (a 14-ton and a 20-ton) and put them on to the tanker's deck with a floating harbour crane. The two cranes were fitted with an extra 152 metres of wire rope in order to reach the ship's engine-room.

Much more delicate was the lifting of George Stephenson's original steam engine, *Locomotive No. 1*, from its pedestal at Darlington Station for its removal to Stockton to undergo repairs, its frail condition being due to exposure to exhaust fumes from diesel locomotives.

Greenham are also, through Greenham Construction Equipment Limited, suppliers of construction equipment in the United Kingdom. Based in Woking, with its principal operating depot at Newcastle from where all parts and services are directed, it is the national distributor for P & H cranes, among the world's best known brand names, and North Eastern distributor for Ford Construction Equipment. The Company is able to sell internationally through contractors working and buying in Britain for use overseas and, by establishing a world-wide base of contacts, a considerable volume of used equipment is shipped away from the United Kingdom.

We are gradually coming down to earth again, to the world of sand, gravel, and concrete in which Nick Greenham was originally interested. In 1960 Greenham Concrete was formed to produce high-quality ready-mixed concrete at a competitive price. In the old days – indeed up to twenty years ago – concrete was generally mixed on site. Now, according to the location, ready-mixed has a 50 to 75 per cent share of the market. The trend has been accelerated by strict standards of quality control in the construction industry. Producing concrete in a central depot enables the contractor to rely on getting the right quality in the exact quantity ordered just when and where he requires it. Greenham Concrete have organized their distribution network so that their fleet of over 100 truck-mixers can cover their sales areas with a maximum journey of five miles. The mix formula is stringently tested in Greenham's laboratory as well as on site. Speed is essential, since chemical changes take place in concrete in transit. Greenham also have a Pump Placing division for supplying mobile pumps to sites: they can pour concrete at an average rate of twelve cubic metres per hour. The largest pour the company has been involved in to date was 1 200 cubic metres, required for the foundations of a site in Bishopsgate, London. This pour lasted for twelve hours – all night from 6 p.m. to 6 a.m.

So let us take an overall world look at the Greenham Group, streamlined in 1973 almost as an independent entity within the Taylor Woodrow Group. Its new dynamism in recent years has much to do with the leadership of Brian Trafford from 1972. Most of its overseas activities are to be found in South and East Africa. It has an associated company, Concrete S.R.L., in Milan, resulting from a partnership (formed in 1965) with Torno, one of Italy's major construction firms; and a construction and mechanical handling equipment company in Denmark, Boeg-Thomsen A/S. One is always discovering new facts about Greenham – such as the Ace Water Skate system, a new way of moving heavy loads, similar to an air-cushion system, by raising them on high-pressure water pumps, and now operated by Lifting Services International, a division of Taylor Woodrow Construction.

Another of Greenham's twenty-four companies, A. & S. Andrews of Ealing, sells Ford cars. The old established Ford main dealer was incorporated into the Greenham Group in 1973. The buildings and workshops were developed and now more than one car per hour of the working week is sold and delivered to customers. Vans deliver parts over a large part of west London and a successful rally car is sponsored, supported by a team of enthusiasts who give up their week-ends and spare time to prepare and service it on competitions.

Among the new Greenham companies are Crane Test and Inspection Ltd., based at Aldridge, who provide a specialist service to users of cranes throughout the United Kingdom, and Greenham Humidity Control Ltd. This company was formed to expand the hire and sales of humidity control equipment which has been in existence for several years but always as a part of other companies. It now includes air conditioners hire and sales, and equipment has been supplied for such varying purposes as drying mink pelts to art treasures damaged by damp as far away as Venice.

The speed of life at Greenham seems to increase daily.

John Watson, chairman of Greenham Plant Hire, which he joined in 1948 as a sales invoice clerk, remembers the time when, on being promoted to salesman, he drove a ten-year-old Ford 10 which used to catch fire occasionally. Now, he says, it's all 'suitcase and airline ticket'. Indeed, the Greenham Group once had its own airline – a scheduled air service from Northolt Airport to Teesside and Newcastle, using a Beechcraft King Air C.90. This mini-airliner, seating eight people, left Northolt every Tuesday at 8.00 am., and arrived in Teesside one hour later and at Newcastle by 9.30 a.m., returning to Northolt the same evening. There was a Monday service to the Manchester area.

In the construction industry, whether you are building a bungalow or a dry dock, you can do absolutely nothing without clay, sand, gravel, and cement. You cannot mix mortar or concrete, you cannot make a humble brick ('the world's first prefabricated module', somebody once called it) without these basic materials. Gravel contains 'sharp' sand which is good for concrete, but not fine enough for mortar, which needs 'soft' sand. And sand and gravel, in particular, are increasingly hard to come by. In the 1970s you are up against pressure groups, environmentalists, and the attitude of local government bodies who are difficult to convince that worked-out pits can nowadays be fully restored to agricultural use or landscaped to prepare them for any other purpose. Greenham reckon they have enough land to last until about 1985; but after that, what? Import aggregate by rail from other parts of the country? Or even from abroad? Think of the cost. 'We are banking on a change of attitude within local government, and we are doing everything in our power to bring that about,' say Greenham. 'Restoration is very important to us, and we have spent considerable sums of money investigating ways in which old pits can be restored to agricultural land of high quality.'

This is less easy than it sounds. You don't just fill up old pits with rubbish and throw down some fertilizer. Greenham consulted soil scientists of Land & Water Management Ltd. about their old pit at Shepperton in 1975, and in October that year invited more than eighty people from the farming industry, local government, and the Department of the Environment to a demonstration there. The visitors inspected two areas of restored land – one of four acres and an experimental one-acre tract which had been restored to Grade 2 agricultural land in only two years.

This really does look like a major breakthrough. The land was originally under water, and the work to fill the pit with inert materials was completed by 1973. The land was then left to settle for two years. In the summer of 1975 the pit was contoured to make an adequate drainage gradient, and subsoil was placed on the prepared top surface and mechanically levelled. Then topsoil (to a depth of one metre) was lifted on to the subsoil layer and levelled in the same way. By mid-August all was ready for planting, and the first result was a crop of radishes. The secret of Greenhams' success lies in their method of handling the soil, allowing no heavy machinery on to the surface (which would damage the soil structure) and using soil which has only recently been removed from another part of the site. The radishes were soon followed by crops of wheat and vegetables. Greenham don't need to hold on to a parcel of land for more than five years. After that it can soon be brought back into use as good quality farm or recreational land. It can even be better than it was before – better drained and more fertile.

In 1975, Greenham could fairly claim that they had filled and restored more land than they had used for extraction. This was the year after the Sand and Gravel Association (SAGA) gave Greenham Sand and Ballast Co. one of their coveted annual awards for – in the opinion of an independent committee of farmers and environmentalists – having restored old gravel workings at Staines and on Stanwell Moor to a high standard. Another award went to Taylor Woodrow Industrial Estates, who had successfully restored a 40-acre site at Ipswich and built twenty factories and warehouses on it.

Greenham actually own Staines Common (using the word in its metropolitan, not rural, sense); or rather they own the minerals underneath it, for the surface belongs to the 'moor-masters' of Staines Moor.

Much gravel is dredged from the bottom of lakes and reservoirs, such as the Queen Mary Reservoir at Staines, which was constructed in the 1920s over 300 hectares of gravel land with London clay underneath it. At the time it was not technically feasible to make the reservoir deeper than twelve metres, and so the gravel lay almost undisturbed. Now, however, there has been another breakthrough. A consortium of companies is dredging up gravel from the bottom and at the same time providing the Metropolitan Water Board with increased water storage capacity. Thus the reservoir's old capacity of 30 000 million litres is being increased by 6 500 million litres. Greenham Sand and Ballast are also members, with eight other companies, of Reservoir Aggregates Ltd., formed in 1969 to work a gravel pit alongside the reservoir to take out some 2 million tonnes of gravel and so provide a space for the disposal of between 1.5 million and 2 million tonnes of silt from the reservoir excavation which would yield about ten million tonnes of gravel. From the start of this operation, a comprehensive landscaping programme has been going on, and the outside excavation area will eventually be handed back to the Water Board in a state suitable for sustaining plant life. Existing belts of trees are being maintained and are even being improved by filling in with new trees and shrubs. All this has been done in consultation with local residents, and no public inquiry has been necessary.

By a joint venture with British Dredging Ltd., Metro-Greenham Aggregates (centred on Battersea) extract gravel from the sea. There is no topsoil on the seabed, so suction dredgers can be used. At Battersea the gravel is processed and sold. The normal method of extraction on land is to strip the topsoil (usually about nine inches) with big scrapers, and then remove about three feet of overburden with dredgers. Underneath is about seventeen feet of sand and gravel.

With old methods of extraction, it used to take about seven years to restore land after gravel has been taken out. That is why the 'delicate slicing' method pioneered by Greenham, and the avoidance of heavy machinery, is something of a revolution: it enables land to be restored in only six weeks.

How do you cope with a divided area, in which pits are close yet separated? At their Hersham pits, Walton-on-Thames, Greenham used dredgers and barges near the river-front area (ninety acres) and excavators and conveyor belt for another fifty acres: the belt is more than a mile long. And during extraction at Kempton Park Racecourse, where they had about 100 acres in five sections, gravel was transported by conveyor belt through tunnels under the racecourse. Not a day's racing was lost, and when it is eventually restored, part of the area will become available for leisure activities.

Enough of gravel. We will end our review of the Greenham Group, restlessly diversifying, so multifarious that a City editor would probably call it the 'traxcavators-to-toilet rolls firm', with half a dozen stories, grave and amusing, that exemplify the never-a-dull-moment atmosphere in which it works. Most of the stories have to do with cranes. New uses for old machines? Twenty years ago they took part in the film, *The Cruel Sea*. Men rowing away in a lifeboat from a sinking ship were shown battling with enormous waves: the lifeboat was in a tank, and the swell was simulated by lifting the whole thing up and down with a crane. Not long afterwards, for *Moby Dick*, another sea picture at Denham Studios, Gregory Peck was seen observing a whale blowing in the distance. The whale was a dummy; the pumps were provided by Greenham.

When, one day in 1976, the practical joking Pete Dulay brought his *Candid Camera* TV programme to Isleworth, he borrowed a forklift and a telescopic crane from Greenham Plant Hire. The first was to raise a dummy telephone box with a would-be caller in it; the second was to enable a joker to ask two ladies with shopping bags the way to London Airport, thank them for their information, flap his arms like wings and disappear into the sky.

Rather more to the benefit of mankind was the summoning of Greenham's largest telescopic crane, which travelled to Llandudno in North Wales to lift a 2-ton kidney machine into position: the unit had to be swung over a row of houses so that it could be placed in the patient's back garden. Early in 1976 a 1½-ton stuffed elephant, complete with a made-to-measure weatherproof plastic suit, was lifted through a taxidermist's roof in London and safely placed into the Royal Scottish Museum in Edinburgh. And, in 1977, Greenham Tool Co. were selling red and white luminous harness for camels to those oil-rich sheikhs who are concerned about conservation. For since Arabia became motorized, camels have become a road hazard to both themselves and drivers. The camel, no longer the ship of the desert in these parts, is now, like the Sarasota alligator, a protected beast.

XIV

A Team is a Team

IN the panelled library of a former stately home, parts of
which date back to 1540 but most of which is Victorian–
Gothic–Jacobean, set in 137 acres of parkland, eighteen
young men and women, happy as children, are building
towers from Lego construction kits. They are split up into
groups or syndicates, and some of them are watching and
commenting on the others. This is Tuesday, the second working day of a Taylor Woodrow five-day Career Development
Course held at Aldermaston Court Conference Centre in
Berkshire. The young men and women, in the twenty-two
to twenty-eight age bracket, are taking part in a planning and
organization exercise. The economic height of each tower
must be established, its building must be costed, and the
imaginary contract must make a theoretical profit. When
each team has planned its tower, it must move round to
another table and build – *another* team's tower.

You do not have to know Taylor Woodrow very well to
guess that this has something to do with teamwork. The
nature of the task is unimportant: it is the *approach* to it that
counts, and the motivation. These young people have been
chosen by their firms – subsidiaries of the Taylor Woodrow
Group – not so much because they are regarded as future
management material as because it is thought that they will
benefit most from the course.

They arrive on Sunday afternoon and spend the evening

Sir Frank Taylor, newly elected first Life President of Taylor Woodrow, receives from Dick Puttick, chairman, a silver replica of David Wynne's sculpture 'Boy with a dolphin' presented to him by his colleagues on the Main Board.

The four joint managing directors appointed on 29 June 1979 – Norman Baker, Bob Aldred, Brian Trafford and Frank Gibb.

The Prime Minister, the Rt. Hon. Margaret Thatcher, M.P., after opening the new Research Laboratories at Southall, with Reg Taylor explaining some of the work on display.

All-weather flying at Fairoaks Airport, Chobham – the first aircraft to take off from the new runway.

The open air market at Newton Abbot.

BNOC's Thistle 'A' platform on station in 530 ft of water 130 miles north east of the Shetland Isles.

Maintenance work by Seaforth Maritime mechanics on the submersible launch and retrieve system of the submersible support vessel *Intersub Three*.

'Team Work' – the original granite sculpture by David Wynne which stands outside Western House.

Re-railing work in the Glasgow Underground railway modernization scheme.

The new grandstand at Cheltenham racecourse opened by Queen Elizabeth, the Queen Mother, in March 1979.

Queen Anne's Mansions, Westminster.

Water skates used by Lifting Services International to move a 240-tonne grain
barge from fabrication shop to launch shipway.

A Taylor Woodrow jack-up platform assisting on salvage work for the Isle of
Man Harbour Board at Douglas.

getting to know each other. Monday is spent in 'written and spoken communication' during which each has to give a five-to-seven-minute talk which is criticized by the others. On Tuesday evening – 'guest night' – Taylor Woodrow directors are entertained to dinner and one course member is elected to make a speech of welcome. An informal party is held in the library after dinner, and this is the opportunity for course members to let their hair down and say anything that is on their minds.

Wednesday morning is spent on another group activity. The day I was there, five volunteers were called for to solve a 'group problem'. Each was given an envelope containing irregular cardboard shapes which had to be fitted together in five *equal* squares. The rules said that nobody was to talk or make signals to anyone else, but that anyone might silently offer a piece to someone else, who *must* accept it. Thus, you may complete someone else's square before your own. The crunch comes when four players achieve equal squares of the wrong size, while the fifth has a fistful of pieces that don't fit anything. . . .

It is all over in thirty minutes, and the conclusions drawn seem to be: (1) Individuals must understand the *total* problem; (2) individuals must understand their own contribution, and (3) be aware of others' contributions; and (4) individuals must be aware of others' problems.

On Wednesday afternoon, another group problem: this time, a town planning exercise, in which you may (indeed, you *must*) talk. You are divided into teams of four, and each team is given a box full of small models – houses, a gasometer, a factory, a church – and is told simply to 'design a model town'. You are not told what kind of town – that is up to the group. What often emerges is that the group starts building its town before it has agreed what sort of town it wants to build or decided its priorities. The one who is keenest to see what is inside the box is generally the *apparent* leader – the man of action; but after a few minutes the rest of the team tend to turn to the one who assumes a *reasoned* leadership by evaluating and selecting ideas.

You hear things like: 'The factory zone must be in the east because the prevailing wind will take atmospheric pollution away from the residential district. . . . You can't have the church in the main street, it's too noisy. . . . Let's have most of the trees in the residential zone so as to provide comfort stations for people's dogs. . . .' At this point everybody bursts out laughing, and the tension is broken (laughter is a necessary part of working with other people).

Again, it's all over in thirty minutes, and participants and observers hold an inquest on what actually happened. Certain lessons have been learnt about 'working together' – that ideas more often gain acceptance when they are presented as questions or suggestions, not as a dogmatic attempt to persuade; that an idea rejected out of hand will be brought up again and again until *reasons* for refusal have been given . . . and many others. 'What did you do at Aldermaston?' 'We played with bricks and Dinky toys.' Well, that is what was literally done; but what was actually achieved was practice in agreeing on an objective, having ensured that it was measurable and attainable.

In between the last two 'group problems' members on the course have been shown a film, *Listening*. This is an instructional comedy about a man who habitually loses opportunities and time by not being aware of what is going on all round him. He is easily distracted (e.g. by his secretary's legs). Or he is so full of his own schemes that he doesn't really want to discuss them ('my mind is made up, don't confuse me with facts'). In particular he doesn't give enough attention to the views of his colleagues and subordinates (allowing for the fact that the subordinates' ideas may be presented rather timidly). Maybe he thinks of two or more things at once, puts up a mental resistance, has a pre-concept of all problems, jumps to conclusions, is cut off from his colleagues by self-importance. Listening is part of a process, the other two-thirds of which are understanding and remembering. Have you *really* remembered something, or has your own personality put in things that weren't there? Exactly what *did* you hear? What conclusions are you entitled to draw from it?

On Thursday you are given practice in how to run a meeting, the art of chairmanship, and how contributions lead to consensus; and on Friday (by which time you are pleasantly tired) you will sum up all you have been thinking about since Monday morning. You will also present a project you have been working on, and finalize your Career Development Sheet (in syndicates of three or four) which is a critical self-analysis hitched to where you expect to be in, say, five years' time, bearing in mind the cardinal Taylor Woodrow belief: 'In business there is no such thing as a setback: a setback is an opportunity not yet recognized.'

You are, of course, invited to criticize the course, and nobody will think the worse of you if your reaction is: 'But this will produce yes-men. If our Founder had bothered about this sort of thing, we wouldn't be here now!' But, despite his intuition and will-power, the Founder *did* bother about all this, many years ago, by being a patient listener and insisting always on politeness and sweet reason as the basis of a relationship between colleagues. The course is *not* an assessment of members: what they do at Aldermaston is not reported to their managers. Indeed, some bosses do not even know what goes on there: one managing director said to a tutor recently: 'I don't know what you do there, but people who have been on the course come back changed.'

The student of Peter Drucker's books and concepts ('management by objectives') and of Edward de Bono's 'lateral thinking' will recognize some of their thoughts in this course, which has been planned by Roy Spiers, Group communications and personnel services director, Mike Watts, personnel development officer, who joined him after a period of salesmanship with Greenham. They are responsible for the training of all but the very top echelon of management – and even top management have been invited by Roy Spiers to attend a course at the London Business School!

There is nothing new in 'sending people on a course', as any ex-soldier knows. The difference here is the extent to which it is being done. If ever there was a man who was grateful for being 'sent on a course', it is Norman Baker, joint deputy chairman and joint managing director of the group and deputy managing director of Taylor Woodrow Construction. Over the past thirty years Norman Baker has earned an enviable reputation as a negotiator of outstanding skill and an expert on planning, estimating, marketing and sales, and above all the gentle art of making a profit. He was company secretary of Taylor Woodrow Construction from 1965 to 1967, and the ease with which he was able suddenly to undertake this new and complex function was, he believes, partly due to his having studied American and international business management at Harvard in 1963. To Harvard he also acknowledges another debt, his ability to 'get on well with Yanks' which has earned him the sobriquet 'the Atlantic Bridge'.

It began, of course, with one of Frank Taylor's hunches. Taylor Woodrow had just gone into partnership with the Blitman Corporation, and Frank Taylor thought that Norman and Howard Blitman would, as personalities, fit well together. The two men, each admits, have taught each other plenty.

The advanced management course at Harvard Business School (which gives a rather frightening idea of what

Aldermaston might become) is probably the toughest in the world. You have to be 40 to 45 and fairly high in the hierarchy to qualify for it at all. From 7.30 a.m. till about midnight, from August till Christmas with only two weekends off, the students, in syndicates (called 'cans'), solve industrial problems of enormous complexity based on actual case histories. They use sophisticated visual aids and make elaborate presentations of their findings at the end of the course. The big surprise came at the very end, when the four best presentations had to be repeated – before the board of the very company whose real-life problems they had been tackling! This was, for Norman Baker, an unforgettably stimulating experience. He has lost none of the friends he made there, and has been heard to say that 'Harvard freemasonry' can sometimes lubricate the acquisition of new business. . . .

It could be said that life at Taylor Woodrow is one long preparation for management if you have the talent, since everything that happens to you has to do with the Group philosophy on human relations. The main or parent board consists of sixteen directors of whom fourteen are engaged full-time in Group trading activities. It takes major decisions, and delegates many matters to the executive board, which is made up from senior executives within the Group as well as main board directors; their appointments are for twelve months. Then there is the Management Development Board, of twelve members who are all up-and-coming executives in subsidiary and associate companies. Its main purpose is to give them experience of thinking both managerially and group-wise, and to pool their ideas. Each member's appointment is limited to eighteen months, and the chairmanship rotates. The Management Development Board does not merely sit and think and talk: at least once a year it goes far afield to explore matters of Group interest. Thus in July 1971 it toured Turkey, visiting universities in Istanbul and Ankara,

and major construction projects such as the Gokcekaya dam
and hydro-electric power scheme, and the new Bosphorus
bridge – the only road link between Europe and Asia outside
the USSR. And in June 1976 members spent a week in
Sweden to study one of the largest timber-processing plants
and its end-products, prefabricated timber houses, schools,
offices, and shops which are turned out at the rate of 2 500 a
year. They also visited two dry docks at Gothenburg, the
new airport at Landvetter, and the Rannebergen Housing
Estate where 5 300 people live. They have been to Montreal
and Toronto to look at Monarch; underneath London to
see the Aldwich-Charing Cross section of the new jubilee
Line underground railway.

The emphasis on 'communications' which we noticed at
Aldermaston simply reflects principles which have been
growing for many years. The problem in an expanding
organization is somehow never to lose the personal touch. At
one end of the scale is a simple form of reporting, which
includes accurate profit and loss accounts for every branch
and every project, large or small, within twenty-eight days
of the end of each month, so that the finance director knows,
every other Monday, the position of every bank account all
over the world. At the other end are house magazines such as
Taywood News, the bi-monthly *Team Bulletin* and Greenham's own magazine, *The Flying 'G'*.

The finance director whose concern is the state of those
bank accounts worldwide is Stan Tribe, main board director
and chairman of Taylor Woodrow Services since 1971. His
knowledge of the Group's financial affairs dates from 1942 –
eleven years before he actually joined the team – when he
went to the Group's wartime headquarters at Kidlington with
the company's auditors, Jenks, Percival Pidgeon & Co – later
Mann Judd and now Touche Ross & Co.

According to Stan the work of the accountant today is to

interpret and comply with the ever increasing and changing laws about accounting, taxation and so on almost to the detriment of his main function, which is the provision of financial information for management.

Having invested a good deal of time and money in studying and developing internal communications, Taylor Woodrow saw it as a possible export, a commodity which could be sold to other firms. In 1976 they established Kadek Vision (an offshoot of Kadek Press, the Group's own printing and design firm), to provide for the Group's own audio-visual programme requirements. As its workload expanded it became, early in 1977, a limited liability company trading in a wide range of audio-visual equipment for industrial and commercial clients. In December 1977 it took delivery at its temporary studio in Beaconsfield, Bucks, of a Sickles Model 3300 pin register rostrum camera, the first to be imported, equipped for Fairchild Synchromatic filmstrip production. This purchase confirmed Kadek's confidence in the Fairchild system, for which it is also an agent. The camera has been a major factor in its expansion from the production of films and audio-visual programmes into the provision of technical services to production companies and photographers. Now in its permanent and well fitted-out studio at Shepperton, Kadek Vision has available one of the few Video 80 production units in Britain.

One important aspect of communications, in a growing and diversifying organization, is the need to understand the other fellow's job – what he has in common with you, how your differences complement each other, and what are the total resources of the Group as a whole which individual companies need to understand. The word 'marketing' is much heard in Taylor Woodrow today, and practically everything we do is part of the process. We may think we are specialized engineers, builders, designers, estimators, scientists, publicists, accountants and so on; but what we are all really doing is making something which we ultimately wish to sell, and the term 'marketing' wraps up the whole process. So, for three days early in 1978, seventy-five directors and marketing executives attended the Group's Marketing Seminar at the Skyway Hotel, Heathrow Airport, to study and discuss a programme developed under the guidance of the late A. J. Hill. The seminar was divided into six sessions, each chaired by a parent board director. The themes were Land Development, Conventional Contracting, Manufacturing, Trading, Specialist and Diverse Skills, and finally 'The Future'. Twenty-four papers were presented and each session ended with about an hour's discussion. The lessons that emerged were a fascinating mixture of old and new wisdom: anticipation of social and economic trends, the supreme marketing value of a satisfied customer, the risks of too much 'hard sell', the need to develop and maintain close personal relationships with clients, to look farther and farther ahead in assessing the requirements of industry, commerce and the community – and to exploit our forecasts through clients who may not yet be aware of their own needs – all these are part of the marketing process.

The demands of a large, dynamic company on an executive can be heavy, especially if they threaten to monopolize his life at the expense of his family. Taylor Woodrow have always been aware of this risk, and a sign of their concern was their Executive Wives' Seminar in June 1978 when some two dozen wives gathered to discuss the Group's work and some of its effects upon their family life. The report of the discussions and recommendations went forward to the executive and parent boards and some changes were made for the future. Initiated by Lady Taylor, the Wives' Seminar was considered well worthwhile and, after a second gathering late in 1978, has become a new feature of Taylor Woodrow life.

Thousands of people all over the world know the Taylor

Woodrow tie with its symbol of four men pulling on a rope. The design, developed from an idea submitted in a Group-wide competition and translated into stone by sculptor David Wynne, appears on every site, every piece of paper or envelope used anywhere in the Group, and has led naturally to Taylor Woodrow's sponsorship of both National and European Tug-of-War championships. The 'school' atmosphere was, until 1975, seen in the annual prizegivings (to which wives and families were invited). Now that the Group is so large, it has been found more practical to hold separate prizegivings for component companies.

Everyone who joins Taylor Woodrow is given a copy of the Team Handbook, which warns against the danger of becoming 'a big unwieldy bureaucratic company' and lays stress on training for all ranks. 'Helping our people to develop and grow is a fundamental Group policy. However, it must be realized that the development of team members is part of a long-term pattern. To help those who are ready to improve their performance and seize the opportunity for promotion, training schemes are operated throughout the Group. These include comprehensive training schemes for graduates, students, apprentices, and trainees as well as general career development schemes. . . . We must have team training schemes for management, trying to bring along the potential future directors and production leaders. We must have schemes designed to help the professional, and all these must have a sense of team spirit in common purpose. Commonsense is most essential at all times.'

The construction industry has for some years had an insatiable demand for trained craftsmen and operations. Taylor Woodrow have had a plant mechanics' training centre since 1953, and in November 1974 opened their permanent building trades centre, at Southall, comprising three workshops, two classrooms, and a practical working area outside.

Presenting completed deeds of apprenticeship, Tom Freakley, president of Taylor Woodrow Construction, said: 'I am privileged to be here today because I myself was once an apprentice bricklayer. Several Taylor Woodrow team members who are today holding positions of great responsibility have risen from craftsmen and supervisors.' Apprentices during the first year of training spend sixteen weeks in the Training Centre and twelve weeks at a college for further education, interspersed with site experience.

Sometimes Taylor Woodrow will sponsor a student civil engineer, say at Salford University, such as Peter Glover, now an assistant engineer at Brighton Marina. After two years in the Design Department at Southall, during which time he passed the Ordinary National Certificate in engineering in one year on day release, and some site experience at Nottingham Victoria Centre and Hartlepool nuclear power station, he became the only four-year 'sandwich' B.Sc. civil engineering student on the 1975 civil engineering course at Salford to gain a first class honours degree.

Less directly geared to careers, but important for character development, is the endowment by Taylor Woodrow of a berth in the *Malcolm Miller* schooner which allows them to make one nomination a year for young team members between the ages of seventeen and twenty-one to spend two weeks on a working cruise. Twenty-year-old David Thomas, a student quantity surveyor with TWC Northern, did this in the summer of 1974, sailing from Plymouth to Corunna, St Malo and Portsmouth, taking part in two of the 1974 Tall Ships Races on the way, and pronounced it 'a most worthwhile and rewarding experience.'

A more recent development, linking Taylor Woodrow with the districts in which they live, is called Young Enterprise. This is an educational charity which tries to provide a link between school and industry by offering boys and girls between the ages of fifteen and nineteen an opportunity to learn how to organize, manage, and operate miniature modern companies. By arrangement with the careers advisers of local schools, about twenty of them from two schools spend two hours of one evening a week for eight months forming and operating imaginary companies. The 'New Horizon Company', for example, produces 'seasonal goods and canvas bags'; the 'Rainbow Goodies Co.' produces 'novelty goods'. Each company works under the guidance of adviser volunteers from Taylor Woodrow Construction, Taylor Woodrow Services, E. & D. Taylor Ltd. (the Group's own insurance brokers) and the Greenham Group. The students elect their own managing director, company secretary, accountant, production manager, sales manager, personnel manager, etc. At the end of the eight-month exercise they present their annual report and balance-sheet and decide what dividend is to be declared to shareholders.

It is not difficult to see this as an attempt to get rid of the 'Them and Us' division in industrial society, particularly under the militant political pressures of the present times. There can also be 'Them and Us' feelings about profits, and so anxious are Taylor Woodrow that every team member should understand exactly how the cake is divided that they not only publish, in all their house journals, explanations every year; but in 1976 began the first of a series of annual films, *Teamwork 1976*, which showed how even taxation benefits each team member through Government, why reinvestment (ploughing back a percentage of profit) is particularly necessary in this industry, why dividends are only one-eighth of profits after tax and depreciation (in a world where millions of workers still believe that *all* profits go to shareholders this cannot be rammed home too hard or too often); and stressing that only competitive free enterprise can yield such financial health.

A new development from this annual report to the team is 'Team TV', a quarterly review in the form of a television video-cassette programme, presented as entertainment by the old B.B.C. *Nationwide* team of Michael and Dilys Barrett, for internal showing to Taylor Woodrow establishments all over the world. Thus 'Spring Review 1978', featuring Dick Puttick as spokesman, analysed financial results and prospects, noted recent achievements in several countries, and ended with a dizzy bit of nonsense at the top of a tower crane at St Katharine's. The programme was made by Kadek Vision in conjunction with Michael Barrett and Group Communications and Personnel Services at Southall.

In November 1975 many salaried team members received a letter from Frank Gibb, now chairman and managing director of Taylor Woodrow Construction and joint managing director of the Group, headed 'Team Consultation'. This was one of the results of the parent board and other directors taking over part of the London Business School ten months before and holding their own 'top people's Aldermaston' to crystallize certain areas of its thinking about industry and the future. The Group philosophy, it was felt, was sound, and had been so for many years, but its application and implementation needed updating. 'Team Consultation' was to begin in and around Southall and be extended to other companies in the Group if successful.

Elected 'team representatives', with only sketchy guidelines, would meet at two levels for consultation – departmental and company. There would probably be ten departmental committees and two company committees, one for head office and one for sites. They would discuss such matters as reports and future plans, legislation affecting the company, safety, health and welfare, suggestions, social and recreational activities. To get the scheme started, directors and managers invited team members to join them on initial departmental committees. It is easy to see, in all this, a strengthening of morale against political pressures, and Frank Gibb's letter ended: 'The Group's policy of a very strong personal relationship being maintained with each team member, enabling them to approach their manager, director, managing director or chairman (whose doors are always open to deal with any problems or important matters of teamwork), will continue unchanged. . . . In this rapidly developing world, social and moral values are increasingly subject to stress, and our way of life to change. We hope that these proposals for consultation will help to strengthen our ability to meet the challenges of the future.'

The scheme had an immediate success, and within months had been extended to Taylor Woodrow Construction in the Midlands, North, and Scotland, and to Myton, Swiftplan, Taylor Woodrow Plant, Terresearch, E. & D. Taylor (Insurance Brokers) Ltd. the Greenham Group, and Taylor Woodrow International.

A logical development from this was the Group's first Team Consultation Conference, held at the Wembley Conference Centre in London on 4 July 1977, which, since it was repeated (and extended to two days) in July 1978, has become an annual event. There 239 team members met to discuss and contribute ideas for the future development of the Group, based on the common aim of 'developing profitable work for the Group and thereby creating more opportunity for members of the Team'.

Having read thus far, the reader will not be surprised to learn that there is not much enthusiasm in the Taylor Woodrow Group for any of the recommendations of the Bullock Commission with reference to worker directors. Taylor Woodrow directors believe they *are* workers anyway, and quite a few of them have come up to the top from manual labour. Because they give everyone the opportunity of

management experience on the way up, from the humblest
levels, they are confident that they are years ahead of most
industrial and all T.U.C. theory.

By the same token, Taylor Woodrow are not disturbed
by the implications of the Equal Pay Act. There is no 'rate
for the job' at Taylor Woodrow: you are paid what management thinks you are worth. 'The Taylor Woodrow Policy',
Dick Puttick replied when asked about this in an interview
in December 1975, 'does not discriminate between men and
women.' The construction industry has often been regarded
as a man's world; yet you cannot go far in Taylor Woodrow
without realizing what important jobs women are doing. In
this the influence of Lady Taylor, herself on the parent board
and the boards of both Blitman and Taylor Woodrow Homes,
is significant. One subsidiary, Taylor Woodrow Services, has
two women directors – Ruth Philip, who was also personal
assistant to A. J. Hill, and Daphne Hyde, personal assistant to
Sir Frank Taylor.

Ruth Philip, with Scottish thoroughness, knows the
industry through and through: 'They made me a director,'
she says, 'the same day that Margaret Thatcher became Leader
of the Opposition!' Her first job was on an Arcon site in her
native Aberdeen, more years ago than she cares to remember.
She was a member of the team which visited Japan in 1973 to
explore opportunities for initiating business through joint
association on a world-wide basis. Daphne Hyde joined
Taylor Woodrow as a shorthand typist in the buying department at Southall in 1947, was transferred to Park Street in
1949 and has been Frank Taylor's private secretary since 1955.
Her first trip abroad, apart from a holiday in Switzerland,
was in 1952 when she went to Taylor Woodrow's Long
Island office for six weeks in exchange for another secretary,
Irene Kaminsky. Since then she has been all over the world
with Frank and Christine Taylor, notably a round trip in

1968 which took her to Australia, Honolulu, San Franciso, and New York. When she isn't travelling, she is making all the arrangements for the Taylors to travel, helping FT to 'do his homework' by getting up-to-date information on all Taylor Woodrow people in the country to be visited and the progress of each contract.

Greenham, too, has a woman director – Gwen Chamberlain, who joined the board of the Sand & Ballast Company in March 1977, having specialized, since she joined the Group in 1960, in personnel and welfare as well as having been personal assistant to the chairman. The comptometer department at Southall is headed by Mrs Stella Smith, née Stella Shepherd – her sister Elsie is secretary to the Group Chairman, Dick Puttick: the sisters have between them fifty-nine years service with the Group. By way of contrast, Brenda Seel, whose background is teaching, is now a personnel services manager. She joined the Group in 1974. Many women in jobs at all levels at Taylor Woodrow are encouraged to visit sites, wade through the mud in wellingtons and get to know people, so that they are not merely voices on a telephone: this policy, too, has been initiated largely by Christine Taylor.

At one time the Publicity Department at Southall had two women journalists, one in words, the other in pictures. Christine Bury, press officer and wife of Michael Bury who works in the research laboratories, was also editor of *Taywood News* until she left to start a family. Jane Bustin, née Coppock (daughter of Emil/Dick), is a photographer: her work has taken her to sites all over the country.

From Christine Taylor to the switchboard girls (at Southall they are a team of five led by Sheila Page), the team is enriched by women who help to make up the corporate personality of the Group.

Marjorie Roberts, planer operator at Swiftplan; Anne Mattock, mechanical engineering graduate working on

machines at Taymech Aviation's refuelling assembly shop at
Feltham; Suzanne Quentric, one of several draughtswomen
in the Atomic Power Division . . . these are no longer matters
of wonder: it is no longer a man's world!

It is not much use joining Taylor Woodrow if you do not
believe in free enterprise and individual initiative, directed to
a common purpose and held together by loyalty – qualities
which, Frank Taylor is fond of saying, 'make the Team
great'. Friendliness is an order; John Rogers has never really
got over his first day at Southall, which convinced him
that he had joined a company that was unlike any other
he had ever worked for. 'I was a new boy,' he says, 'and
complete strangers rang me up asking if they could *help* me!'

Taylor Woodrow's 'good neighbour' policy, wherever
they may be, at home or abroad, is well-known. At Christmas they decorate the bleakness of scaffolding with Christmas
trees and fairy lights. They were the first construction firm to
think of 'observation platforms' so that passers-by could
indulge the fascination of watching other people working.
They pioneered 'apologetic notices' in which they expressed
their genuine regret at having to make so much noise and
mess in public places. They invented the Pilemaster to lessen
the noise. . . . We have given examples of small helpfulnesses
towards members of the public, and two more, one from
Nigeria, the other from Brighton, may complete the picture.

Every major Taylor Woodrow site has its own power
generator. At Sokoto, northern Nigeria, the wedding
between a local bank manager and a young lady teacher was
almost ruined by a local power failure. The wedding dress
had not been pressed because there was nowhere to plug in
an electric iron. So Eric Adams, the project manager, yielded
his office to the seamstresses, saying: 'I thought I had done
every possible job on a construction site in my time, but
pressing a wedding dress isn't one of them!'

And on 2 September 1974, Harry Godden and Dick Klanceweiz, looking out to sea from the main office block at the Brighton Marina site, saw a group of men in an inflatable life raft which had been tossing on the waves for several hours after a storm. Going out to investigate, they found they were rescuing survivors from the crew of Ted Heath's yacht *Morning Cloud*. Mr Heath thanked them personally, and the next day's newspapers were full of them.

But we were speaking of politics, and in the 1970s the civil engineering industry cannot stay aloof from politics. Shareholders know this when they receive their annual reports. Those beautifully produced booklets take shareholders into the confidence of the board, who share their triumphs and misgivings about the future with them as if they were members of the Team (which of course they are). It may be Frank Taylor pleading for industrial peace – 'action of this nature [i.e. strikes] carried to its logical conclusion would lead not to more work and higher wages, but less of each, if clients came to think they could no longer rely on this great industry of ours.' Or it may be Dick Puttick's exasperation with the Industrial Democracy Bill 'for trade union representation on supervisory boards ... at a time when industry is fighting inflation on an unprecedented scale, facing intense international competition and experiencing disruption by politically motivated extremists.'

The annual report is very much a team effort, produced under the direction of Nat Fletcher, parent board director who heads up Publicity and Marketing, and Robin Christie, parent board director and company secretary. A shrewd, forthright, and humorous son of Sunderland, Robin is the only man in the Group who has seen Frank Taylor almost every day for thirty years. On the parent board he has special responsibility for Australian interests but, his main activity is, of course, deep in the complex realm of company law, currency controls and stock market procedures at home and overseas. Robin joined the Group in 1946 after demobilization from the Army, having previously worked for a firm of chartered accountants and solicitors in the north east of England.

His close friend and, indeed, neighbour, Nat Fletcher has guided the development of Group communications, both internal and external, since he founded the Taywood News in 1945. Nat is a 40-year-service man, who came into the team as an assistant buyer having travelled south from his Yorkshire home in the mid-30s to pursue his career as a journalist.

Every letter you receive from Taylor Woodrow comes in an envelope with the 'four men' symbol and the 'Free Enterprise' sign. This is Frank Taylor talking, but it might just as well be Dick Puttick or practically anyone else you stop in any corridor of Taylor Woodrow. 'Our Group was founded and has prospered on the principle of free enterprise and we believe it is the right of every legitimate business that it should be able to go about its activities with the minimum of State interference,' said Dick Puttick in his 1975 letter to shareholders.

The threatened nationalization of the building industry, clearly stated in the Labour Party's 'policy background paper' *Building Britain's Future – Labour's Policy on Construction* (October 1977), produced vociferous opposition from Taylor Woodrow. It is sometimes expressed with a wry smile, as when Sir Frank Taylor told the *Financial Times* that 'today, the British industrialist has to spend too much time trying to keep his business from falling into the hands of those who would steal it.' But more often it is said in outright anger: 'We have in this country fine men who are prepared to work and produce, but we are hindered by the worst type of militant element in the trade unions, the Communist type.

What saddens me is that they never say "if we get our form of government you will be slaves, you will have the secret police watching you, you won't be able to go overseas, you won't be able to worship where you like".'

For many years Taylor Woodrow – and Sir Frank Taylor in particular – have been closely associated with two 'freedom' movements: Aims for Freedom and Enterprise (formerly Aims of Industry) and the Freedom Association (formerly the National Association for Freedom). Brian Trafford is a council member of the former, and Lord De L'Isle, an old friend of the Group, is chairman of the latter. The policy of Aims for Freedom and Enterprise has been summed up by its chairman, Sir John Reiss, BEM, thus: 'We have fought for free enterprise and opposed unnecessary nationalization and state control of industry. We have always accepted that there is a relationship between a responsible free enterprise economy and political and individual freedoms. We will continue to stress the importance of free enterprise and we will oppose any extension of nationalization and unnecessary state ownership and control of industry. But we will place increased emphasis on the importance of other individual and group freedoms which we believe are being increasingly threatened.'

The Freedom Association concerns itself even more widely with *all* freedoms, not merely political and industrial, and its manifesto includes freedom of worship freedom to belong to a trade union or not to, freedom from 'confiscatory taxation', the right to 'live under the Queen's peace', the right to be 'defended against the country's enemies' – a general reassertion of the Bill of Rights, the Atlantic Charter, and almost every statement of human liberty that history can show.

It follows naturally that Taylor Woodrow stoutly supported CABIN, the Campaign Against Building Industry Nationalization, of which Frank Gibb, chairman and managing director of Taylor Woodrow Construction, was a Council member. CABIN started off with a national opinion poll which, ignoring the 'Don't Knows' (who included 23 per cent of Labour voters), showed that 85 per cent of the public were *against* nationalization, and so were 87 per cent of construction industry workers and 74 per cent of Labour's own supporters. CABIN pointed out the inevitable proliferation of civil servants in the event of nationalization (two new public corporations, three new public agencies, two new public boards to control and regulate every builder, and all supplies to be obtained from a national building materials corporation!).

There are nearly two million people employed in the building and construction industry. Seventy-four per cent of those interviewed in the survey thought that nationalization would result in less profitability and less efficiency. Summing up, Sir Maurice Laing, leader of the CABIN campaign, said: 'The lessons the Government have learnt from their other 'lame duck' nationalized industries, taken together with the strong views expressed in the survey, must surely persuade the members of the Labour Party's National Executive that their proposals to nationalize the building and construction industry should now be dropped for all time.'

In 1976 Sir Frank Taylor's work for freedom was recognized when, at a luncheon at the London Press Centre on 'Free Enterprise Day', 1 July, Robert Strausz-Hupe, Permanent U.S. representative to NATO, presented him with a cartoon of himself by Richard Wilson. In an interview afterwards, Sir Frank said: 'I wish more people in business would realize that in addition to keeping their companies solvent and expanding their business as much as possible, they have a duty to add their voices to those who are trying to oppose nationalization and creeping socialism. Free enterprise and a free society go together. Threaten one and you threaten the other.'

XV

Into the 1980s

ONE of the questions which nobody at Taylor Wood-row takes very seriously is: 'When is FT going to retire?' Towards the end of 1976 he told me: 'Well, I *was* going to retire in 1975, but the Board urged me to stay until after Britain's economic crisis.' The crisis, of course, is with us yet, and likely to continue at least until the end of the decade.

It is difficult to imagine him living otherwise than the way he lives now. Non-drinking, non-smoking, diet-conscious and a great keep-fitter, he and Lady Taylor, sometimes accompanied by his personal assistant, Daphne Hyde, spend about four months of the year visiting contracts all over the world, and his reports (on cassettes of tape) are sent home immediately. In one sense, he has retired already, or so he says. By an unusual manœuvre, he stepped aside from chairman to managing director of the parent company in 1974 so as to allow a younger man, Dick Puttick, to become chairman. At the same time, Frank Taylor insisted that his office door (for the eight months of the year when he is not travelling) is 'ever open' to any member of the team who has something on his mind. As we have seen in the opening pages of this book, there have been further changes among the personalities at the head of this great enterprise.

Brian Trafford, whose ability to harness enthusiasm was seen during his years with the Greenham Group (of which

he is still the chairman), is a hater of red-tape who believes
more in the shredding machine than in the filing cabinet, the
telephone confrontation more than the long memorandum.
He started the Marketing Division at Greenham to sell
Greenham as much to the Group as to the outside world.
Like most senior management, he believes in 'fighting
nationalization to the end', and that the Taylor Woodrow
Group has a 'phenomenal' future if only industry can stay
free. 'But trading in the 1980s will be as different from
trading in the 1960s and 1970s as *they* were from the 1940s.'

This defiant optimism draws strength from the Group's
profits. How can a huge international company go on, almost
monotonously, announcing 'record profits' year after year?
These words are being written in mid 1979, and bingo! it's
happened again: '. . . These activities, coupled with earnings
from our property investments, made a considerable contribution to group turnover and with the achievement of not
unsatisfactory profits, I am pleased to report that for the
eighteenth consecutive year we have improved on the results
of the previous year.' The £24 million profit, an increase of
£1·6 million over 1977, would have been at least £600 000
more but for movements in exchange rates.

The results two years before caused *The Sunday Times
Business News* to say, on 17 April 1977, 'In the middle of the
worst recession to hit the construction industry since the war,
Taylor Woodrow has just produced some astonishingly good
figures from its export drive . . . two thirds of those profits
came from abroad, earned on much less than half the turnover.'

It is going to be harder to fill the home order book, and
it is going to mean trying harder so as to get a greater share
of a smaller market – and to do it without under-tendering.
The small job often turns out more profitable than the jumbo.
'The Government used to be our biggest employer,' says Tom

Freakley, president of Taylor Woodrow Construction. 'Now that there has been so much cut-back, I think we're looking for a supply of work as much as for expanding profits.' At home, at any rate until the 1980s, it looks like consolidation rather than growth. Could there be, after all, a road-building programme in spite of Government cut-backs? Some quarters of the construction industry have suggested that, as happens on the Continent, motorways could become toll roads, and finance could be raised, for example, from the hundreds of European juggernauts who use our motorways for nothing.

The spectacular expansion of Taylor Woodrow International over the past decade leaves little room for doubt that the overseas trend is likely to become a permanent feature of the civil engineering scene. Which countries? At the moment Taylor Woodrow have a great many – hopefully not too many – eggs in the Middle East basket; and in the Middle East we include the whole of Arabia and round the Gulf. In February 1977 Taylor Woodrow International signed a contract with Sheikh Hamad Al Khalifah and his brothers to design and construct the Bahrain Sheraton Hotel for £20 million. Scheduled to open in the spring of 1980, it will be the third Sheraton Hotel in the Gulf area. It will have 350 luxury guest rooms, four restaurants, a main ballroom accommodating 500 for banquets, a health club, squash courts, and an adjacent commercial centre which will include a cinema and a bowling alley, and a 16-storey office tower as an extension of the original contract.

The Bahrain Sheraton features a new development pioneered by Swiftplan Ltd. – ready-assembled bathroom units manufactured at Southall and exported in containers so that they were literally dropped into place beside bedrooms. Self-contained, needing only connections to their copper water pipes and waste disposal units, tiled and complete almost to the last toilet-roll, they measure about 10 × 7 feet. The variable layout comprises bath, shower, lavatory, bidet, marble basin unit, mirrors, tissue dispenser and robe hooks, and the whole, on a concrete floor, is solidly contained in a wood frame treated for tropical pests. It is not difficult to see this as a future trend in hotel-building.

Taking the most pessimistic view, it could be argued that oil-wells eventually run dry, and, in the shorter term, populations of Middle East countries are still too small to support many more schools and hospitals. Thus the Middle East market might begin to tail off by the mid-1980s. Egypt needs industrial development but lacks capital: Libya is rich but, under its present government, unpredictable.

Bob Aldred, chairman of Taylor Woodrow International, says his job includes 'looking ahead for our business in five and ten years' time, as well as our immediate future of continuing our expansion abroad with caution'. Such expansion, despite the umbrella of Export Credit Guarantees, should be in economically *stable* countries.

In the Far East, Taylor Woodrow are well established around Singapore and Malaysia, and have even entered Vietnam. Arcon Building Exports, it was announced in February 1977, won a large share in the first major British capital goods contract to be signed with the Socialist Republic of Vietnam since the end of hostilities there. Working closely with James Mackie & Sons Ltd., the Belfast machinery manufacturer, a complete jute mill is being built at Thai Binh, a city on the Red River Delta, fifty miles south-east of the capital, Hanoi. Arcon Building Exports are responsible for the design and supply of all materials and equipment for the steel-framed buildings, mechanical and electrical services and steel reinforcement for foundations, and management the local construction, including civil engineering works. Thus the whole project draws on the skills of several Group components, from Octavius Atkinson to Terresearch.

Yet it is in the Far East that some of the stiffest competition must be faced – from countries needing foreign currency and construction firms some of which are believed to be subsidized by their governments – the Japanese, the Koreans, the Vietnamese. In which countries will they compete? How far outside their respective spheres will they attempt to go?

Which brings us to Sarawak, the former realm of Rajah Brooke and now, no longer addicted to head-hunting, part of Ron Whitehouse's equatorial hunting ground. Here, in partnership with Tengku Arif Bendahara (chairman of Teamwork Malaysia and also of the United Asian Bank), Taylor Woodrow are in the timber business, cutting down tropical forest (which renews itself every twenty-five years) and exporting it to Far Eastern countries (including Japan), also to Europe and America.

Bob Aldred is one of several senior people at Taylor Woodrow who look to an ultimate turn-around of fortunes in Australia. Australia has had most of our own problems in recent years, including inflation and unemployment. So it was encouraging to note that, in March 1977, Taylor Woodrow International added a new contract to the many they have carried out in Western Australia – a £1 million marine berthing facility at Stirling Naval Base, Garden Island.

The success of the Romanian irrigation contract points to the possibility of further work in Eastern Europe. There are perhaps signs of this in other contracts in Russia, worth about £3½ million, awarded to Arcon Building Exports for 90 panel-construction buildings as part of a gas pipeline – the huge 600-mile Tyumen-Chelyabinsk pipeline in Siberia. The first contract, placed by the 'Coberrow Consortium', was for forty-two buildings to house Rolls-Royce engines and Cooper Bessemer compressors at pumping stations; the second for forty-eight 'skid-mounted' buildings. All are steel-framed and insulated, and have been designed for a temperature range from +40 degrees to −40 degrees centigrade. All have snow-porches, which are essential in Siberia.

Still further east, China beckons, with the growing financial independence and autonomy of the provinces suggesting opportunities for co-operation. Bob Aldred went there in 1978 as a member of a Trade Mission led by Mr. Edmund Dell, then Secretary of State. 'The trip was very useful, but as may be expected will take time to become productive,' he said later. 'I found myself answering numerous technical questions and since every appointment had to be arranged through my hosts – the foreign trade ministry – there were the necessary waiting periods between useful meetings. But, by going with the Minister, I was helped through the political barriers and met the all important end-users.'

He went on to say 'we will seize any proper opportunity to demonstrate our ability in China. Taylor Woodrow has the necessary experience and technical competence and will be able to meet the necessary period of waiting for acceptance, This is a well known basic requirement when looking at a new area such as China, and numerous companies today bear witness to the time and money spent in acquiring satisfactory results.'

Having made overtures to the Chinese about their wide experience particularly in irrigation and marine work. Taylor Woodrow joined in the British Energy Exhibition in Peking in June 1979, demonstrating their involvement in opencast coal, conventional and nuclear power stations, off-shore oil exploitation and alternative forms of energy. Many of the 350 or so other exhibitors had been associated with Taylor Woodrow in the past, and Bob Aldred declared 'I believe there is great scope for joint venture operations. The funds and the expertise are available. We would like to take part in vertical consortia concerned with the design, construction and equipment – and where applicable the training of operatives – for manufacturing or secondary industrial projects.'

In the last twelve or fifteen years, Taylor Woodrow have been offering more and bigger 'package deals' – built-in management as a service, as well as their basic construction skills, plus electrical design and equipment, plus the very knives and forks and toothpicks that go to make up, say, a modern hotel. There will, most directors agree, be more joint ventures for 'jumbo contracts' in faraway countries where only very big civil engineering groups can draw on skills and equipment from bases around the world and mobilize labour forces both locally and from within a reasonable distance, thus saving the client time and money. For these reasons, it makes sense for a major civil engineering group to diversify into industries *allied* to construction; which is why, among many examples we have quoted, Taylor Woodrow happen to be linked with a Swedish firm, Svenska Vaeg A.B., in a joint venture for underground oil storage, actually floating the oil on water in rock caverns so that the ground surface is not disfigured and can be used for other purposes.

Expansion abroad obviously means that more team members must *work* abroad for fairly long periods. Anyone who wants to make his career in civil engineering and construction must be prepared for this, and from what we have seen in the course of this book, it really isn't such a hardship. Unless you are uncontrollably addicted to *Coronation Street* and *The Generation Game* you won't miss television after a time, and you will meanwhile have discovered the pleasures of home-made entertainments in a social community where people are dependent on each other. After a year's overseas service you pay no income tax as long as you are abroad; and there is even a risk of getting too used to foreign service, so that coming home is an anti-climax after the standard of life you have been enjoying abroad. In Oman and Dubai people tell you, with a wry grin, 'it's tough in the Gulf but you'd be mad to refuse the money!' And you know they don't really mean it. As unemployment threatens to become a semi-permanent feature of life in the United Kingdom, there may well be more volunteers for service abroad than there are jobs available. A Taylor Woodrow International recruiting film shown on television in the Newcastle-upon-Tyne area produced overnight 2 700 inquiries for work on overseas projects.

In a highly competitive industry, one of the most effective ways to progress beyond merely getting a share of the market is to develop special skills, experience, capabilities. Speaking mainly of Taylor Woodrow Construction, of which he is chairman and managing director, but also by implication of the Group as a whole, Frank Gibb says: 'What we are seeking are opportunities to build up our experience and skill in several new fields, mostly related to energy and natural resources. We hope to extend our capability to cover all oil and gas areas, including exploration and production, both onshore and offshore. We wish to provide services which extend right through from initial exploration to processing and refining.' This means teaming up with experienced part-ners 'to help us extend our own skills'.

Frank Gibb can see Taylor Woodrow doing the same thing in the fields of metal and mining, both surface and deep, in which the Group already has experience of large projects. 'Again, I would like to see our capability expanding from the original exploration for minerals or coal through mining and on to the refining process.'

At times when there is less work at home and more abroad, it makes sense for Taylor Woodrow Construction to spread the geographical load by looking abroad for work. 'At the moment we're looking at the Central and South American countries,' Frank Gibb says. 'It's a fairly lean area unless you're prepared to invest there. . . . We have opened our local office in Caracas, Venezuela, and are looking at various projects – industrial plants, especially harbours, airfields and mining work – which Taylor Woodrow know a lot about, and the skills of which are rooted in the basic task of earth-moving. There is an enormous need for housing and infra-structure work.' South America is not an easy area to operate in (Taylor Woodrow International have discovered this over the years), but Frank Gibb has faith that 'if we take on certain jobs that are more selective we should be able to succeed.'

Success is already in hand for several Group companies in North America, as we have seen, and in January 1979 Taylor Woodrow Construction announced the establishment of three new companies in the USA. The principal company, Taywood Energy Services Inc., is seeking work in all fields of energy – oil, gas and coal, and is based in Houston, Texas. The other companies are Taywood Minerals Inc which acts as the mine property and asset owning company, and Taywood Mining Inc. which is the operating company in coal and other minerals mining. These last are based in Lexington, Kentucky.

The first opencast mining project is being undertaken at Pineville in East Kentucky. It involves removal of the moun-tain tops and reforming the valleys whilst extending the various coal seams encountered.

Another Taylor Woodrow speciality, we have seen, is tunnelling. It can be one of the trickiest jobs in civil engineer-ing. 'We started in 1957 with the cooling water tunnels for Hinkley Point nuclear power station,' says Frank Gibb. 'We either had to develop tunnelling skills ourselves or sub-contract them, and we decided to do it ourselves.' Other tunnels at other nuclear and thermal power stations followed, all under the sea because of the water cooling systems. From each something new was learnt. 'We couldn't have carried out the cargo tunnel at Heathrow in 1966–68 without first having done the various tunnel jobs on nuclear power stations.' Frank's own personal contribution to this expertise has been of outstanding importance. He instances 'a fairly complicated job at Fawley power station in 1964, with all compressed air working driving tunnels through silt, sands and silty clays. (This was for the cooling water tunnels into the Solent and the two-mile transmission tunnel under Southampton water.) We gained our experience under some of the most difficult conditions – hardly any job has been straightforward. This however enabled us to develop the shaft-raising method for the seaward end of the tunnel. We proposed the method to avoid expensive coffer dams in the North Sea and developed it first by models and then by full-scale land trial at Sizewell, and finally the real thing. It was a controlled and safe way and it saved a tremendous amount of time and money, another piece of pioneering of new methods.'

Taylor Woodrow's disappointment at the abandonment of the Channel Tunnel is all the more understandable in the light of this experience. 'Together with three other companies in the joint venture, Cross Channel Contractors, we put to-gether one of the best tunnelling teams that ever existed,' Frank Gibb sighs. Will the Chunnel ever be resumed? 'If it isn't built in the next five years, I very much fear it never will be. There are so many alternatives – ferries, hovercraft, short-range aircraft and so on – and yet we *do* need a rail link between Britain and Europe.'

Many people at Taylor Woodrow are full of advice for the young man contemplating civil engineering as a career. There is such a strong measure of agreement in what they say that we will let Frank Gibb speak for all of them. 'If you're pre-pared to move around where the work is, if you enjoy wrestling with problems, solving them, and seeing something constructive being achieved, then engineering and construction could be the job for you. Almost irrespective of academic attainments, there's a first-class opportunity for the great majority of people in a construction organization, taking part in work onshore and offshore all over the world.'

The Group has faith in its ability to grow its own timber. Those 'academic attainments', for example: often you can acquire them while working. Frank Gibb again: 'There's no doubt our system of training poeple inside the Group has proved, time and time again, that this is where our best source of people lies. Whether we take them on from school, or universities, people who have worked their way through the organization are generally our best people, the most reliable and hard-working, the ones who get results.' How does Frank Gibb's own life fit into this pattern? 'I was at Loughborough College, where I did mechanical engineering. Due to Government direction at the tail end of the War, I specialized in aeronautical mechanical engineering. I later joined Handley Page at a time when we were changing from a large aircraft industry building military aircraft to an undetermined size of industry building civil aircraft.' Uncertain whether to stay in aircraft, his mind was made up for him by a fortunate meeting with Frank Taylor, with his uncanny flair for talent spotting. 'He was enthusiastic about his team and invited me to join to gain experience – and here I am, still gaining experience. I started on opencast coal and soon learned that there was a major difference in outlook and attitude.

Frank Gibb's (and Taylor Woodrow's) view of the industry's future is closely bound up with ecology. The engineering and construction industries have a grave responsibility for the environment. We have seen examples of this at Butterwell and other opencast mining sites, with the need to restore the workings back to agricultural land; and in solving the problem of noise pollution, where Taylor Woodrow's 'silent piledriver' has made such a contribution.

We have to work *with* nature as far as possible, not *against* her. We need to pay attention to the natural life of the area preferably at the design stage. This is becoming an important part of major works, in the responsibility both for the company and the individuals.' It means thinking far ahead. 'I hope this is one of the factors we shall invariably take into account when deciding how and where to undertake a project, what the natural vegetation and wildlife is, how we can preserve as much of it as possible. We can't just destroy it and forget about it. And I think this can be often done without much effect on the economics of the project. We do this for people, after all – we try to have the best possible industrial and human relations, we try to foster a good spirit in our team. We shouldn't just say "The environment is the client's responsibility" and look the other way.'

In stepping down, or sideways, as managing director, Sir Frank Taylor has gracefully made way for future management without in any way relaxing his behest to love one another which has always been part of his policy. Nor have basic attitudes in the Group changed much in the last half century:

'If we, in this country, are to prevent our present standard of living falling, we shall have to increase production. . . . Higher production all round is the only solution to the nation's difficulties. We are living beyond our means. . . .' Thus Frank Taylor in 1951.

'The joy and satisfaction in life is creating things, doing our allotted tasks efficiently; then we can enjoy leisure that has been well earned. If this policy is put into effect, then the present low level to which British prestige has, unfortunately, sunk in many parts of the world, will be restored to the high level we all desire.' Thus Frank Taylor in 1931.

'There is nothing wrong with the people of this country, they're the salt of the earth. We are up against a Communist minority trying to seize power, but we shall defeat them.' Thus Frank Taylor, 1977.

'The most important priorities to get our country's economic recovery restarted are to switch effort and resources from bureaucratic overheads into greater production and marketable goods and services.' Now it is Dick Puttick talking, in January 1977. 'The construction industry is very flexible and its operations do not require a big establishment. We are an essentially mobile industry and, therefore, can quickly set up new operations wherever the opportunities present themselves.' In the search for those opportunities Taylor Woodrow senior executives put in an estimated million flying miles a year (the figure is George Hazell's).

The reiteration of the word 'team' in the daily speech of all Taylor Woodrow people puzzles some outsiders, but it is utterly genuine. Into the Taylor Woodrow vocabulary there has lately crept another word, 'synergy' which has been defined as a united effort in which 'the whole is greater than the sum of its parts.' It means, of course, the same thing. 'The team must be a blending of a variety of people rather than that everybody shall conform to one pattern. We need steady and solid types, highly skilled types, imaginative types, energetic types, resolute types, tactful types, aggressive types....' That was the late A. J. Hill, first president of Taylor Woodrow Construction talking: 'There have been huge social changes since 1971. We have to encompass them without losing our purpose. And, of course, we shall. We are still after all, the same people.'

There is just one snag that could dent the optimism with which the men who run Taylor Woodrow are imbued: the threat to Free Enterprise. The usual reason why industries are nationalized is because they are inefficient. Frank Taylor quotes the examples of Rolls-Royce and Leyland: 'You have to go back to the origins of the trouble. At RR they made the grave error of becoming dependent on government subsidies and handouts. . . . They ought to have brought one or two good accountants on to the board. British Leyland was built up in the wrong way, with a conglomerate of companies many of which were very good in themselves.' He quotes Peter Parker of British Rail: 'There's nothing in nationalized industry to replace the fear of going broke.' And he awards generous praise to other free businesses in totally different fields from his own.

Frank Taylor feels that 1977 was in many ways a 'turn-around' year, just as 1971 was a 'watershed' year. To him, the Silver Jubilee was 'almost as good as a referendum. It showed that people have their hearts in the right place. I am positive that this country will be able to face up to the challenge ahead and put the "great" back into Great Britain.'

And Taylor Woodrow? The Team? 'If I died tomorrow,' Frank Taylor said in a press interview in February 1978, 'the Team would go on, because the philosophy of a square deal, integrity and service is now deeply imbedded in the 160 directors of our company who joined us as bricklayers, carpenters, accountants, estimators, civil engineers, mechanical engineers and so on. It's absolutely marvellous!'

Illustrations — Acknowledgments

3. Burne House, the Post Office's new multi-million pound telecommunications centre, was designed by the Property Services Agency in conjunction with C. B. Pearson, Son & Partners. The structural engineers were W. S. Atkins & Partners; mechanical engineers, Department of the Environment and Edward A. Pearce & Partners, with quantity surveyors, Frank N. Falkner & Partners.

4. Architects and consulting engineers (services) for the town hall were the John S. Bonnington Partnership, formerly Sir Basil Spence, Bonnington and Collins who were responsible for the original design. Consulting engineers (structural) were Ove Arup and Partners and quantity surveyors, Reynolds and Young.

5. The Eagle Centre, financed jointly by C.I.N. Properties Ltd. and Derby Corporation, was constructed by Taylor Woodrow Construction (Midlands) Ltd. to a design by C. H. Elsom, Pack & Roberts. The structural engineers were Clarke, Nicholls and Marcel with quantity surveyors, Crosher & James. The Corporation's consultant quantity surveyors were Carter & Glover & Partners.

6. Houghton-le-Spring is just one of many sewerage work contracts completed by Taylor Woodrow Construction (Northern) Ltd. D. Balfour & Sons were consulting engineers to the Houghton-le-Spring Urban District Council.

7. On 20 May 1977, Her Majesty, Queen Elizabeth II opened the Town House extension, built by Taylor Woodrow Construction (Scotland) Ltd. for the City of Aberdeen. The architect was Mr I. A. Ferguson, ARIBA, ARIAS, FRTPI, AMBIM, City Architect, Aberdeen. Structural engineers were W. A. Fairhurst & Partners with quantity surveyors, Anderson Morgan Associates.

8. Redevelopment of brewery premises for Courage (Eastern) Ltd. by Taylor Woodrow (Arcon) Ltd. to provide new keg warehouse and tanker filling facilities.

9. The motor scooter assembly plant at Jakarta, Indonesia, was constructed using Arcon structural steelwork supplied by P.T. Arcon Prima Indonesia. Client: P.T. Danmotors Vespa Indonesia. Architects and Consultants: International Design Consultants.

11. Taylor Woodrow International Ltd. are providing 'management and technical advice' to Iraq's State Constructional Contracting Company for the construction of the Panorama tourist project.

12. As project managers, Taylor Woodrow International Ltd. provided the overall planning and programme co-ordination for the six schools; procurement services for plant and materials; management and technical advice for the construction work carried out by the Guyana Builders Consortium Co-operative Society Ltd.

13. Client: Commonwealth of Australia. Architect/Engineer: Commonwealth Department of Works.

14, a, b, c. Construction work at Brighton Marina has been carried out for the Brighton Marina Co. Ltd. by Taylor Woodrow Construction Ltd. The architects were The Louis de Soissons Partnership in association with Overton & Partners. The quantity surveyors were G. D. Walford & Partners. Consulting engineers (marine work) were Lewis & Duvivier; (lock) Bertlin & Partners; (inner basin, etc.) Ove Arup & Partners; (mechanical & electrical services) Steensen, Varming, Mulcahy & Partners.

17. Staples Corner Interchange, built by Taylor Woodrow Construction Ltd. for the Department of the Environment, was opened in 1976. W. S. Atkins & Partners were project consulting engineers to the DOE's Eastern Road Construction Unit, Bedford. Quantity surveyors were H. J. G. Samuel & Partners.

18. Built by Taylor Woodrow International Ltd. for Academy Entertainment Pty. Ltd. Australia's largest entertainment centre is a venue for all forms of entertainment and indoor sporting activities. The architects were Hobbs, Winning, Leighton & Partners with structural engineers, P. G. Airey & Associates, and quantity surveyors, Rider Hunt & Partners.

19. Completed three and a half months ahead of schedule by Taylor Woodrow International Ltd. to a design by Swan & MacLaren, Singapore.

21. This residential development in New York was designed by Horace Ginsbern & Associates and Unger/Napier & Associates. Main contractors were Blitman Construction Corporation.

23. Developed by the Monarch Group, the scheme, which also includes a medical centre, is extensively landscaped and all stores front on to a covered walkway.

25. Southgate House was completely refurbished by Myton for use as office accommodation by Legal and General Assurance Society Ltd.

26. In addition to the construction of the building for Brador Properties Taylor Woodrow Construction (Northern) Ltd. were responsible for the internal finishes of the C. & A. Modes store while Myton Ltd. carried out the finishings for British Home Stores. The architects were Leach, Rhodes & Walker with structural engineers, Leonard and Partners, and quantity surveyors, Banks Wood & Partners.

27. Constructed in the Taylor Woodrow-Anglian industrialized building system with some *in-situ* concrete and traditional brick construction, this project for the City of Westminster is one of the largest housing schemes of its kind to be carried out in London. Some 1 500 homes were provided.

28. Restoration and reconstruction of ornamental plasterwork at No. 13–15 Carlton House Terrace, London, under the direction of Messrs Cluttons for the Crown Estate Commissioners.

29. In 1977 the 'Rochester' design won Taylor Woodrow Homes Ltd. an award in the 'New Home of The Year' competition organized by *Homefinder* magazine.

31. Taylor Woodrow of California Inc. owns this shopping centre in California. It has been developed in conjunction with Sutter Hill Ltd., experienced shopping centre developers of Palo Alto, nr San Francisco.

32 a, b. The development at St Katharine's, being carried out by St Katharine-by-the-Tower Ltd. a subsidiary of Taylor Woodrow Property Co. Ltd., already includes the riverside Tower Hotel, the London World Trade Centre, the restored Ivory House and Dickens Inn, together with the St Katharine's Yacht Haven. This project also includes housing for the Greater London Council,

33. The Tono project is being constructed by Taylor Woodrow International Ltd. for the Government of Ghana.

34. Teamwork Malaysia Sdn. Bhd. built these premises to a design by Mr Chong Kum Kwan for Intel (Malaysia) Sdn. Bhd.

35 a, b, c. Taywood-Santa Fé assisted Burmah Oil Development Ltd. in the management of the design and construction of an oil-drilling platform and related services, including those required for: the steel jacket construction; onshore module fabrication; offshore support operations; marine pipelaying systems and a single point mooring tanker loading facility.

36. Hartlepool Nuclear Power Station – designed and under construction for the Central Electricity Generating Board by The Nuclear Power Company, of which Taylor Woodrow Construction Ltd. is the civil engineering member.

37. This opencast contract from the National Coal Board, Opencast Executive, is the largest ever civil engineering contract undertaken by Taylor Woodrow in the United Kingdom.

38. Investigations being carried out by members of the Research Laboratories at Southall.

40. The seabed sampler has been developed by Taywood Seltrust Offshore in association with Terresearch Ltd.

41. The aviation fuel dispenser refuelling Concorde was manufactured and supplied by Taymech Aviation Equipment Ltd.

42. Design and erection of mechanical and electrical services by the Mechanical, Electrical & Process Division of Taylor Woodrow Construction Ltd.

45 a, b. These dry docks were constructed for the Dubai Dry Dock Co. Ltd. by the Costain-Taylor Woodrow Joint Venture.

49. The sculptor was Mr Parackal Chacko Sebastian, an Indian artist employed by Taylor Woodrow International Ltd. as a carpenter in Salalah. As a result of producing a ½-scale sculpture in plaster which stands outside the team's Salalah offices he was invited to London to produce a life-size sculpture in

resin bronze. Members of the Taylor Woodrow team were models for the figures. The figures were cast in large pieces in vinyl moulds, made by Jonathan James Ltd.'s craftsmen, from a model-in-plaster prepared by Sebastian working in an annexe of the Taylor Woodrow Construction Materials Laboratory at Southall.

53. Taylor Woodrow Property Company's shopping centre and office development constructed by Taylor Woodrow Construction Ltd. Architects: Leslie Jones and Partners; quantity surveyors: Rider Hunt and Partners.

54. All-weather flying from a new black-top runway provided in only eight weeks by Taylor Woodrow Construction Ltd. for Fairoaks Airport Ltd.

58. The south turnout chamber with turnout ramp, part of the work carried out by Taylor Woodrow Construction (Scotland) Ltd. in the modernization of Glasgow underground railway for the Greater Glasgow Passenger Transport Executive. Consulting engineers: Sir William Halcrow and Partners.

59. Constructed by Taylor Woodrow Construction (Scotland) Ltd. for The Steeplechase Company (Cheltenham) Ltd. Architects: Howard V. Lobb, Ratcliffe, Leather & Partners; quantity surveyors: Langdon & Every.

60. Queen Anne's Mansions, built on one of London's most prestigious sites in Westminster by Taylor Woodrow Construction Ltd. for The Land Securities Investment Trust Ltd. Architects: Fitzroy Robinson & Partners; consultant architect: Sir Basil Spence; consulting engineers: Bylander Waddell Partnership; quantity surveyors: Gardiner & Theobald.

Index

AGB Research Limited, 144
Abu Dhabi, 84, 86
Agrimeco, 107
Agro-industry, 98–109; purposes of, 99
Aims for Freedom and Enterprise (formerly Aims of Industry), 219
Aldermaston Court Conference Centre, 200 ff
Aldridge, 185–6
Alexandra, H.R.H. Princess, 159, 165, 167, 169; visits Port of London Clipper Regatta, 159, 165; inaugurates wharf extension, Port Harcourt, 167; opens new terminal building, Aberdeen Airport, 169
American Home Owners' Warranty, 113
Andrews of Ealing, 194
Anne, H.R.H. Princess, 169; opens Royal Borough of Kensington and Chelsea's new town hall complex, 169–70
Arcolprod, 52; associated names, 52
Arcon (Building Exports), 22, 48, 63, 105, 224; contracts secured in Vietnam, 224–5; contract in U.S.S.R., 225–6
Arcon (Singapore), 17; contracts secured in Far East, 17
Ardyne Point, Argyllshire, timber breakwater at, 59–60
Arrol, Sir William, 57
Atkinson, Guy F., 25
Atkinson, Octavius, 86, 225
Atomic Power Construction Company Limited, 42–3
Australia: Garden Island Causeway built, 17; various projects completed, 141
Avu Keta agricultural project, 106

Babcock & Wilcox Ltd., Messrs., 42; building constructed for, 14, 179
Bandar Abbas, 92
Barker-Mill Trust, 146
Baxter, Raymond, 105
Bayah, 74, 82–3

Bear Brand Ranch West, Laguna Beach, 115
Beatty, Balfour, 25
Beecham's Pharmaceutical penicillin factory, Juron, Singapore, 17, 62; opened by H.R.H. Princess Margaret, 167
Bendahar, Tengku Arif, 107–8, 225; chairman of United Asian Bank, 107–8, 225; chairman Teamwork Malaysia, 225
Biba store, Kensington, 19, 181
Birmingham, New Street shopping centre at, 14
Blankevoort, 86–7
Blitman Construction Corporation, 20, 23, 125, 204; refurbishing jobs completed by, 128; award presented for 'splendid record as equal opportunity employer', 129
Boeg-Thomson Holding, Denmark, 17–18, 194
'Bombardon' structure, 59
Booker, McConnell, 105
Breakwaters, floating, 59; development of, 59–60; Ardyne prototype, 60
Brent Cross Shopping Development, 16, 183
Brighton: new Marina at, 15–16, 55, 210; American Express building, 55
British Airports Authority, 189
British Aluminium Company, 62
British Dredging Limited, 198
British Energy Exhibition, 226
British Engineering Exhibition, Hong Kong, 167
British Exports Centre, 150, 154
British Home Stores Limited, 20, 179, 181
British National Oil Corporation, 33
British Nuclear Associates, 43, 45
British Nuclear Design and Construction Limited, 43; consortium, 14, 43
British Oxygen Company Limited, 189
British Standards Institution, 54–5
Builders Supply Company, see Swiftplan
Bullock Commission Report, 213

Buraimi Oasis, 76
Burgess, Professor R. A., tribute paid to Sir Frank Taylor by, 24, 50
Burmah Oil Developments Limited, 33–4
Burmah Oil Thistle oilfield, 24, 33
Burns, T. F. and Partners, 57
Butterwell, Northumberland: site of largest civil engineering contract in United Kingdom, 29, 47; Charity Association, 49

CABIN (Campaign Against Building Industry Nationalization), 219
Calder Hall nuclear power station, 24, 42, 167
California, shopping centre developments in, 143
Cambrelle, see Terram
Campbell of Eskan, Lord, 114
Canadian Safeway Limited, 139
Canalside project, 128
Capital and Counties Property, 14, 17
Casas de Seville development, California, 116, 127
Central Electricity Generating Board, 62, 177; power station at Pembroke built for, 18–19; nuclear power stations for, 42
Channel Tunnel project: abandonment of, 25, 230; disappointment by company at abandonment of, 230
Charles, H.R.H. Prince, 168; visits Tono irrigation project, Ghana, 168
Chartwell Shopping Centre, Toronto, project, 133 ff.
China, potential in, 226
Churchill, Sir Winston, 166, 170
Cluthen, Hungary, project at, 105
'Coberrow consortium', 225
COBLA, see Blankevoort
Community Land Act 1975, 114
Computer programming, 64
Concrete Society, 65
Concrete S.R.L. Milan, 17, 194
Continental Oil, 84
Corby Development Corporation, 116
Corrosion, instruments for measuring inside concrete, 55
Costain-Taylor Woodrow Joint Venture (Costay), 26, 87, 90–1, 93 ff. Guest-House, 91; Club, 93; Country Club, 93
Cousteau, Jacques, 84
Coventry, project in, 19
Craigends, housing scheme at, 112
Crane Test and Inspection Limited, 194
Crosland, Anthony, 25
Cwm Bargoed Disposal Point, 47
Cymru Buildings Limited, 118; RAPID system specialists, 118

Damman, Riyadh, 120

Dalgety Agricultural Development International Ltd., 106
Danchelesco Trading Company, 92
Daqqaq, Ali, 76
Dhofar, 70, 73; projects in, 26; Development Department, 72
Dounreay, Caithness, nuclear reactor at, 44
Dowlais, 46
Drucker, Peter, 43
Duane, Frank, 136
Dubai, 9–10, 20, 84 ff.; road built in, 26; dock gates idea mooted by company, 57; dry dock, 85 ff.; projects in, 85; Offshore Sailing Club, 90–1; religious holidays in, 91; life and leisure activities in, 92 ff.
Dubai Dry Dock Company, 9, 20
Dubai Petroleum Company, 84

Elizabeth, H.M. Queen, 164 ff.: opens Brighton Marina, 16; opens Dubai dry dock, 85; visits St. Katherine-by-the-Tower, 164–5; visits and opens many Taylor Woodrow projects, 166–7; visit to Aberdeen, 169; visit to Nottingham, 170; opens Piccadilly line tube extension, 171
Elizabeth, H.M. the Queen Mother, 19; opens Oxford Central Library, 19
EMI Electronics, 34–5
Energy, alternative sources of, 66 ff.
English Electric Company, 43, 76
Eton College, project at, 19
Euston Station development opened by H.M. Queen Elizabeth, 167–8
Exeter, St. Thomas Comprehensive School, conversion of, 117

Fenston, Felix, 131, 178
Ferodo factory, Caernarvon, opened by H.R.H. Princess Margaret, 167
Financial Times, The, 44, 159, 218; Architecture Award given to Group by, 44
Finlay, James Group, 40
Fleischmann, Dr Arthur, 164
Floating Breakwater Limited, 59, 168–9
Florida Boom, 121
Florida Mortgage & Investment Company, 121
Ford Construction Equipment, 193
'Fulham Study', 147–8

Garzaiz irrigation system, 107
General Electric Company, 45; electrical projects, 103
George Cohen Machinery Limited, 186
Ghana, Tono irrigation projects, 27, 100 ff.
Gloucester, H.R.H. the Duke of, 170; opens National Association of Boys' Club headquarters, 170

Grangemouth Docks, new lock at, 14
Greenham Concrete Limited, 23, 193
Greenham Construction Equipment Limited, 192
Greenham Crawler Crane Division, 191
Greenham Electric Limited, 189–90; specialization of, 189–90
Greenham Group, 20, 28, 185 ff., 213; acquisition of S. V. Newbold Limited, 186; acquisition of S. R. Walsh Limited, 186; acquisition of Andrews of Ealing, 194; diversification of lines, 187–8, 198; supplies polythene sheeting to Syria, 187–8; suppliers of construction equipment in United Kingdom, 192–3; Pump Placing division, 193; overseas activities of, 193–4; Ace Water Skate system, 194; own airline, 195; operations in land recovery sphere, 195–6
Greenham Humidity Control Limited, 194
Greenham Plant Hire, 190 ff.; fleet of Manitowoc cranes, 190–2; example of operations, 191–2
Greenham Sand and Ballast Company, 23, 196–8, 214; award to, 196
Greenham Tool Company Limited, 185–7, 199; activities in Arabia, 199
Greenham Tyre Company, 189–90; branches of, 190
Grimethorpe Colliery project, 64
Gulbenkian Foundation, 151
Gulf General Atomics, America, 62

Halcrow, Sir William & Partners, 10, 85–6, 91
Hall, Matthew, 118
Harbison Development Corporation, 143
Harris & Sutherland, Messrs, 59
Hartlepool nuclear power station, 43, 45, 63
Harvard Business School, 204–5
Havi, 106
Head, Wrightson Teesdale, 53–4
Heath, Edward, 18–19, 216
Heathrow Central Station, 15
Hebron, 49
Heron's Hill Homes, Scarborough, Canada, 135; Chartwell, Shopping Centre at, 139
Heysham nuclear power station, 14, 43, 45, 63
Hinkley Point 'A' power station, 43, 229
Hochtemperatur Reaktorbau GmbH (H.R.B. German Nuclear Company), 44, 62
Hodge, Julian S. Bank (Isle of Man) Ltd., 181
Housing developments, dates and venues of, 112–13

IBM, 19, 62

International Ports and Harbours Association, 154
Inverforth, Lord, 174
Invergordon, aluminium reduction works at, 14
Irrigation schemes, 100; Romania, 103 ff., 171, 190; Tono River, 100 ff.
Isle of Man, contracts completed for Myton Ltd., in, 181

James, Jonathan Ltd., 30, 139, 183; plastering work completed at Queen Anne's Gate, 182–3; awarded Plaisterer's Trophy, 183, work done in City of London, 183; contract awarded for Brent Cross Shopping Centre project, 183
Jebel Qara, 70–2, 80–2
Jebsen U.K., 39
Jordan Phosphate Mines Company, new plant for, 27

Kadek Vision, 165, 207, 212
Kemevor, E. D., 168
Kensington Borough, new town hall, 19
Kent, H.R.H. the Duke of, 168–9; visits stand of Floating Breakwaters Limited in Caracas, 168–9
Kew Public Records Office, 19
Khalifah, Hamad Al, Sheikh, 223

Laguna Beach, California, 115–16; houses to be built at, 127
Land & Water Management Limited, 196
Land Securities Investment Trust, 29
Legal & General Assurance Society, 27, 174, 177
Leicester, 19
Lifting Services International, 194
L'Isle, Lord De, 219
London Airport, 14, 24; Ariel Hotel, 15, 167; Queen's Building, 15
London World Trade Centre Association, 148, 154–6, 165
London World Trade Institute, 155
Longleys of Crawley, architects, 157

Mackie & Sons Limited, James, 224
Mactaquac Dam, 130
Margaret, H.R.H. Princess: visits Singapore, 17, 167; opens Beecham's Pharmaceutical penicillin factory, Jurong, Singapore, 167; opens British Engineering Exhibition, Hong Kong, 167; opens Ferodo factory, Caernarvon, 167
Marsa el Bregha, 76, 89
Matsumoko, Gaku, 154
Materials Research Laboratory, 56
Meadows Country Club, 125
Meadowood Management Company, 125
Medinat Qaboos, 26, 69, 78–9

Metro-Greenham Aggregates, 198
Mohammed, Ahmed Abdulla, Sheikh, 82
Monarch Group, 26, 125, 129–30, 132 ff.;
Industrial Development Division, 133;
Chartwell Homes Division, 136; projects and developments, shopping centres, 137 ff.
Morgan Grenfell, bankers, 10–11; finances project in Dubai, 11
Mount Miriam Hospital, Penang, 30
Mowlem, John, 25
Mulberry Harbours, 31, 55
Multi-functional Service Vessel (MSV), construction of, 40
Mutrah, 75, 77, 79; Hotel, 77
Myton Limited, 14, 19, 142, 174 ff., 213;
building for Messrs. Babcock & Wilcox Limited, 14, 179; project completed for Dorothy Perkins Limited, 19; refurbishing Northmet House, 27; Colleges of Technology, Commerce, and Arts, Birmingham, visited by Queen Elizabeth 166; Reading University Faculty of Letters building visited by Queen Elizabeth, 167; Ariel Hotel opened by Queen Elizabeth, 167; joins Taylor Woodrow Group, 178; involvement in property development, 174 ff.; development of complexes in Brighton and near the Clyde, 178–9; refurbishing of Glasgow Stock Exchange, 179; housing and office development, York Gate, Regent's Park, 179; hotels built by, 179–80; work done for British Home Stores, 180–1; contracts in Isle of Man, 181; restoration of Covent Garden, 181–2; examples of refurbishing, 182; 'revitalization' of local authority housing by, 184

National Association for Freedom, 219
National Association of Boys' Clubs, 170;
association with Taylor Woodrow Limited, 170
National Coal Board, 27, 46 ff., 64; recovering coal for, 27
National Coal Board Pension Fund, 140
National House Building Council, 113
National Nuclear Corporation, 45
Naval Construction Research Establishment, 27, 58; high-pressure test chamber built for, 58
Newbold S. V. Limited, 186
Nigeria, projects in, 17
Nizwa, Qaboos Boarding School, 80
Norwich Union Insurance Company, 14
Nottingham Victoria Centre shopping centre completed, 17
Nuclear Inspectorate, 46
Nuclear reactor, controversy over design for next nuclear programme, 45–6

Nuttall, Edward, 25

Occidental Oil Company, 191
Ocean Thermal Energy Conversion (OTEC), system, 66
Offshore Energy Technology Board, 65
Offshore Technology Conference (OTC), 53
Ogilvy, Hon. Angus, 165
Oman, 28, 69 ff., 107, 119; projects in Dhofar province, 18, 71, 73; joint company formed by Group in, 20; refurbishment of historic buildings in Muscat, 26, 79; Yacht Club formed in, 79; desalination of water supply, 81–3; religious holidays in, 91
Oman International Development Company, 78
Opencast mining, 46–7, 229
Oxford Central Library, 19; opening by H.M. the Queen Mother, 19

P & H Cranes, 193
Palm Springs, 116; houses to be built at, 127
Parafill synthetic, 51–2
'Parallel working', 174–5, 179
Parker, Sir Peter, 234
Pembroke, Central Electricity Generating Board power station, 18–19
Perez of Venezuela, President, 169
Perth, Australia: City Arcade complex in, 14; 'Channel 7' Edgley entertainment centre, 26
Petrolina-Juazeiro Agro-Industrial Development, 105
Philip, H.R.H. the Prince, 24, 165, 167; invests Sir Frank Taylor with doctorate, Salford University, 24
Phillips Consultants Limited, 86, 177
Plummer, Sir Desmond, 154
Port of London Authority, 161
Port of London Clipper Regatta, 165
Port Rashid, 9; extension of docks at, 27, 85 ff.
'Project 2' computer programme, 37
'Promod' system, 57
Pwll-Dhu, Blaenavon, opencast coal mine, 46

Qaboos bin Said H.M. Sultan, 26, 28, 70 ff.,
Qaboos Boarding School, 80
Queen Anne Mansions, building of, 29–30
Queen Charlotte Islands, 129–30

Rancho Mirage, southern California, 116; ground-breaking ceremony at, 127
Ras Musandam, 81
Raschid, Mohamed, 83
Rashid bin Said, Sheikh, 10, 84

Rauma Repoli, 41
Ravenseft, 178
Redpath Dorman Long, Messrs, 57
Reservoir Aggregates Ltd., 178–9
Rhymney, 46
Richardson, Sir Ralph, 142
Rig Design Services, 191
Ringling, John, 121
Ringling, Mabel, 121
Rio Tinto Zinc Development Enterprises, 25
Risut, 70–1
Riyadh, 28, 119–20
Romania irrigation project, 103 ff., 169, 171, 190
Rosyth, test chamber built at, 27, 58
Royal Free Hospital, Hampstead, project, 25–6
Rutherford, Professor Sir Ernest, 65
Ruwi, 78, 79; hospital, 78

SAGA (Sand and Gravel Association), 196–7; award to Greenham Sand & Ballast Company by, 197–8
Said ibn Maktoum, Sheikh, 84
St Katherine-by-the-Tower, 148 ff., 163, 171; Tower Hotel at, 19, 63, 154; hotel at, 142; Docks, 148; Yacht Haven, 156 ff., 164; Ivory House, 156, 158, 162; 'G' Warehouse, 157–8; Dickens's Inn, 158; regatta at, 159; International praise bestowed upon, 160; 'B' Warehouse, 161–2; 'C' Warehouse, 161; conservation of, 162; trees planted at, 162–3
St Katherine-by-the-Tower Ltd., 148
Sajad Vine, 91
Salalah, 26, 69 ff.
Salmesbury, new brewery at, 15
Samuel, Lord, 178
Sante Fé International, 34
Sante Fé Overseas Inc., 39
Sante Fé-Pomeroy Services of America Inc., 24, 32
Sarasota, 20, 115–16, 121 ff.; visit by Sir Frank Taylor to, 115; Meadows development in, 143–4; Meadows Estate golf course, 123–4, 126; condominium at, 124 ff.; model homes, 125–6
Saudi Arabia, Swiftplan units in, 119
Seabed sampler, development of TSO, 60–61
Schmehausen, reactor at, 44
Seaforth Maritime Ltd., 39, 40, 41; member of James Finlay Group, 40
Seaforth Taywood Ltd., 39, 40, 41
Seatek, 34
Seeb International Airport, 78
Selection Trust finance company, 60
Selfridge, Gordon, 138, 181
Shaw & Partners, Archibald, 59

Shell Expro, 40
Shimmon, Don, 34; praise for Thistle platform installation, by, 34
Sigmund Pulsometer Pumps, 103
Singapore, 89; container berth built at, 14; ecclesiastical building in, 30; pharmaceutical plant for Messrs, Beecham at, 62
Sizewell, 43, 68, 230
Solar energy: uses for, 65; sea as reservoir for, 66
Solomons, Dr Barnet, Group's medical adviser, 23
Southgate, Northmet House, 27
Spence, Sir Basil, 29, 169
Standard Life Assurance Company, 178
Staples Corner, Hendon, 16, 183; traffic problems eliminated by Group, 16–17, 29
Sunday Times, The, 25, 151–2
Superior Oil Company, 84
Sutter Hill Ltd., Messrs. 143
Svenska Vaeg A. B., 227
Swiftplan Ltd., 48, 80, 116 ff., 213, 223; specialists in 'system', 'method' or 'modular' buildings, 116–17; 'decant' units, 118; new development pioneered by, 223

Tate & Lyle Ltd., Messrs. 106; joint venture with Taylor Woodrow International Ltd. on pilot farm scheme and sugar estate, 106
Taylor, E & D. (Insurance Brokers) Ltd., 211, 213
Taylor Woodrow (Arcon), 23
Taylor Woodrow (Arts/Loi) S.A., 141
Taylor Woodrow Blitman Inc., 128
Taylor Woodrow (Building Exports), 22
Taylor Woodrow of California Ltd. ('Taycal'), 115
Taylor Woodrow (Canada), 129
Taylor Woodrow Construction Ltd., 15, 17, 19, 21, 27, 32, 39 ff., 45, 50, 53, 61, 62, 147–58, 167, 170, 174, 204, 209, 210, 213, 220, 228; civil engineering work completed on Heathrow Central Station, 15, 171; projects in England completed by, 19; joint venture with Jebsen U.K., 39; 'M.E. & P.' division, 62–3; Lifting Services International division 194
Taylor Woodrow Construction (Midlands), 17, 40, 213
Taylor Woodrow Construction (Northern), 210
Taylor Woodrow Construction (Scotland) Ltd., 177
Taylor Woodrow Developments Ltd., 142
Taylor Woodrow Energy Ltd., 39
Taylor Woodrow Group, 20, 32, 166, 194; involvement in civil engineering industry, 11; Golden Jubilee of company, 12,

Taylor—*cont.*
14; tunnelling a speciality, 15, 229–30; North Sea oil platforms designed by, 18; various projects in England completed, 19; involvement in seeking alternative sources of energy, 41; involvement in 'power game', 42; commendation given by *Financial Times* Architecture Award, 44; inventors of Pilemaster 'silent pile-driver', 48, 57, 232; researching offshore engineering field, 52; development of floating breakwaters, 59; mission to Oman, 69 ff.; involvement in agro-industry projects, 100 ff., 108–9; projects in Eastern Europe, 103; irrigation system at Garzaiz completed, 107; 'speculative building' by, 110–11; founder members of N.H.B.C. and American Homes Owners' Warranty, 113; strength of company in Middle East, 119; homes built at Palm Springs and Laguna, California, 127; projects in eastern American states, 127–8; building in Canada, 129–30; developments in California, 143; honoured by seven Royal occasions in Jubilee Year, 168; Career Development Course organized, 200 ff.; constitution of Board, 205; Management Development Board, 205–6; emphasis on communications, 206–7; Marketing Seminar, 207–8; Executive Wives' Seminar, 208; distinguishing tie of, 208; sponsorship of European and National Tug-of-War championships, 209; apprentice training centre, 209; sponsorship of student civil engineer, 209; Young Enterprise development, 210; Teamwork Video review development, 211; 'Team Consultation', 212; Team Consultation Conference, 213; views on Bullock Commission Report, 213; 'good neighbour' policy, 216; opposition to nationalization of building industry, 218; associated with Aims for Freedom and Enterprise, and National Association for Freedom, 219; support for CABIN, 219; profits of, 222; in timber business, 225, 231; future in China, 226; attitudes toward future, 226 ff.

Taylor Woodrow Homes Limited, 20, 22, 110–12, 113 ff., 122–3, 147, 214; areas of building development, 111–13; expansion abroad, 115

Taylor Woodrow Homes (Scotland) Limited, 112

Taylor Woodrow Industrial Estates Limited, 14, 22, 23, 144 ff.; projects developed, 146–7; award to, 197

Taylor Woodrow International Limited, 10, 17, 18, 21, 30, 31, 42, 59, 63, 75, 86, 93 ff., 105 ff., 169, 213, 229; contracts secured in Far East, 26, 224; completion of 'Channel 7' Edgley entertainments centre, Perth, 26; contracts secured in Singapore, 30; Queen's Award for Export Achievement, 2, 171; expansion of, 223; contract to build Bahrain Sheraton Hotel, 223–4; contract to build marine berthing facility, Sterling Naval Base, Garden Island, 225

Taylor Woodrow Irrigation Group (TW-IG), 103 ff.; Brazil, 105

Taylor Woodrow Plant Company, 48, 213

Taylor Woodrow Property Company Limited, 18, 22, 112, 140 ff., 143, 147, 148; developments by, 141, 143; Standard Life Assurance, partnership with, 142; Teignmouth Council, partnership with, 142

Taylor Woodrow Research Laboratories, 54 ff.; first to be accepted under British Standards Institution's system for registration of test hours, 54

Taylor Woodrow Services, 170, 210, 214

Taylor-Woodrow-Towell, 26, 69, 78, 82; refurbishing historic buildings in Muscat, 26; building Qaboos Boarding School, 80; water scheme completed by, 80 ff.

Taylor-Woodrowisms, 6

Taymech Aviation, 63, 216

Taymech service vehicles, 48

Taywood Club, 72, 79

Taywood Energy Services Incorporated 229

Taywood Engineering Limited, 44, 61

Taywood Minerals Incorporated, 229

Taywood Mining Incorporated, 229

Taywood-Santa Fé Limited, 32, 36, 37, 39; project management task faced by, 36 ff.; Promap, 38

Taywood Seltrust Offshore, 60

Taywood Wrightson Limited, 62

Taywood Wrightson Offshore Organization, 54

Teamwork Malaysia Sendirian Berhad, 107

Teamwork Saudi Arabia Limited, 28, 120

Telford, Thomas, 150

Terminal Towers (Hamilton) Limited, 130 ff.

Terram (formerly Cambrelle) material, 187

Terresearch, 60–61, 213, 225

Thatcher, Rt Hon. Margaret, 67

Thistle North Sea Field: 'jacket' scheme and operation, 27–8, 32 ff., 37–8, 50; 'A' platform, 32, 138; *see also* Burmah Oil Thistle oilfield

Thistle Partnership, 33

Thomas, Alderman Charles, 19

Tobruk, 76

Tono River irrigation scheme, 100 ff.; visit by H.R.H. Prince Charles to, 168
Torno, 194
Toronto Chartwell Shopping Centre, 26
Towell, W. J. Company Limited, 20, 28, 77, 78
Tower Hamlets, 149 ff.
Trecatty, 46–7
'Tricentre', 144
Trollope & Colls, Messrs, 178, 183
Trucial States, 70; Council, 84–5
TWINGS aircraft service, 28, 73, 81

U-Thant, 156
United Kingdom Atomic Energy Authority, 42
United Nations Food & Agricultural Organization, 102
Urban renewal, 163; St Katherine-by-the-Tower at, 163; Surrey Docks at, 163

Vea irrigation works, 168
Vickers, Messrs, 103
Victoria, Queen, 167

Victorian Society, 148, 161
Visalia, projects at, 116

Walsh S. R. Limited, 186, 188
Wave motion, study of, 58–9
Wind Energy Tests, 66
Wind energy, use of windmills for, 67; feasibility study, 66
Windscale, reprocessing of nuclear fuel project, 27, 44
World Trade Associations, 155
World Trade Centre, 154, 161, 164
World Trade Centres Association, 154 ff.; educational and language facilities at, 155–6
World Trade Institute, 155
World Traders Club, 156
Wylfa, Anglesey, power station, 43–4, 89
Wynne, David, 7, 162, 209

Yorkdale, Canada's most spacious shopping centre, 138–9

Zeckendorf, William, 138